The
Beekeeper's
Lament

The Beekeeper's Lament

HOW ONE MAN AND HALF A BILLION HONEY BEES HELP FEED AMERICA

Hannah Nordhaus

HARPER PERENNIAL

NEW YORK • LONDON • TORONTO • SYDNEY • NEW DELHI • AUCKLAND

HARPER ● PERENNIAL

Grateful acknowledgement is made to the following for the use of photographs:
p. 26: copyright © 2010 Linda Stander; p. 54: courtesy of USDA; p. 84:
copyright © 2010 Singeli Agnew; p. 142: copyright © 2000 Kate Ihle; p. 254:
copyright © 2010 Melody Owen. All other photographs courtesy of the author.

Excerpt from "Fourth Georgic" from *The Georgics of Virgil* translated by
David Ferry. Copyright © 2005 by David Ferry. Reprinted by permission of
Farrar, Straus and Giroux, LLC.

HarperCollins books may be purchased for educational, business, or sales
promotional use. For information, please e-mail the Special Markets
Department at SPsales@harpercollins.com.

Designed by Betty Lew

Library of Congress Cataloging-in-Publication Data is available upon request.

ISBN 978-0-06-187325-6

15 OV/RRD 10 9

To Jeanele, who gave me words

What god was it, O Muses, who devised

An art like this? Where was it that such strange

New knowledge came from and was learned by men?

—"FOURTH GEORGIC," *THE GEORGICS OF VIRGIL*

CONTENTS

The
Beekeeper's
Lament

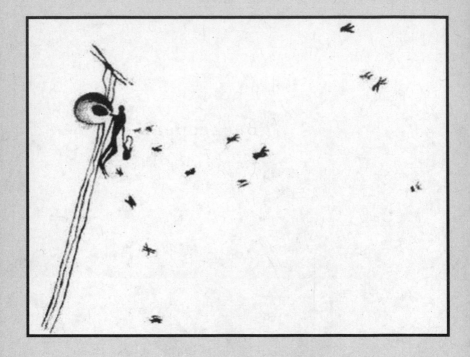

Chapter One

Fast Cars and Big Trucks

JOHN MILLER ISN'T FOND OF DEATH. HE TAKES IT PERSON-ally. A few years ago he even bought a Corvette, as if that could stave it off. It was a red C-5, number 277 produced that year, brand-new. He purchased it just before he turned forty-six, as the days lengthened to summer's zenith. Then he promptly fled California. East of Reno the highway emptied, and he inched the speedometer faster—90, 100, 120, 170. He passed a souped-up Cadillac STS as if it were a dawdling tractor; the driver didn't even have time to turn his head and gawk. Miller likes numbers, so he clocked himself and did some silent math. Even going 90, the sucker in the STS had to wait forty-five seconds for a mile to pass. Miller? Twenty-two and a half seconds per mile. And just like that, he was nine hundred miles away, in Hudson, Wyoming. He stopped there for a meal at Svilar's restaurant with his old friend Larry Krause.

John Miller is a migratory beekeeper, and so is Larry Krause. They travel the country with thousands of hives, chasing blooms and making honey. Miller and Krause have been friends for a very long time, as is often the case with beekeepers. They are a dying breed, figuratively speaking. There are fewer and fewer of them, and they tend to a breed—*Apis mellifera*, the European honey bee—that is literally dying. Yet they persist, against all logic and pecuniary sense, because beekeepers—who have, after all, chosen careers involving stinging insects—are not terribly rational people. They are loyal people, however. Miller loves Larry Krause. He is the kind of guy, Miller says, that they don't make anymore: kind, gentlemanly, solid, unassuming—"a guy you would introduce to your mother." Krause and Miller help out with each other's bees and eat nearly every meal together whenever they attend the same beekeeping conference.

Once a year, as Miller drives from California via Wyoming to meet his bees in North Dakota, he and Krause go to Svilar's for a good steak. Then they head down the street to a bar "littered," Miller says with good-humored disdain, "with signed, framed pictures of dead liberals"—Roosevelt, Kennedy, even Truman. They end the night at Krause's house, where they feed the leftover steak to the dog and Miller crashes out in the guest bed. The next day, he continues on to North Dakota. Beekeepers, like bees, observe predictable rhythms, and the trip on the cusp of Miller's forty-sixth birthday was little different: steak, bar, doggy-bag, bed. Except this time, the car was faster. In the morning, he hopped back in the Corvette, and by nightfall he was in North Dakota. Another thousand miles, another day saved by the speedy sports car, one less calendar square crossed off on the march to death.

John Miller would probably agree if I said that the Corvette wasn't simply a way to go fast, or to intimidate other beekeepers, or to impress women. Rather, it was a symbol—a crude effort, as purchases made during midlife crises often are, but a symbol nonetheless: of a life unfettered, an existence unencumbered by bees and hives, by constant death, by protective suits

and smokers and pasture and comb and feeders and hive tools,
by semis and pallets and forklifts and other utilitarian vehicles.
The Corvette was not utilitarian in the least, although it handled
much more easily than a semi.

Semis are tippy and carry a lot of things. Sometimes they
carry supplies, like corn syrup to feed bees during fallow times,
and forklifts and pallets to lift them, and ropes and netting to
tie them down, and a case of honey "for goodwill at all times,"
Miller says. Sometimes they carry bees loaded four hives high,
which is too much for a flatbed but is stable enough on a drop-
deck trailer. Most of the time. In 2004, which was the first of a
series of bad years for John Miller, his brother Layne was driving a truck full of bees on Route 287 near Bear Trap Canyon
west of Bozeman, Montana, when he misjudged a curve, sloshed
side to side, and overturned—512 beehives, 60,000 bees per hive,
30.7 million bees smeared across the pavement. Layne's elbow
was scraped to the bone and he had to kick out the windshield
to escape. He was lucky, though, because some passing drivers
helped him out before the bees were fully aware of what had happened. He walked away with the injured arm and only twenty
stings. Soon the bees emerged from their hives and coated the
outside of the truck and its honey-slicked cargo so thickly that
you couldn't see the wreckage under all the layers of distressed
insects falling to the ground in big black gobs. It would be fourteen hours before a squad of emergency beekeepers could capture them, the road crew and firefighters could clear the wreck,
the state transportation department could clean up the last pools
of honey, and the road could reopen. Traffic returned to normal,
but the lives lost that day were beyond comprehension.

Miller likes to think he's equipped to handle death. If he
weren't a beekeeper, he says, he'd be a mortician, with a "black

suit and a synthetic smile." He knows how to deal with human mortality. When a neighbor dies, he is often moved to write eloquent if overwrought tributes. When a bee colony dies, though, he lacks the tools to describe his feelings. The loss is so profound. Many people believe that a beehive exists to support its queen—that social insects like bees are motivated by blind, cult-like devotion to a charismatic leader. But the queen also serves the hive, chasing some blind imperative to lay egg after egg, thousands a day, until the end of her productive life, at which point she is set upon and stung or ripped to death. The worker bees forage for supplies to keep the queen alive, but their first job is to care for the young. So really, they are tending to the future.

A typical beehive is a rectangular wooden box, usually painted white. The top of the box comes off, and that is the way beekeepers gain access to their bees, though they usually need a hive tool, a ten-inch, wedge-like steel implement that looks like a caveman's crowbar, to disengage the flat wooden top from all the gunk that has accumulated underneath. Within the body of the hive—also called the brood chamber—lie ten top bars, wooden strips that rest across the rimmed edges of the box and hold the frames, which are rectangular planes of wax comb that hang like folders in a file cabinet. Each frame is filled with hundreds of wax cells—small interconnected hexagons in which queens can lay eggs and worker bees can store honey and pollen. Because the frames aren't attached to each other or to the hive, the beekeeper can easily remove them one by one as a file clerk would remove a hanging folder, pulling the frames straight up and out of the hive to examine the bees or harvest honey. When a colony is healthy, the frames are teeming with thousands of bees, crawling and hatching and eating and working. The workers—the female bees who do all the cleaning, feeding, gathering, storing, and guarding—clamber over and under each other with purposeful direction; the paunchy drones—larger male bees whose sole task is to be available to impregnate a queen—wander around looking for handouts. Amid all this chaos, the queen sits like a rock star in a mosh pit, laying eggs, encircled by fawning workers who tend to her every need.

That's what a healthy colony looks like. But when a colony collapses—when the population dwindles, when the incubating larvae get too cold, when the workers expire in a huddled, fluttering mass inside the hive or crawl out the entrances to die away from home, and when the queen finally dies, too—then it is an entirely different scene: empty brood cells, scattered disheartened survivors, plundering robber bees and mice and wax moths, filth and rot and ruin and invasion and death creeping in, like a neighborhood abandoned to the junkies. And when that happens, the real tragedy is not simply the loss of 35,000 or 60,000 or even 80,000 insignificant and perhaps soulless individuals, but of the future—the colony's and Miller's. That sort of loss is harder to comprehend. It leaves Miller wordless or, more accurately, overflowing with words he is not supposed to use. The death of a hive is both mind-numbingly ordinary and mind-blowingly sad. How do you describe that sort of bereavement? It is not so easy.

🐝

PREMATURE DEATH IS NEVER PART OF A BEEKEEPER'S PLAN. Nonetheless, it is a way of life for him, because the best-laid plans are more like faint suggestions when your livelihood depends on the well-being of insects. We know this now. In the last half decade, a third of the national bee herd—about a million colonies—has died each year, often under mysterious circumstances. Miller is accustomed to losing bees on a large scale. "The insect kingdom enjoys little cell repair," he says. "Humans relate poorly to this truth." If a bee is sick, she doesn't get better. If she breaks a leg, it doesn't heal. If she ruptures her exoskeletal protection, she dries out and dies. If her wings are too worn to fly, she dies. Even when things are going well, a hive can lose a thousand bees a day as a matter of course. So each year, as wings and bodies wear out and one generation replaces the next, Miller oversees the deaths of billions of bees.

But the extent of these recent losses has defied even his insect-borne realism. It began, for him, in February 2005, soon after his bees awakened from a short winter dormancy to commence pollination season. He had trucked his fourteen thousand beehives from their winter quarters in the potato cellars of Idaho and unloaded them at his farm in Newcastle, California, as he does every winter. He'd left them alone for a few days while they dropped three months' worth of "yellow rain"—little mustard-colored spatters of bee feces that drizzle onto beekeeping suits and baseball caps and windshields and car finishes and take three runs through a car wash to remove. Then he'd delivered the bees to holding yards around Newcastle, and from there to the almond orchards in California's Central Valley, where he'd loaded their feeders with corn syrup and waited for the trees to blossom. They did, as they do every winter, right around Valentine's Day. But then a horrible thing happened: his bees did not rise to the occasion.

February is the moment commercial beekeepers wait for all winter, when 740,000 acres of almonds flower simultaneously in the Central Valley. Almond pollen is too heavy for the wind to transport, so the trees depend instead on such pollinators as bumblebees, ground- and twig-nesting bees, beetles, bats, and especially honey bees to introduce pollen to stigma, male to female, to create nuts. Three quarters of a million acres of blooming trees make a lot of flowers, too many for any ordinary local pollinator to visit, much less for the wild insects and birds that once lived full-time in the Central Valley but have been driven to near extinction by pesticides and habitat loss. Instead, almond farmers rely on beekeepers like John Miller, who descend with billions of hardworking bees to accomplish the onerous but glorious task of turning almond blossoms into nuts and thence into money. Most commercial beekeepers spend the whole year keeping their bees alive and healthy for this three-week pollination extravaganza. Miller does, anyhow. Farmers will pay up to two hundred dollars for a hive of bees to visit their blossoms, and with honey prices depressed, that's the way he counts on turning a profit. So February was the time when his bees were expected to invigorate not only the almonds, but also his bank accounts. His hives should have been singing with activity, plump brown bees working doggedly to carry pollen from blossom to blossom. Instead they emerged sluggish and wandered in drunken circles at the base of the hives, wingless, desiccated, blasé.

At the time, Miller had set himself the modest goal of "total global domination" of the beekeeping industry. His family's business was among the top twenty operations in America, and he was well on his way to meeting a five-year plan of expanding his hive count by 50 percent, to fifteen thousand. And then, suddenly, he wasn't. In a matter of weeks, Miller lost four thousand hives—somewhere around 150 million bees, about 40 percent of his operation. He wasn't the only one. Some of his colleagues lost more than 60 percent of their hives. It didn't seem to matter whose bees they were, how they'd been nurtured, or where they came from: "the population just cratered." There was nothing for a beekeeper to do but throw up his hands, take out another loan, and start again. It was, Miller says, a "profound collapse."

Still, nobody outside the bee world really seemed to notice the frightening decline in the nation's herd until late 2006, when a Pennsylvania beekeeper named Dave Hackenberg lost more than two thirds of his bees. One day in November 2006—November 12, to be specific—Hackenberg, a gangly, dark-haired man with a weathered face and a pronouncedly beaky proboscis, went to move 400 hives he had left on a gravel lot south of Tampa, Florida, and found 360 of them oddly empty. Full of honey, yes, and wax and honeycomb and brood—bees in various stages of development from egg to nearly imperceptible worm to white bee-like mass to baby bee. All that was left in most of them was a lonely, unattended queen and a clutch of attendants roaming the empty hives—just a pocketful, a cup of bees, not the teeming garbage-bin-sized load he expected. There were hardly any adult bees to be found. Nor could Hackenberg detect any sign of the opportunists who might under normal circumstances be expected to raid the honey stores of collapsed colonies: no robber bees, no wax moths, no hive beetles. There weren't even any dead bees at the entrance to the hives. The entire adult population of the colony had simply flown out en masse and vanished.

Bees don't do that. They are creatures of routine, sticklers for order. Their short lives revolve around tending and cleaning and feeding the queen and the young. Bees are single-minded. They do not ditch their queen just because they feel like it. They do not get restless and leave their young. They do not go on flights of fancy. They do not enroll in semesters abroad on a whim or grow dreadlocks or get tattoos or go on extended vacations. They do their jobs. When they leave the hive, it's a short-haul commute. They venture to flowering trees or bushes or flowers that may be a few yards away or a mile or two or even three, but they stay close enough that they can make it back with the pollen and nectar they collect to help sustain the hive. They don't linger on the job. They gather their bounty and hightail it—"beeline" it—home. They are predictable, reliable. They are, in short, not in the business of wandering off for no apparent reason. And yet, in late 2006 and 2007 and again in the winter of 2008, that's exactly what they did. The strange disappearances left many of Hackenberg's apiaries almost completely devoid of adult bees. The hives did not appear outwardly diseased; rather they waited, fully stocked with pollen, honey, and larvae—like ghost ships—for their inhabitants to return. But the bees never came back.

Perhaps that's why the world was so taken with the mass collapse of 2007. It was creepy. Hackenberg was the first to witness and report a loss, but others soon followed. The scientific community initially gave the strange new malady the name "Fall Dwindle Disease," but as fall turned to winter and winter to spring, and as beekeepers across the country and then the world began to report similar inexplicable losses, they renamed it Colony Collapse Disorder, or CCD. More than a third of the nation's hives collapsed in thirty-six states, and losses were reported in parts of Europe, India, and Brazil as well. Some beekeepers saw up to 90 percent of their colonies fail that year and the next. Hackenberg lost 2,000 of the 2,900 hives he had shipped to Florida that year.

Still, it wasn't, after all was said and done, much worse than the die-off of 2005, when John Miller and many of his colleagues lost lots of bees. What was different was that the disease looked like nothing anyone had ever seen. Not Hackenberg in his forty-five years of beekeeping; not John Miller, whose family had been keeping bees for four generations; not the army of entomologists and geneticists and nutritionists and agricultural extension agents called in to investigate the problem. There is nothing like a calamitous mystery to pique the interest of the public. After years of invisibility, beekeeping had become suddenly, exquisitely interesting. Newspapers, magazines, and websites reported every theory bandied about to explain the puzzling malady, from pesticides to bad weather to bad corn syrup to high-voltage electric transmission lines to cordless phones to various viruses, bacteria, and fungi to the first sign of the coming "rapture," when worthy souls—like bees—would be recalled to heaven.

When reporters called Miller for quotes, however—which they often do, because he gives awfully good ones—he usually let them down. He placed the blame for CCD on a related disorder he called "PPM," shorthand for "piss-poor management," or "PPB," for "piss-poor beekeeping"; some variation of the acronym swept through the beekeeping community as quickly as the disease itself. Miller believed that the afflicted beekeepers simply hadn't taken good enough care of their bees. And that's what he told the clamoring media.

I sympathized with the disappointed press corps. I was working on a magazine article about John Miller, one that had been in the works long before CCD had arrived, and I admit it would have been wonderfully convenient for my purposes had his bees disappeared as well. But that winter wasn't shaping up to be a particularly bad one for Miller—no worse than normal, anyhow. Millions of his bees died, because that's what bees do these days. But they did not disappear in romantic and disturbing ways. They just died, en masse, of various ailments, as they had every year since Miller's miserable February of 2005. I kept emailing him, hoping he'd report something terrible. He kept emailing back, offering me the latest beekeeper gossip—blaming genetically modified corn syrup for the deaths, or a new strain of an old fungal infection, or, most likely, a massive dose of PPM. Then Miller would change the subject to something far more interesting to him, like a dying neighbor, or a new truck.

JOHN MILLER LIKES TO EMAIL. HE ALSO LIKES TO PONTIFI-cate, joke, write, say incendiary things, tell stories, drip with sarcasm. Most of all, he likes to talk. The first time I spoke with him, in 2004, I phoned him for an article about Honey Stinger, a honey-based energy gel company in which he is a partner (along with Tour de France champion Lance Armstrong, who became an owner of the company in 2010). Miller told me he had been up all night for nearly two weeks straight, moving bees into almond orchards in California. "We all need to take a nap," he said. That sounded worth a follow-up, so I called him again and asked him a few questions about his work. We spoke for an hour and a half, and I sent him an email thanking him. He responded not long afterward. It was a surprising email, written in stanza form, and I kept it, because it was funny and also somehow touching. I realized that I had stumbled onto someone who had taken an unusual and thorny route through life, someone who cared passionately about something strange and had a talent for expressing it. I had, perhaps, crossed paths with the email poet laureate of the beekeeping profession. I pasted his missive into a file, and later the next one, and eventually accrued hundreds of pages of free-verse emails that, in aggregate, form something of an epic poem—an Arial ten-point ode of Homeric proportions.

"I am Mormon; though I only have one wife," he wrote in his first email, and he continued:

I have taken public speaking courses.

I am a Toastmaster of some rank, though no longer a member.

I believe, but am not sure, I am the only subscriber in this industry to the Wall Street Journal, Harvard Business Review, and Fast Company Magazine.

This does not make me better than anyone else.

It does not make me worse than anyone else, either.

I am curious, and probably read a bit more than the average bee guy.

I spend 300 days a year outside, so my idea of camping is

mid-town, say the Drake, 17th floor, room-service. THAT IS CAMPING!

no bugs, no sleeping under the truck in a sleeping bag.

When I get out of the bee yard, I want OUT of the bee yard.

I like speaking to bee guys, and I think I have something to say to them. . . .

Beekeeping, he concluded, is

a mystery to me, and I love talking about it.

People are always willing to listen to a fool, for some length of time,

just for the entertainment value.

I owned you for an hour and a half the other day . . .
see?!

He did. He had. I booked a ticket and in February 2006 flew
from my home in Colorado to visit him as the California almond bloom unfurled toward its peak. He picked me up in the
Corvette. The car was well loved and well kept, even though it
was seven years old by then. It rode smoothly and close to the
ground. We drove not much faster than anyone else—this being California and the highways being clogged with cars—from
the Sacramento airport east to his home in Newcastle, where
the Central Valley begins its slow ascent toward the Sierras. The
house perched on a green hill overlooking three acres of mandarin groves and below them a few aluminum outbuildings, a fleet
of trucks and forklifts and syrup tanks in various stages of ob-
solescence, a U-shaped assembly of trailers and modular homes
for employees, and hundreds of rectangular white bee boxes
grouped and stacked hither and thither, what Miller described as
a "mad Jed Clampett scene." "Bee guys," he says, "shouldn't be
allowed to own property."

Such an assessment is not entirely fair to him, and certainly
not to his wife, because his house was spotless, a model of order.
It was still newish, with lots of windows and white furniture,
walls adorned with family photos, impressionistic landscape
paintings, and one blue-eyed, slightly angry Jesus illuminated in
gray-edged clouds. We got there in time for supper with friends
from church and Bill Miller, no relation to John, but rather the
father of Alan Miller, a high school beau of Jenny Miller—John's
daughter. Bill was soft-spoken and recently divorced, and he
was there not only for dinner and fellowship, but also to buy
the Corvette.

It was time for John Miller to move on. ("Three years passed, and I hadn't had a speeding ticket," he wrote. "What's the point of owning a fast car?") We're not sure if Bill Miller took the car home that night. I like to think he did. John Miller's wife, Jan, is pretty sure he didn't. Jan is a slender, fit, and quietly agreeable microbiology teacher with auburn hair and big, astonished-looking blue eyes. She grew up in Blackfoot, Idaho, with John. They knew each other in high school, though they ran in different crowds. They started dating when they were twenty-two, and both agree that "he hasn't grown up any since." Jan tolerates her husband with amused exasperation—"sometimes amused, consistently exasperated," Miller says. She keeps a clean kitchen and if my estimation is right, she is the one who tracks family details, so she is probably correct that they sold the car a few days later. John Miller neither remembers nor cares, but he's not afraid of a little embellishment, so he won't mind if I conclude that the car did go home with Bill Miller that night—and so I was there for a passage in John Miller's life, a small player in his large story.

It's a good thing to be part of John Miller's story, because he tells it well. Miller is smart and engaged, a master of details. He remembers everything, though not always as it actually happened. He is also very funny—even in the face of the many unfunny things that happen to a beekeeper these days. Bob Koehnen, a queen-rearer and almond farmer who is not terribly funny but is very friendly and sturdy and thorough, once said to me that he didn't know how John Miller could have a sense of humor when so many things in his business are not humorous at all. Yet he does. The wit is mordant; the humor gallows. He jokes and "yarns" and speaks out and joins boards and cares for the future of his industry, but most of all he cares about the loyal, industrious, sometimes violent, always fragile insects that die by the dozens every time he opens a hive. He doesn't mind making a fool of himself to make that point: "I am the blabber-mouth you've been seeking," he told me.

Miller was born in 1954. He has a pointed nose, quizzical arched eyebrows, an orderly crown of receding salt-and-pepper hair, a reassuringly sonorous, Jimmy Stewart–like voice, and an eternally bemused expression. He is a fallen Mormon, and it is agreed in his family that he won't take the sacrament when it is offered, because he has a lot of work to do before he ascends to Latter-day Sainthood. For starters, he often uses "cowboy words," especially when he gets stung, which is a daily event for him, although each time it happens—as much as fifty times on a bad day—he seems somehow affronted. He has also been known, at times in his life, to down a supertanker of coffee or a six-pack of Coors Light in a sitting—vices forbidden by his church. He isn't proud of it. "Church," he likes to say, "is for sinners," and his frequent mutinies make him all the more deter-mined to reform. Still, reverence is not his thing.

If he isn't the picture of a perfect, observant Mormon, neither does he look the part of the traditional flannel-and-rubbers-clad beekeeper. His usual uniform includes surf shorts, a baseball cap, running shoes, and a footrace souvenir T-shirt. He has run twenty-five marathons. His four kids—two boys, two girls—are grown and starting their own families, and some of them run races with him. None plans to be a beekeeper; they're too sen-sible for that. Miller's oldest son works for Apple in Silicon Val-ley; one daughter trained as a nurse, another as an accountant; his youngest son recently finished his Mormon mission and is contemplating law school. Miller suspects, and Jan agrees, that all four have surpassed him on the maturity front, the decision to forgo a life in beekeeping being one sure sign of a more evolved state. If you looked at a family tree, he says, he'd fall closer to the Neanderthals; his kids fall closer to Jan.

Miller is wiry, though middle age has thickened him slightly around the waist. He never stands still; he veritably bounces. He gets excited about lots of things. He gets excited every time he pries the top off a beehive. He got excited about the BEEKEEPERS FOR OBAMA pin he'd bought at a charity auction, even though— or precisely because—he didn't support Obama in the least. He gets excited when people he knows are in the news. When he comes across their names, he mails them copies of the articles with a self-addressed envelope, to be signed and mailed back. He gets ideas, and he gets excited about them, and then he starts calling other people to get them excited, too. He wants all the bee advocacy groups to talk to each other. He wants beehives at the White House. He wants his employees to do things differently. Sometimes his ideas are good ones. Sometimes they wreak havoc. He likes that, too.

He loves spreadsheets—loves them. If he were a mortician, he would log all the pallbearers into a database—he is serious about this because, remember, he feels strongly about death, but also because he believes that "numbers matter." He keeps detailed records for every bee yard—spreadsheets galore—and knows the exact bloom date for every type of plant his bees visit. He knows all his friends' phone numbers by heart. He loves his friends. A few years ago, Miller bought an old grocery store in his North Dakota summer hometown and turned the space into Miller Honey's False Hope Gym, stocking it with exercise equipment and leaving it open 24/7 for the locals to use, no fees required. He believes in lost causes.

He is not patient. He often disappears without goodbyes. He

rarely sits through a church service or a party or a beekeeping meeting without an abrupt and unexplained departure and return. He can be very, very peevish. He relishes saying things that make you cringe. He likes you to be complicit in his fun. Even un-fun things can sound fun when he describes them.

Although he disapproves of dying, Miller doesn't wear a seat belt. He once flipped a ten-wheeler on Interstate 80 in California, just west of the Riverside exit, a couple of days after Christmas. It was full of corn syrup meant to keep his bees alive until the almonds bloomed. A kid in "a hulk of an old Camaro" who had just repaired his brakes—or tried to—passed Miller's truck. Just as Miller said to himself, "piece of junk," the kid put on the brakes and nothing happened. He went thisaway and thataway across the freeway in front of Miller, and then the Camaro's tires popped and the car came screaming crossways to hit Miller's ten-wheeler behind the spindle on the front axle. The steering wheel spun out of Miller's hands, the front axle went airborne, and when it landed the truck commenced an elegant 180, tipped over, and sheared the straps that held a thousand-gallon tank of syrup on the back. The tank rolled down the highway like a bowling ball and lodged against a guardrail. The steering column and shifting tower pushed past the dashboard into the spot where Miller would have been sitting had he been wearing a seat belt. Because he wasn't, he was thrown to the floor between the seats as the cab crumpled to a space just large enough to fit a "fat, bald guy," as he likes to describe himself—although he is not fat at all and not entirely bald yet.

Miller sat there, in the hive-like cavity of his crumpled cab, contemplating the unfavorable aspect of things. The state troopers were not going to be happy with him. The highway department would have to shut the road and sand down the slick of

corn syrup to prevent further carnage. Miller would have to replace a $45,000 truck and pay an extra $1,200 for enough corn
syrup to get the bees through the month. It was winter, and
there was nothing in bloom, and there wasn't enough honey to
keep his bees alive until the almonds came into flower. There
were orchards to visit and hives to place and pollen patties to
lay. He had a whole lot of bees to feed before he was to leave on
a Caribbean cruise four days later, one of the very few vacations
he and his family had taken in all his years as a professional beekeeper. So here is what this particular brush with destiny taught
him: never, ever wear a seat belt.

YET NO ONE SHOULD WEAR THEM MORE, BECAUSE AS A MI-
gratory beekeeper he is on the road more often than not. The
American Beekeeping Federation estimates that there are probably 1,200 other roaming bee guys in the United States—like
Larry Krause, Miller's friend in Wyoming, and Dave Hackenberg, who first noticed the symptoms of CCD. It is a profession
uniquely suited to the diversity of the American landscape, the
bigness of American agriculture and industry, and the restless-
ness of the American people. Like retirees in Winnebagos, migratory beekeepers winter in warm places—California, Texas,
Florida—and in summer head north to the clover and alfalfa
fields of the Dakotas and other rural, northern states. Miller likes
to call the annual flight of the beekeepers the "native migrant
tour," because he and his colleagues are among the few migrant
agricultural workers these days who were born in this country,
and he likes to call himself the tour's "padrone"—because, well,
there's no one within earshot to disagree. If traditional beekeepers are like European bees, single-minded and docile, migratory

beekeepers might better be compared to Africanized "killer" bees—itinerant and aggressive, traveling in swarms.

Miller is not the biggest beekeeper in the United States— South Dakota's Richard Adee, with his eighty thousand hives, wins that distinction. But like the gentle, dark Carniolan bees he tends, Miller does have impeccable breeding. He is descended from Nephi Ephraim Miller, a Mormon farmer known as the "father of migratory beekeeping." In 1894, N.E., as he was called, traded a few bushels of oats for seven boxes of bees and parlayed those seven boxes into a Utah beekeeping empire. "He was curious," Miller says. "He was a gifted man, and he grew to understand the honey bee." N. E. Miller pioneered the practice of migratory beekeeping, shipping his hives from the clover fields of Utah to the orange groves of California each winter, and he is famed for producing the nation's first million-pound crop of honey. His sons and grandsons and great-grandsons followed in his footsteps, as have most of today's commercial beekeepers, hoisting hundred-pound hives onto pallets and pallets onto semis that chase honey flows and pollination contracts north and south across the country.

Bees organize their lives around seasons of plenty and want. So does Miller. Like his bees, he is frequently on the move, his life a series of numbers- and date-driven bursts of activity. Winter is a time of quiet, of loss, when bees cluster for survival in the hives, some stored near his home in Newcastle and some in leased potato cellars in Idaho, where 40-degree temperatures and well-ventilated darkness ensure a brief period of dormancy for the bees, to reserve their energy for the coming spring. Miller too hunkers with his family over the holidays, preparing for the busy year to come.

Spring is a time of bustle, birth, rebuilding. It starts early for

Miller and his bees. On January 19, he inspects and feeds the 2,700 hives he has stashed in fields and clearings near his house in Newcastle. On January 20, he begins shipping the rest of his bees—7,000 or so hives—from the Idaho cellars to California. From January 26 through the first two weeks of February, he roams a two-hundred-mile range from south of Modesto to north of Chico, placing colonies in almond orchards. During that time, he visits lots of taco wagons. On March 1, the bloom peaks, and from March 9 to 13, almond farmers "release" the bees that have been placed on their property from their con-tractual obligation, and Miller is free to take them away. He's got to get them out fast then, or risk their starvation in the now-blossomless desert of the orchards and exposure to the variety of agricultural pesticides loosed on the Central Valley in spring. Pollinating crops is like being a hooker, Miller says: "I come in the night; I wear a veil; they give me their money; a few weeks later they call me and tell me to get out of there."

So he does. In late March, he ships 3,000 or so hives home to Newcastle to prepare them to receive new queens; 3,000 travel to Washington to pollinate the pink lady apples; 1,600 go to the cherries around Stockton. On April 2, he divides his Newcastle hives and buys new queens for them; on April 5 the Stockton bees leave the cherries for Newcastle, where they too receive new queens. On May 5 he ships his apple bees from Washing-ton to Gackle, North Dakota, his summer home, for the honey season. On May 10 he flies there, too, and plants a garden in the backyard of his summer home. As he plants, he assesses the promise of the northern spring: the subsoil and topsoil moisture levels, how warm the dirt is, the blooming of the lilacs next to the garden, the early health of the honey locust and apple trees nearby. He notices if the spring wheat has been sowed on surrounding farms, and for how long. This tells him how much supplementary feed he may need to keep his bees alive until the clover starts blooming in late June. By then all of his bees will have arrived in North Dakota. He will stay there for the summer, with brief visits home to see his wife in California.

The summer is a season of bounty, harvest, work. The honey-producing season begins June 20. The first crop is yellow sweet clover, whose flow typically coincides with the first big mosquito hatch. When the mosquitoes become obnoxious, Miller knows the clover is set to bloom. Yellow sweet clover usually blooms a few days before the alfalfa and peaks around July 4, when, if the weather has been auspicious, it can be truck-mirror high. The white sweet clover peaks ten days later. The dairy guys cut down their first alfalfa crop before the end of June; beef guys, looking for more tonnage, wait until the first week of July. Miller likes beef guys, because he prefers flowers over shorn and useless stalks. If the rains are good and the stars align, there may be a second crop of alfalfa, peaking from late July to August 4—but a smart beekeeper should never bank his honey crop on a second alfalfa bloom, because there's no guarantee that by July 15 the flowers won't be scorched. After the clover and alfalfa go, there's buckwheat and gumweed, which make darker honey, and goldenrod.

August 20 marks the end of honey production. In a good year, Miller may wait until after Labor Day to begin "robbing" his harvest boxes, which are shallow wooden rectangles stacked two or three high above the main body of the hive. Those harvest "supers" contain all of the honey bound for sale. The stores in the double-deep main hive chamber at the bottom of the stack, where the queen lays her eggs, are for feeding future bees—that honey is always left alone. Bad years, he may start stripping the harvest boxes as early as August 15. The goal is to have all the salable honey off the hives between September 25 and October 5. By the autumnal equinox, around September 21, the first hives will be loaded into trucks bound for Idaho, where they will sit in big holding yards and wait until daytime temperatures drop to around 45 degrees. It takes eight weeks for Miller's crews to get all the hives out of North Dakota. By November 25, they're all in Idaho, where it's finally cold enough for the bees to go "to bed"—hunker down in the climate-controlled potato cellars. A smaller batch of bees is sent to Newcastle, where they get another feed before dormancy. And then, on January 25, the almonds begin to bud and the year starts again.

This annual bee migration isn't just a curiosity; it's the glue that holds much of our agricultural system together. Without the bees' pollination services, many of our nation's crops would produce only a small fraction of the harvest they generate with the help of the honey bee. Farmers depend on honey bees to pollinate ninety different fruits and vegetables, from almonds to lettuce to cranberries to blueberries to canola—nearly $15 billion worth of crops a year. Although wind and wild insects pollinate some plants on a small scale, only bees promise the levels of production needed to meet the needs of the nation's grocery shoppers. Like every aspect of American agriculture, beekeeping has, by necessity, joined the global economy of scale. Bees are pollination machines, and many of America's farmers need them just as much as they need their tractors, threshers, and combines. For problems with water, labor, pest control, and soil quality, there are irrigation systems, big machines, pesticides, and synthetic fertilizers. Today the biggest factor limiting the amount of produce grown is, for many crops, the number of bees available.

"To make a prairie it takes a clover and one bee," Emily Dickinson wrote.

> *One clover, and a bee,*
> *And revery.*
> *The revery alone will do,*
> *If bees are few.*

She could not have anticipated the state of apiculture today. It is no longer so simple as bee, flower, honey. The millions of acres of intensely and singularly planted crops at the center of the American agribusiness machine simply cannot produce without the help of the beekeepers' pollinating army. Without the itinerant bee and the migratory beekeeper, we would have to forsake one in every three bites of each summer's harvest. We would say goodbye to many of the most delectable piles of fruits and vegetables at the supermarket. Without the honey bee, the American diet would be a far more lackluster affair.

But without the honey bee, John Miller's life would be a far more agreeable affair. Since he was a young man, he has left his wife and children for eight or so months each year, keeping company with a rotating cast of migrant workers, farmers, landowners, and beekeepers. Even before the calamities that began in 2005, the keeping of bees could be likened to a continuous economic and natural disaster: infections rage, queens die, droughts wither, semis jackknife, equipment rots, prices plummet, competitors undercut, employees disappoint, bankers demand, neighbors complain, vandals, bears, and skunks raid. Miller's income is uncertain, his predicaments constant.

In the century since N. E. Miller ushered in beekeeping's industrial revolution, the occupation has become commercialized,

rationalized, and preposterously complicated. John Miller's bees
ply some of the same fields that hosted his great-grandfather's
hives. He sells his honey on a handshake to the same proces-
sors his grandfather sold to and competes with the sons of the
very same men his father competed against. But the business
of beekeeping today requires more than just a comprehension
of bees. It also requires a command of botany and molecular
biology and chemistry and genomics and meteorology and aca-
rology and accounting and immigration law and truck-buying
and truck-driving and truck-fixing and marketing and public
relations. Where N.E. used trains and telegraphs to conduct
his business, John Miller's tools are now semitrucks and email,
spreadsheets and amortization schedules. Where Nephi made
his income from honey, Miller now derives his profit from pollination fees.

Nor could Nephi have anticipated the kind of nationwide,
devastating losses that John Miller and his colleagues have
experienced. In 1990, there were 3.3 million bee colonies; in
2006, fewer than 2.5 million remained. In the wild, honey
bees have disappeared entirely. The unschooled public tends
to think the recent apiary apocalypse began in 2006. In reality,
it started twenty years before that. Bees have been on life
support for decades now, kept aloft only by the efforts of
determined—perhaps imprudent—men like John Miller. "The
past twenty years have been the most tumultuous years in the
history of man's relationship with bees," Miller says; the past
five, a bloodletting.

> *It's true for bees as it is for human beings:*
> *Life brings sickness with it. You can see*
> *The signs of it in the bees, without any doubt:*

Their color changes as soon as they fall ill;
Their bodies are all disheveled and there's a dreadful
Emaciation in the look of them;
And then you can see the other bees as they carry
Out from the dwelling places the bodies of those
From whom the life has gone; and you can see
The sick ones not yet dead that hang almost
Motionless around the doors outside,
With crossed and tangled feet; or still inside,
Listless with hunger and shrunken from the cold.
And then you can hear a mournful long drawn-out
Whispering rustling sound like the sound of the cold
South Wind as it murmurs in the woods, or like
The agitated hissing of the sea
As the waves draw back, or the seething noise of a fire
Eating its way as it burns inside a furnace.

Virgil wrote this, not John Miller. Bees have been dying since bees have been living. Miller has labored to keep his bees healthy in the face of various parasites and pathogens for years. But in that fateful February of 2005, he realized that the job description of a beekeeper had changed inalterably. He was no longer a mere keeper of bees. He was steward and shepherd of a species teetering on the edge of survival. Not even a Corvette can make you feel better about that.

Chapter Two
....
Beekeepers' Roulette

IF YOU SPEND ANY TIME WITH JOHN MILLER, YOU WILL SPEND much of it in cars. Or rather, trucks—big trucks: two-ton Fords, and 515-horsepower Freightliner Cascadias, and lately, against his every inclination, an un-American Toyota Tacoma (the "yoda," he calls it), which he bought with patriotic reluctance but calls "the finest pickup I have ever owned." When he backs into a ditch to catch a swarm, he knows that if he's driving his Toyota, his "little black mamba," he'll get out. It can also do airport pickups. In January 2009, Miller picked me up at the Sacramento airport in his black Toyota, a stash of almonds, mandarins, and Honey Stinger bars tucked in the console to keep us going. We sped due west, heading to the annual American Beekeeping Federation conference in Reno. There, Miller told me, "twelve hundred of the least competent people in America" would gather to discuss their role as gatekeepers of America's food supply and contemplate why their bees are dying. We climbed through steep snow-clogged river valleys, topping out among the genteel granite crags of the high Sierras, then raced down through towering conifers and the foothills' stunted shrubs to a russet desert and a boxy city. We pulled off the highway straight into the parking lot of John Ascuaga's Nugget, a monstrous casino and convention center that covers an entire city block. The parking lot was full of other beekeeping outfits; Miller could identify each owner by his rig. "There's Krause's truck!" he said. We parked right beside Miller's good friend and headed to the conference.

Inside, we rode an escalator away from the slot machines, music, flashing lights and bells and beeps, emerging into a cavernous conference hall with movable walls and a bold-patterned carpet. The beekeepers sat on folding chairs, wearing plaid shirts and baseball caps, looking alternately bored and befuddled as one skinny scientist after another spoke of mitochondria and morphology, single nucleotide polymorphisms and marker-assisted selection. Miller wore a bee-striped polo shirt and rarely managed to sit through more than one presentation at a time, disappearing into the hallway and reappearing five or twenty minutes later. Others lasted longer, staring bleary-eyed at the PowerPoints, listening politely to a diminutive Croatian who spoke of bee "dee-arrhea."

In the hallway, beekeepers hovered, chatting. Zoologist Karl von Frisch discovered some fifty years ago that bees return to the hive to perform a "waggle dance" communicating the location of nearby flowers. Beekeepers go to conferences for similar reasons—to share essential information about the bounty that might be expected from the blooms. They don't often dance, at least not well; but they talk. Incessantly. "We swap canning tips and recipes," Miller jokes, though they don't. What they do is trade gossip, debate the merits of orange or red hive tools, and compare balance sheets, hive losses, pollination fees, and honey prices. They pay too much for honey at the silent auction. They buy raffle tickets from the wholesome, if less than glamorous, "honey princesses" who wander the halls in skirt suits and shoulder sashes. Both the princesses and the bee guys looked terribly out of place at the Nugget, a monument to artifice and quick cash—quick cash has never been a defining characteristic of the beekeeping profession. And beekeepers work outside. In the enormous Nugget you could spend the entire convention without once exiting the climate-controlled interior.

✦

BEING TERRIBLY OUT OF PLACE IS NOT A NEW EXPERIENCE for beekeepers in this country. Honey bees are not, after all, native to North America, and neither are beekeepers. The nation's first bees and beekeepers came from England around 1620 on the same boats that brought the nation's first colonists and their crops, as much a tool of European conquest as the muskets, microorganisms, and ambitions that also debarked from the settlers' ships. The insects did fine—did great—in their new environment, taking to the wooded eastern forests with aplomb. Escaped swarms spread quickly across the frontier, working their way westward toward the Great Plains at a rate of forty or so miles a year. "The bees have generally extended themselves into the country a little in advance of the settlers," Thomas Jefferson wrote in 1788. "The Indians, therefore, call them the 'white man's fly,' and consider their approach as indicating the approach of the settlement of the whites." Domesticated since before the Egyptians built their first pyramid, bees have traveled the paths of human migration over the millennia from Africa to Europe and Asia, then to North America, thriving wherever they went. No surprise then, that the New World proved an entirely agreeable place for the European honey bee.

The European beekeeper, on the other hand, found the going rougher. The first recorded professional apiarist on American shores was a man named John Eales. He was induced to move from Hingham, Massachusetts, north to Newbury in 1644, according to local court papers, to run a communal apiary, "with ye expectation of his doing service which the Towne was not acquainted with." By 1645, he was also among the town's first recorded paupers. "Being found unable to get his living," he was remanded to the town's constable "until this Courte sh'ld determine the waye to dispose of him." After some deliberation, a judge determined that Eales "should be placed in some convenient place where he may be implied in his trade of beehive making, etc.; and ye Towne of Newbury to make up what his work wanteth of defraying ye charge of his livelyhoode." Eales was the first known American beekeeper to lose his shirt; he certainly wasn't the last. "It takes longer to go broke keeping bees than in any other business," John Miller says—he stole that maxim from another California beekeeper. Yet it didn't take Eales long at all.

Miller's banker once told him that a beekeeper should be prepared to fail two out of every seven years. That's today, with all of our modern technologies and economies of scale. It was even easier to go broke a couple of centuries ago. Beekeeping had been, in its first two and a half centuries on the American continent, a cottage industry and a sideline. Farmers bartered crops for bees and traded or sold what little surplus honey they couldn't use. They didn't dream of making a living from it. That changed, however, after a talented but melancholic minister from Andover, Massachusetts, got into the business. Lorenzo Lorraine Langstroth was born in 1810. Dignified, with a broad, open face and a shock of thick hair, he developed a love of insects early, studying the movements of ants on the ground until, he wrote, he wore out the knees of his pants. In 1833 he took up beekeeping, in part to help with his "head troubles," serious jags of depression and "hysterical muteness"—most likely bipolar disorder—from which he suffered his entire life. He acquired a colony in a log hive, and then another, and another, and soon had hundreds and was spending every spare moment caring for and observing his bees.

It was not a propitious time to take up beekeeping. The nation's hives had been besieged by a mottled grayish brown pest called the wax moth, whose larvae fed on wax comb and hive debris and left behind a sticky white web of discarded cocoon shells and a sickly-sweet smell of rot. The bees were also increasingly at the mercy of a deadly new bacterial disease called American foulbrood, which killed young larvae and was highly infectious in hives. There was, moreover, no easy way to rid colonies of such pests and pathogens, because at the time, even the typical activities of beekeeping exacted a dismal toll. Most beekeepers still used traditional round straw skep baskets or hollowed-out log "gums," and they could not open their hives to examine the colonies without destroying vast sections of comb. The only way for a beekeeper to collect honey was to cut the comb out of the hive and in the process kill its bees. The only way to increase his colony count was to build a strong colony with lots of healthy workers, and then capture a natural swarm of bees as it departed the hive to find a less crowded home. By the time Langstroth came along, scores of observers, from Aristotle to Columella to Virgil, had described the life of the honey bee. Still, Langstroth wrote, "the interior of a hive was to common observers a profound mystery," and this ignorance compounded beekeepers' problems.

Hoping to do better with his own bees, Langstroth began reading. He quickly concluded that there were no American beekeeping manuals worth examining and so turned to the Europeans. He read Charles Butler, England's "father of bee-keeping," whose *Feminine Monarchie* was the first full-length beekeeping guide written in the English language, and who was among the first to posit that the large bee that controlled the hive was female. He read the seventeenth-century Dutch biologist Jan Swammerdam, who spent every daylight hour for five years examining his bees, "all the while exposed in the open air to the scorching heat of the sun, bareheaded, for fear of intercepting his sight." Swammerdam's exhaustive treatise *Historia Insectorum Generalis* featured the first near-perfect drawings of bee anatomy and "proved so fatiguing a performance, that Swammerdam never afterwards recovered even the appearance of his former health and vigor." The book was published posthumously in 1737.

Langstroth then turned to more contemporary musings. He learned about François Huber, a blind French scientist who, with the help of devoted servant François Burnens, carried out a number of experiments to divine the mysteries of the bee. In 1789 Huber designed a "leaf hive" with frames that opened like the pages of a book, the first beehive that allowed observation of the interior of a colony without requiring its total destruction. He read the Englishman Edward Bevan, whose classic 1827 text described a hive with multiple honey boxes stacked atop it. He read Johann Dzierzon, a Silesian pastor who, in the 1840s, contrived a hive design that featured removable honeycombs supported by grooves in the hive's side walls. With increased command over his combs, Dzierzon was able to increase his stock to 360 hives and produce six thousand pounds of honey in one season, despite "frequent reverses"—theft, fire, flood, and a fatal attack of foulbrood.

Dzierzon's and Huber's and Bevan's leaf and top-bar designs were vast improvements on the traditional skeps and gums. But they still required significant mangling of comb in order to break the frames apart. Without a better hive, Langstroth believed, beekeepers would be "unable to remedy many of the perplexing casualties to which bee-keeping is liable." A better hive would minimize damage to combs when beekeepers inspected the bees and harvested honey, improving bees' survival and beekeepers' economic viability. "In short, I felt satisfied that beekeeping could be made highly profitable, and as much a matter of certainty, as most branches of rural economy." Langstroth decided to design his own hive.

To allow access to a colony without destroying honeycomb, Langstroth needed to prevent the bees from attaching comb to the hive's sides, top, and bottom. Bees, he had come to understand, were exacting creatures: they left a specific gap—three-eighths of an inch, to be precise—for flying and maneuvering between combs. If the space was narrower than a fifth of an inch, they would fill it with propolis—a sticky, resinous substance collected from tree buds and sap, which bees use to fill small gaps and seal and reinforce their hives. If the space was wider, they would bridge it with additional honeycomb. He termed that ideal gap "bee space," and mulled how to design a hive that would incorporate it throughout. One afternoon in 1851, he found his answer:

> *Returning late in the afternoon from the apiary which*
> *I had established some two miles from my city home,*
> *and pondering, as I have so often done before, how I*
> *could get rid of the disagreeable necessity of cutting*

the attachments of the combs from the walls of the hives . . . the almost self-evident idea of using the same bee-space . . . came into my mind, and in a moment the suspended movable frames, kept at a suitable distance from each other and the case containing them, came into being. Seeing by intuition, as it were, the end from the beginning, I could scarcely refrain from shouting out my "Eureka" in the open streets.

Langstroth promptly filed a patent. His improved hive is little different from the rectangular white box with hanging frames that beekeepers use today. Among the long list of advantages offered by his simple invention, beekeepers could take out and examine the combs "at pleasure" to look for moths and destroy moth larvae, and "permit the surplus honey to be taken away, in the most convenient, beautiful, and salable forms." They could remove old, tattered combs and furnish empty combs to allow bees to focus their energies on the production of honey rather than wax. They could move their hives more easily to follow pollen flows and protect them against heat and cold. Langstroth's new hive also made it easy for beekeepers to divide one hive into two or three when the bees were preparing to swarm, increasing their numbers and preventing productive colonies from flying off. And they could do so without angering the bees. "Many persons have been unable to suppress their astonishment," he boasted, "as they have seen me opening hive after hive, removing the combs covered with bees, and shaking them off in front of the hives; forming new swarms, exhibiting the queen, transferring the bees with all their stores to another hive; and in short, dealing with them as if they were as harmless as flies."

In 1853, he published *The Hive and the Honey-Bee,* which

described the benefits of his hive and provided practical advice on bee management. The book is still in print. After millennia of uneasy domestication, Langstroth's invention promised to transform the beehive into a fungible unit of production, rendering bees as tame as any other farm animal. His hive endowed the bee—or rather, its keeper—with a level of control and mobility that transformed the hive into an implement of modern agriculture. "It must be manifest to every reflecting mind," he wrote, "that the Creator intended the bee, as truly as the horse or the cow, for the comfort of man."

But even such an enormous technological breakthrough— and it was, and remains, the transformative technology of modern beekeeping—couldn't ensure a life of ease for the aspiring apiarist. The Langstroth hive was no panacea. It possessed no "talismanic influence which can convert a bad situation for honey into a good one," Langstroth wrote. It couldn't supplant hard work and vigilance: "If many colonies are kept, a competent person should always be on hand, in the height of the season, to attend to the bees. Even the Sabbath cannot be observed as a day of rest." It promised "no splendid results to those who are too ignorant or too careless to be entrusted with the management of bees." Despite the superiority of his hive, the greatest threat to the world's bees was still the incompetence of their keepers.

Nor could it guarantee prosperity. "There never will be a 'royal road' to profitable bee-keeping," Langstroth warned. "Like all other branches of rural economy, it demands care and experience; and those who are conscious of a strong disposition to procrastinate and neglect, will do well to let bees alone." Indeed, despite the "handsome profit" he promised, most bee-keepers, even the most diligent, continued to struggle to make a profit. Langstroth was among them. He patented his hive in

1852 but found it impossible to enforce. Entrepreneurs quickly brought their own versions of the hive to market, and although he initiated a number of lawsuits to enforce his rights, the mental energy required to litigate sent him into an enervating bout of "head trouble." "While under its full power," he wrote of his depressive spiral, "the things in which I usually take the greatest pleasure are the very ones which distress me the most. I not only lose all interest in bees, but prefer to sit on that side of the house where I can neither see nor hear them." At his lowest moments, he added, "I would see the letter 'B' and it would push me deeper into darkness." He died in Dayton, Ohio, in 1895, supported by his daughter and the surrounding community, but not, in any meaningful pecuniary way, by his bees.

STILL, LANGSTROTH'S INVENTION SPURRED AN OUTPOURING of compatible technologies. According to Tammy Horn's *Bees in America* (a comprehensive academic history of beekeeping), a short span of twenty years in the mid-nineteenth century produced four innovations that transformed the industry from hobby to commercial endeavor. First, in 1851, came Langstroth's hive. Then, in 1857, Johannes Mehring invented wax-comb foundation sheets that attached to the movable frames used in the Langstroth hive. These premade honeycombs gave bees a head start in building the hexagonal cells that house honey, pollen, and brood, allowing them to focus their energies on making honey rather than beeswax. In 1865, an Austrian beekeeper named Francesco de Hruschka invented the honey extractor, which used the centrifugal force of a drum spinning inside a barrel to pull honey from cells without destroying the comb and forcing bees to continually repair and rebuild. Moses Quinby's smoker, invented in 1873, added a more reliable bellows to the traditional firebox used to calm bees when working in hives. At the same time, two new national publications were launched. The *American Bee Journal* began publishing in 1861. A. I. Root's *Gleanings in Bee Culture: Or how to Realize the Most Money with the Smallest Expenditure of Capital and Labor in the Care of Bees, Rationally Considered* started up in 1873 and is still the nation's predominant beekeeping journal (though now it has a slightly pithier title: *Bee Culture*). Both helped disperse and popularize those innovations among American beekeepers.

Suddenly it was possible, for a handful of beekeepers at least, to consider quitting their day jobs. Quinby, a contemporary of Langstroth's who developed not only the bellows smoker but also his own variation on the Langstroth hive, kept 1,200 colonies in New York's Mohawk Valley. He was a prolific writer and inventor and is considered among the first Americans to support himself exclusively as a beekeeper. Another early commercial beekeeper, Dr. C. C. Miller (no relation to John), was a trained physician who took up beekeeping as a hobby in 1861. In 1878, he closed his medical practice and turned full-time to bees, gathering material for *Fifty Years Among the Bees*, a memoir and practical guide that explained how he had successfully made the production of honey his "sole business." On the heels of the Gold Rush, an entrepreneur named John Harbison imported thousands of colonies from the East Coast to California by sea, by train across the Isthmus of Panama, and then by steamer to Sacramento, where he sold them for thousands of dollars in profit. Harbison's success sparked a "bee-fever" that brought an estimated 10,000 hives by the sea-and-isthmus route to California. Harbison kept 2,000 colonies in the sage and buckwheat fields of Southern California, and was, during the

1870s, the biggest honey producer in the world. Likewise, John Miller's great-grandfather N.E. harnessed a restless nature to emerging technology and a dream of apiary greatness. At his peak, N.E. managed 10,000 hives; 30,000 if you count those owned by his children and the former employees he launched in the business.

N. E. Miller was born in 1873 in a log cabin in Cache Valley, Utah, the fifth of fifteen children of Mormon immigrant farmers from Germany. As a youngster, he found a hollow tree in the woods that harbored a swarm of bees. It sparked a lifelong interest; in the fall of 1894, at the age of twenty-one, he persuaded his father to allow him to trade five bags of leftover oats for seven colonies of bees owned by a neighbor. He discovered that he had a gift for handling bees, and his apiary grew rapidly as he captured swarms and purchased colonies wherever he could find them. In 1904, after a disappointing grain harvest, he extracted four five-gallon cans of honey from ten colonies of bees and made twelve dollars—the best day's pay he had ever received. The next day he did it again. He soon concluded that the production of honey could be more profitable than farming, if only he could keep enough bees to produce it in quantity. He quit his job on a wheat-threshing crew to focus exclusively on beekeeping, and in 1906, with three hundred hives under his management, he moved his growing family to Logan, Utah, to be closer to shipping routes. He placed hives on local farmers' land throughout the area and northward toward the Idaho line.

In 1907, he heard that a California beekeeper had developed a promising new method for processing beeswax. "So in December, 1907 I borrowed $107 from Orval Adams at the bank in Hyrum, Utah, and went to Southern California," he wrote. (His stories were collected in *Sweet Journey*, a biography by

John Miller's great-aunt Rita Skousen Miller, who married
N.E.'s son, Woodrow.) In California, N.E. saw that the bees
were still flying and gathering nectar long after those in Utah
were huddled in their hives against the cold. Until that point,
he had placed his hives in cellars for the Utah winters, covering
them on three sides with straw and dirt to protect them, but he
lost dozens of colonies each winter. If he shipped his bees somewhere warm in the cold months, it occurred to him, he might
halve his winter losses and double his honey and beeswax production. He might even be so lucky as to double the number of
his colonies. The San Bernardino area seemed perfect for winter
forage, with vast stretches of flowering orange groves and sage
fields and nearby railroad stations that would provide easy access to market. So the following winter, Miller took to the rails
with his apian cargo to pursue his endless summer, chasing the
blossoms and pollen flows from the clover fields of northern
Utah to San Bernardino and back.

N. E. Miller wasn't the first migratory beekeeper. In ancient Egypt, beekeepers transported small numbers of colonies
by boat up and down the Nile River. Fifty years before N.E.'s
first migratory eureka, Lorenzo Langstroth wrote of a man in
Germany who moved his stocks throughout the honey season:
"Sometimes he sends them to the moors, sometimes to the meadows, sometimes to the forest, and sometimes to the hills." In the
1870s, a man named C. O. Perrine enlisted a fleet of barges to
bring one thousand colonies up and down the Mississippi River.
His staff of fifteen men may have known something about river
navigation, but they knew little about beekeeping. They timed
landings poorly, missing the honey flows and losing many bees
to starvation, drowning, and the toppling of hives overboard.
Perrine gave up after one abysmal season, advising a group of

attendees at a meeting of the North American Beekeeping Association to "keep as far as possible from large bodies of water." This didn't dissuade O. O. Poppleton—nineteenth-century beekeepers had a thing for initials—who moved hives up and down the Indian River in central Florida with some success at the turn of the twentieth century. Both John Harbison and the aptly named Migratory Graham hauled colonies around California, moving them dozens of miles by rail or wagon to take advantage of shifting honey flows. N. E. Miller's contribution was to adopt these practices at an industrial level, using trains to pioneer the large-scale interstate movement of beehives.

N.E.'s first step was to approach the Union Pacific Railroad, which made a cattle car available. He purchased six hundred California colonies for his first "test flight" from California to Utah. The bees, labeled as "livestock" so as not to scare railroad employees, survived the trip, and N.E., who already had six hundred hives in Utah, doubled the numbers he had available to ply the clover fields. In the winter of 1909, he shipped his entire operation to California. That too proved successful, and in 1910 he brought his family with him. His sons traveled with the bees for the four-day journey, sleeping with the hives on the floors of the railcars, using wagons and Model Ts to deposit the colonies in the San Bernardino bee yards. The interstate shipments promised more honey and money but brought with them an entirely new set of hassles: Hives had to be stacked, braced, screened, and plugged so the bees could neither escape from the railroad cars nor suffocate; colonies were hauled to the trains by horse and wagon (or in winter, sleds) manned by drivers equipped with veils, gloves, and rudimentary knowledge of the behavior of bees. There needed to be enough bees and brood in each hive to gather a honey crop on arrival, but not so many that they would asphyxiate en route; enough honey to feed the bees until they were able to forage in the fields, but not so much as to incur unnecessary shipping costs. The trains had to run quickly and on time: in the summer, traveling over the sands of the Mojave Desert, engines stopped and broke down frequently. When they did, the beeswax would melt and run to the bottom of the hives, killing the bees. In early shipments, losses often exceeded 50 percent. But Miller persisted, experimenting with boxcars, cattle cars, automobile cars, refrigerator cars, various methods of stacking and bracing the hives, even spraying the hives with water in transit to keep them cool. His perseverance paid off. By 1911, he had three thousand colonies.

N.E. was restless and grandiose, an "extremist," said his daughter Florence, John Miller's great-aunt, with a "galloping personality." Like John Miller, N.E. was prone, Florence said, to "sudden strokes of ideas." He was also meticulous. His honey warehouse was spotless. His trucks received oil changes every thousand miles. As a practicing Mormon, he consumed neither tea nor coffee nor alcohol nor tobacco. He would hire no one who did. "Profanity was unknown to him," wrote Rita Miller in *Sweet Journey*, though he "sometimes used the expression, 'By the hell fires and damnation' to express utter disgust or disappointment." He would always look a man in the eye before selling him honey; if he deemed him worthy, he would then ship thousands of pounds to him on open account. Particulars mattered to N.E.: "A successful manager watches all details," he wrote in a company manual, "because the honey business is a detail business if success is obtained." The manual included instructions on nearly every aspect of beekeeping, from the proper hand to lay on the hive when prying it open (the left), to where to place the cover while working the bees (in front of the entrance).

N.E. was a gifted beekeeper, but aspired to more. Like many of his contemporaries in other fields, N.E. believed he could make a proper industry of commercial beekeeping. It was the era of scientific management. Barons of business, from Henry Ford to John D. Rockefeller, were developing meticulous procedures to render their employees and operations more efficient. Systems were essential. Mass production was key. N.E. applied the same principles to his beekeeping operation. He was, according to John Miller, the first commercial beekeeper to ship bees on a huge scale, the first to buy a carload of honey jugs and jars for a year's harvest, the first to ship a carload of honey to eastern markets. When large trucks became available, N.E. quickly abandoned the rails. With a truck, two drivers could make a nonstop haul from California without the frequent, bee-killing layovers required of trains. N.E. believed that, with a few good systems and forward-thinking ideas, beekeepers could, Rita wrote, "accomplish in the honey industry what Henry Ford had done in the auto industry: namely, to put honey in the price range so the people living in large cities and in thickly populated sections could afford to use it as a regular food."

Such ambitious expansion required breathtaking debt, which N.E. accrued liberally in search of an ever-elusive economy of scale. "Debts could always be paid by increasing his production," Rita wrote, "more branches—more bees—more honey to sell." When finances began to look shaky, N.E.'s response was to take out a loan and buy more bees, dispatching his sons across the West and Midwest to open new honey territory. John Miller's grandfather Earl opened a branch in Blackfoot, Idaho. Earl's brother Dell also opened an outfit near Blackfoot, moving to California later. Their brother Woodrow opened an ill-fated branch in Nebraska. Another brother, Ray, ran an operation in

Salt Lake City. When N.E. moved to California full-time, Ray took over all of the Utah holdings.

But in 1917 N.E.'s debts began to overwhelm him. A pile-on of bad luck—the loss of an entire shipment of bees in refrigerated fruit cars, a poor honey crop, a raft of accounting problems, and a World War I labor shortage—made matters worse. "He had bills stacked high on his desk that he was unable to pay," John Miller's grandfather Earl recalled, "in addition to heavy notes at the bank, on which the bank was demanding payment." N.E. briefly contemplated filing for bankruptcy, but decided against it. Instead he melted all the beeswax from the colonies that had perished and sold it off, along with some land he owned in Utah. Over the course of three years he managed to pay off his obligations.

Then he bought more bees. By 1926, the company had rebounded. With thirty-two thousand colonies, N.E., his sons, and their associates—men who had worked for N.E. and whom he later helped set up in business—produced the nation's first million-pound crop of honey. It filled thirty-eight railcars. The triumph was short-lived, however. The Great Depression soon destroyed demand, and the price of honey dropped below the cost of producing it, destroying the prospects of those who made a living selling it. Scores of commercial beekeepers left the business. Hives went without repair; comb was eaten by mice and moths; colonies starved and died. In the fall of 1933, N.E. traveled to Kansas City, St. Louis, Chicago, Milwaukee, Council Bluffs, Iowa, and Omaha and Lincoln, Nebraska, to market his honey. He returned without selling a single carload. Again the debts piled up. In a return to the cottage-scale economics that N.E. had so long plotted to leave behind, the Miller sons traveled door-to-door selling honey to individual families. N.E. put everything up for sale, but there was no one to buy it. "We just had a cold banker threaten to take away all that water stock for a measly $350. It is worth or cost about $2,440," he complained in a letter to Woodrow, who was on a Mormon mission in Canada. When a grandson, Clinton, inquired about getting into the bee business. N.E. urged him instead to pursue "the fields of commerce, communications, and public utility." Woodrow, upon completing his mission, went to Washington, D.C., to work for the Department of the Interior, where he learned that "there was only one agricultural pursuit that was financially worse than beekeeping, and that was the raising of goats."

In the end, Miller's was one of the few commercial honey production companies that squeaked through the Depression. N.E. died in 1940 at the age of sixty-six, leaving to Woodrow, who had returned from Washington to help his ailing father, a business burdened with debt. For a time, Woodrow continued to travel with the bees. In 1941, he was the largest honey producer in the world, and the next year, his operation gained national repute when an article, "Woodrow Miller's Traveling Bees," appeared in *Reader's Digest*. But after his father's brushes with insolvency, Woodrow came to conclude that the business of keeping bees would always be precarious. The money, he reckoned, was in honey packing and distribution. He gradually rented out, then sold off, his colonies, focusing instead on bottling and selling other people's honey. In 1954 he and a fellow honey packer invented the first plastic honey bear. Like Langstroth, they made little money off their invention, which they never patented. N. E. Miller's company is today run by Woodrow's descendants, who purchase honey from beekeepers across the West and sell it in eight-ounce bottles and forty-five-thousand-pound tanker trucks to retailers, bakeries, and markets in the United States, Europe, the Middle East, Japan, and the Philippines. Developers burned N.E.'s original honey production house in San Bernardino in 1962 to make room for a luxury residential development called Honey Hills.

NOT EVERY BEEKEEPER, HOWEVER, HAS ABANDONED THE field that N.E. pioneered. Like N.E., beekeepers have continued to harness new technologies in the hopes of making a consistent profit. In the 1960s, they began using forklifts and hardwood pallets that could hold four to eight hives, lifting the entire unit onto trucks, moving more bees faster. They also began making sugar syrup in three-hundred-gallon galvanized tanks, siphoning syrup to drip cans, which sit on top of hives and look like hamster-cage water dispensers, or in-hive feeders, which John Miller prefers—deep, narrow, rectangular plastic troughs that slide into a hive in the place of two frames. The feeders allowed beekeeping outfits to nourish and move their bees without worrying about the immediate availability of forage on the other end. They could truck them to, say, a holding yard in California for two weeks, feeding them syrup while they waited for the almonds to bloom. They could haul the bees to North Dakota in early May, knowing that the major honey flow didn't start until late June. These supplementary feeding techniques permitted the growth of the twenty really big bee outfits in America today—John Miller's among them.

Even the biggest outfits, though, have kept it mostly in the family. John Miller grew up in Blackfoot, Idaho, and from the age of six, helped his father, Neil, work the bees. In 1996, he and his brother Jay bought the family business from their dad, who had bought it in 1957 from his father, Earl, who had bought it from his father, N.E. Almost every industrial-scale beekeeper in the business has a similar story: beekeeping may, in fact, be one of the nation's last aristocracies. This is due in part to the imposing start-up costs. It's easy enough to run a backyard hive or two, but to make a living, most beekeepers believe you need a minimum of six hundred hives. "You need three hundred thousand dollars to just get going with a frumpy old truck and a thousand hives," Miller says. "You can't just wake up and say, I'm going to be a bee guy." Even if start-up funding weren't an issue, it's all but impossible to find good pasture in the nation's prime beekeeping territories. The land has to be accessible, offer sufficient nectar and pollen, and not be covered with asphalt, shopping malls, or trophy homes. Miller keeps many of his bees on the same land his father and grandfather did. Orin Johnson, another California beekeeper I spoke with, places hives on property his family has used for more than sixty years. The same goes for Larry Krause. If an aspiring commercial beekeeper doesn't have the patrimony, his best bet is to cozy up to "some geezer on his way out" whose kids are not interested in taking over the business, says Miller, and who might be willing to pass his equipment and bee yards on to an eager protégé. Otherwise, his bees will have a difficult time finding enough to eat.

Bee guys are sensitive about pasture. "Locations," says Miller's good friend Pat Heitkam, another California beekeeper, "are the most dear things we have." They don't like it when other bee guys horn in. Placer County, east of Sacramento, is John Miller's winter "territory." He shares it begrudgingly with a couple of Russian beekeepers and Bob and Joan Seifert, who are far enough away and keep few enough bees not to be a threat, and his friend Larry Krause, willingly, because he loves

Larry Krause, and because Krause's father bought those wintering grounds around the same time John Miller's father did, and he has every right to claim them as his own.

Though it's somewhat easier to find bee land in the less developed Dakotas than in California, a "dirty dozen" beekeepers, as one North Dakota bee inspector has termed them, have locked up most of the prime bee territory in the most desirable beekeeping states. In North Dakota, Miller has claimed sixty miles to the west of Gackle, twenty to the north and east, and twenty-five to the south as his summer digs. His friend Zac Browning operates out of Jamestown, forty miles away—far enough to keep their bees apart and their operations cooperative. Browning runs nearly fourteen thousand hives. He grew up in Blackfoot, Idaho, too, and is married to the sister of Miller's manager, Ryan Elison. Such intermingling wasn't always the case: Miller's and Browning's grandfathers hated each other.

In Wyoming, the law forbids commercial beekeepers from setting up apiaries within two miles of a bee yard run by somebody else's outfit. Larry Krause has three thousand hives. His assistant, Jim Niezwaag, has seventy-three but can acquire no more hives unless he finds new yards. The two-mile rule limits his access to nearby pasture, though Krause, who is, remember, the nicest guy you'll ever meet, lets Niezwaag use his yards— "We just want to keep those big migratory beekeepers from, say, North Dakota out of our state," Krause explained. A similar law holds in South Dakota. In North Dakota, they did away with it because the big bee guys had so many hives spread so widely across beekeeping country that no one else could keep any bees. "Bee guys don't play well together and with society in general," says Miller. "That's why bee guys are bee guys." They like bees; people are another matter. "A honey bee only has a nine-hundred-thousand-neuron brain, so if I conduct my-self within the framework of the bees' limited understanding, they're fine," he says. "If I go outside their ability to understand what's happening, things go south. I understand bees. I don't understand people very well."

Beekeepers are not, typically, "people people." They like to be outside, working with their hands, alone. After World War I, the U.S. and British governments promoted beekeeping as a ca-reer for disfigured or shell-shocked veterans because they could work on their own. A bee yard is a good place to hide from other people, and for that reason beekeepers are often secluded souls. This is ironic, because the creatures that they tend are so existentially social. Bees live and die in communities. "Honey-bees can flourish only when associated in large numbers, as in a colony," Lorenzo Langstroth wrote. "In a solitary state, a single bee is almost as helpless as a new-born child, being paralyzed by the chill of a cool Summer night."

Bees differ from their keepers in other ways as well. Honey bees are the epitome of organization and collaboration. They have defined roles, and they perform them with alacrity. "So work the honey bees," wrote Shakespeare. "Creatures that, by a rule in Nature, teach / The art of order to a peopled king-dom." The peopled kingdom of beekeepers, however, has a hard time keeping things ordered and unified. There are two major beekeeping organizations, the American Honey Producers As-sociation and the American Beekeeping Federation. The Honey Producers are strictly a domestic commercial beekeeping group, full of "dads and lads" who have run the family beekeeping business for generations. The Federation is an umbrella group of commercial beekeepers, sideline beekeepers, backyard beekeep-ers, honey packers and importers, queen-breeders, back-to-the-earth types, and, Miller jokes, "people who have actually ridden in flying saucers." The two organizations were one until 1969, when a bitter feud over the question of proposed tariffs on imported honey prompted the Honey Producers to swarm off into their own organization. "They took their double-knit polyester and stormed off," Miller says—although today "no one knows what we're fighting over anymore."

There are also plenty of similarities between the bee and its keeper. Bees' and beekeepers' lives are both governed by climate. When the weather is propitious, the beekeeper and the bee are both out working. They are steadfast. Bees would do anything for their queen, including die. They are even loyal to specific blooms, a trait that is known as "constancy," visiting the same flowers until the bloom is over. Beekeepers are also creatures of fidelity and habit. John Miller eats the same lunch of chicken salad—add relish, mayo, and pickled veggies from his North Dakota garden—most every day. At beekeeping conferences, he and Larry Krause eat at the same restaurant every meal. Miller and Krause rely on long-standing relationships with honey packers and almond ranchers. Good beekeepers rarely jump ship for a better deal, a sweeter bloom. They save leftover hives to help out their beekeeper friends when they fall on hard times. They offer each other tips for dealing with pests. They share leads on new pollination contracts.

Commercial beekeepers are throwbacks that way—"knuckle-dragging Neanderthals," Miller would say. In an era of constant career change, beekeepers still work in family businesses; many have never done anything else. They don't blog; Larry Krause doesn't even email. They never throw away anything, not a hive tool, not a tattered veil. Bees are confused for a few days when their environment changes, when their hive is moved or their queen replaced, but they soon forget their old circumstances and adapt. Beekeepers, not so much. They are profoundly disoriented when the world around them changes. They tend to be stubborn. "I am well aware how difficult it is to reason with beekeepers," Langstroth wrote, "who stigmatize all knowledge which does not square with their own, as mere 'book knowledge unworthy [of] the attention of practical men.'"

Miller considers himself something of an innovator in the beekeeping industry. He reads business journals and speaks to beekeeping groups about such perplexing concepts as the cost of funds, proper depreciation decisions, long-term versus short-term acquisitions, and nonperishable versus perishable consumables. He realizes that what makes a good beekeeper— a love of bees, a respect for life, a sense of stewardship—is not necessarily what makes a good businessman, and he strives to be good at both. He believes passionately in reinvesting in the industry, in research into bees and into new technologies, but he fears that his field is "infested with small thinkers." Like his great-grandfather N.E., he doesn't believe himself to be a small thinker. Successful beekeeping, he says, requires a willingness to adapt and change. But most beekeepers like to do things the way they always have done them.

There's no one way to do it. There's the John Miller model: go south to pollinate, divide and multiply the hives, move to the northern plains to participate in summer's abundance, make honey, put the bees in the Idaho potato cellars for two months, start over again. There's the Richard Adee model, which is the John Miller model on steroids. Adee runs about 80,000 hives between operations in Mississippi and South Dakota and California, acquiring other outfits as they go out of business: 5,000 here, 15,000 there, achieving unheard-of economies of scale.

There's the Orin Johnson model: Johnson runs 700 hives, keeping his numbers down and trying to manage well what he has, placing most of his bees in the wild sage fields within fifty miles of his home in Hughson, California. There are those who, like Miller, pollinate the almonds and oranges in California, but then send their hives to other bee guys in the northern plains for the summer. There are the northern bee guys who eschew the hassles of the almonds altogether and stay put for the winter, letting their bees die and restarting their hives from "packages" of mail-order bees the next spring.

However they do it, it still isn't easy. Fifteen years ago, Miller estimates, there were 5,000 commercial beekeepers—defined as those who manage more than three hundred hives and make their living primarily from beekeeping, producing at least six thousand pounds of honey per year. Today, the number of guys, and a few women, who live and die by the bee has dropped by more than three quarters. There were 468 commercial beekeepers in North Dakota in 1979; 178 in 2009. The commercial guys have been driven out of business by pesticide kills, droughts, and poor honey prices; by strip malls, mega-malls, mini-malls, and subdivisions swallowing up their bee yards; by the hassles of buying, renting, and coordinating forklifts, syrup tankers, and semis; by missed birthday parties and family events; by nights and weeks and months on the road; by the annual "trauma and drama" of finding employees who don't mind working in a maelstrom of stinging insects and are willing to leave their families for months at a time; by disagreeable competitors who dilute their honey with water or syrup or don't take good care of their bees; by thieves who pilfer hives; by invasive insects, parasites, and diseases. There are few leisurely vacations; few golf club memberships—in 1988, after back-to-back droughts in

North Dakota, Miller sold his house, lent all the money to the honey business, and moved his family into a trailer nearby. He likes to joke that someday, he will change the name of his bee outfit to "Aggravation Apiaries."

Most beekeepers are, like N. E. Miller, like John Miller, like Lorenzo Langstroth, obsessive types. The beekeeper, wrote Langstroth, must be sure that "he fully understands and punctually discharges the appropriate duties of each month, neglecting nothing, and procrastinating nothing to a more convenient season; for, while bees do not require a large amount of attention, in proportion to the profits yielded by them, they *must* have it at the *proper time* and in the *right way.*" These days, the details are grim—poor economics, thorny logistics, and a plague of disappearing bees. "So generally, beekeepers are unhappy people," Miller says. "We're so vulnerable, so dependent on the vagaries of nature." Perhaps that was always the case. The honey bee, after all, is an introduced—at times invasive—species that boosts the productivity of other introduced species—almonds, for instance—and has now fallen on hard times because of the introduction of still more nonnative invaders—humans, shopping malls, parasites, monocrops. Langstroth once countered critics who objected to his manipulation of bees and comb: "Those who object to this, as interfering with nature, should remember that the bee is not in a state of nature."

Neither are bee guys. In an eminently practical nation, they are hopeless romantics, dancing on the razor's edge of failure in order to do something they love. Of all N. E. Miller's descendents, John Miller and his estranged brother are the only ones left who work with bees for a living: "Everyone bailed out, became accountants, lawyers, and honey packers," he says. "Why don't I get out? I love bees. They work hard; they're well behaved; they're selfless; they're generous." Signs of his apian affection are everywhere, from the bee-striped rug in the entryway of his home to his Salt Lake Stingers baseball cap to the yellow-and-black-striped German felt-tip pens that he encountered in an office supply store. When they were discontinued because of their propensity to leak, he bought out what remaining stock he could find. He carries them wherever he goes, and his fingers and shirts are often stained with ink. The love of the bee is an impractical passion.

"This calling feels good," says Miller. It used to feel better. There were, he says, three major revolutions that changed American beekeeping. The invention of the Langstroth hive was the first, making it possible to earn a living from beekeeping. Migratory beekeeping was the second, making it possible to run beehives as a modern business. The third, in 1987, was cataclysmic, and it rendered life among honey bees—already a trying assignment—even more difficult.

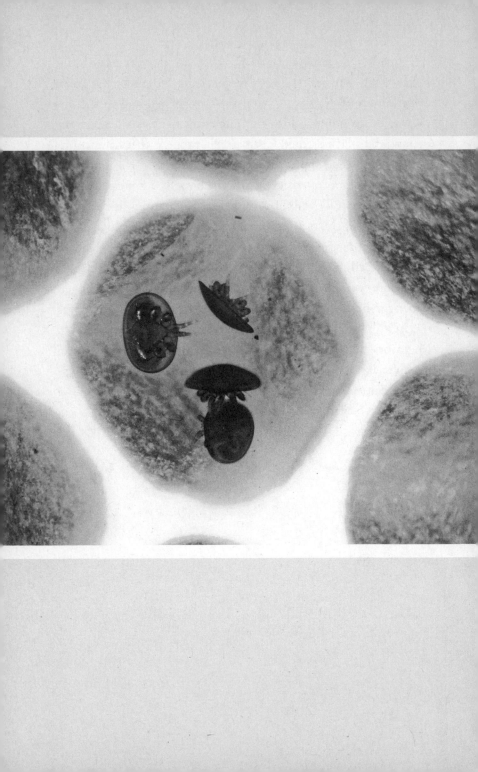

Chapter Three

....

The Tiny Leviathan

THE FIRST TIME JOHN MILLER SAW THE DIMINUTIVE PEST that would loom large over the rest of his career was in the early 1990s. He doesn't remember the year, but he remembers the week. It was in early April, and Miller's crew had just broken the top off a robust hive teeming with healthy bees. One of his employees glanced at a drone cell that had been mangled when the hive top had been pried off, and noticed a small, reddish-brown creepy-crawly thing tucked inside.

No one present had ever seen such a creature. They had seen pictures, though, and knew that the barely visible tick-like bug was something called a varroa mite, which had first been spotted in the United States in 1987. Its presence in this one hive boded ill in the extreme, not just for that particular colony, but for the entire Miller outfit. Everyone in the yard stopped their work and gathered, speechless, looking at the mite. Miller uttered a few choice cowboy words and ran around "in an autistic loop" for about an hour. Then he went out and bought some chemicals to kill the mites. They were the first pesticides he would ever use inside a hive.

Later, he would receive two official letters. The first was

from the North Dakota Department of Agriculture, explaining that a state bee inspector had found a varroa mite in one of his bee yards. The second, the following winter, came from Placer County, his home base in California, also proclaiming the reality of his infestation. Miller was lucky. Had a single mite been found in one of his hives just a few years before, the state of California would have insisted that he kill his entire outfit, poisoning each colony and burning the equipment in which his bees lived. But the state had given up on that, because it was expensive and because, although the policy had wiped out beekeepers left and right, it had done nothing to stanch the mite's spread.

The letters didn't impart any earth-shattering news. Miller already knew he had mites. But the fact that the agriculture authorities—ostensibly impartial third parties—in two states had publicly declared him infested was, he says, "like a stain." Miller was once a "prideful" beekeeper. Other people's outfits might suffer from foulbrood and varroa mites, but Miller's were always clean, well tended, expertly managed. He was, he says, in a "delusional state of self-righteousness"—under the acute misperception that he was too good a beekeeper to fall prey to such pitfalls as the varroa mite. But the mite didn't distinguish between good and bad beekeepers. It infested every hive it encountered, riding on the backs of bees from failing hives to infect healthy ones. Although the mite, which is the size of the head of a pin, might be small enough to overlook if you weren't terribly observant, its oversized effects were hard to ignore. "This varroa mite," says Miller, "swaggers like a colossus across beekeeping in North America."

THE VARROA MITE IS A BLOODRED-TO-BROWN, TICK-SHAPED creature, about 1.8 millimeters long and 2 millimeters wide. It has eight legs, a hairy, shiny dark shell, and a sharp, two-pronged tongue designed to pierce a bee's exoskeleton and suck its hemolymph—what serves as blood in bees, who don't have circulatory systems, hearts, arteries, and veins as we understand them, but rather blood-like tissue that flows osmotically between body segments. The mites jump onto adult bees like fleas onto dogs, in an instant, and set up camp on the bees' backs or between their abdominal plates, where they are nearly impossible to spot. A pregnant foundress makes the first foray into a colony. She rides into a hive on an unwitting adult bee and jumps into a cell destined to raise the incubating bees—the brood—that will become the hive's next generation. She times it perfectly, burying herself in the bottom of the cell during the period of larval feeding, before the worker bees cap the cells with wax to allow the larvae to incubate. Once the brood cell is capped, it is impossible for either bees or humans to spot or smell a varroa mite. The only way to find one is to open the cell, which kills the baby bee.

Ensconced now in the cell, the foundress hunkers down and lays four to six eggs—one male, the rest female—and after five to eight days the eggs hatch into juvenile mites, which feed on the hemolymph of the bee larvae and pupae. The mites mate, then emerge with the immature bee to colonize a new cell. Bees whose brood cells hosted mites often emerge damaged and ill, surviving only hours, rather than weeks. They suffer a variety of disabling defects—crumpled or disjointed wings, undeveloped glands, shortened abdomens, insufficient proteins, reduced sperm quality. They also weigh less than healthy bees, and fly less often. The sickest ones are quickly evicted from the hive, where they crawl helplessly at the base until they die. With all the disabling viruses mites bring along with them, even a single mite can cut an adult bee's life span by as much as half. When mite populations grow, they sap the strength and vigor from entire hives.

The varroa infestation is, cruelly, a malady of prosperity. The mite preys most effectively on colonies that are thriving. A beehive's population peaks in the middle of July, when honey flows are at their strongest and a queen can lay thousands of eggs a day. Miller calculates that on July 16, a healthy colony may house almost 80,000 bees—which means his total population of bees, across all of his ten thousand hives, is approximately 776 million bees, "or half the number of rats in Manhattan." That's a lot of bees, and initially, the mite has little impact on a colony, because in spring and summer a hive's ability to replenish population lost to age and roadkill is almost infinite, while each varroa mite can lay only four or five or six eggs every seventeen days.

In August, however, queen bees begin laying fewer eggs as they prepare for the scarcity of winter, and as bee populations drop, the mite populations continue to grow—at this point, exponentially, thousands of mites each laying multiple eggs, now a mind-boggling rate of increase. The varroa population reaches its full strength in late fall, just as the bee population hits bottom. In winter, the population in any one hive drops to fewer than thirty-five thousand individuals—"or one-tenth the number of roaches in Manhattan," Miller says. When these two elegant population curves—of bee and mite—intersect, a hive, even one that was brimming with honey and brood and worker bees in June and July, will falter. With fewer healthy workers available as summer turns to fall and winter, honey, pollen, and brood production decline, and the hive becomes more vulnerable to starvation, predation, disease, and ultimate collapse. When the varroa mite population overwhelms the ability of a hive to recover, the colony "crashes."

The varroa mites, meanwhile, move on, riding into new colonies with drifting or robbing or absconding bees. Then they begin reproducing all over again, one pregnant foundress turning into many, to similar calamitous effect, creating a ripple effect of crashing hives, crashing bee yards, and all too often, crashing beekeeping operations. Since 1987, the mite has been *the* major cause of honey bee mortality across the United States. The nation's CCD losses pose no comparison. In Miller's grandfather's day, a beekeeper's major problem was American foulbrood infection, spread when beekeepers moved frames between hives and hives between apiaries. But the varroa mite moves from hive to hive on its own, at a speed that has confounded beekeepers' ability to react to it. "This is going to be the challenge of my career, there is no question about that," writes Miller. "My grandfather never heard of it; my dad was barely aware of it; it occupies much of my problem-solving time."

Varroa destructor is the official name.

Varroa works just fine for me.

Given its eerie resemblance to a garden variety tick,

deer tick, goddamn tick, Lyme Disease tick,

I often lapse into "tick" mode.

Call the thing whatever you want, it is a plague.

The varroa mite's disastrous appearance in American hives was presaged by the arrival of another parasitic affliction. The tracheal mite—a microscopic parasite that lodges in bees' breathing tubes and interferes with their respiration—was found in the United States three years earlier. Unlike the varroa mite, which is hard to miss once you've suffered an infestation, the tracheal mite is impossible to spot with the naked eye. To see it, a beekeeper—or more likely, an entomologist or bee inspector—must dissect a bee, extract its trachea, immerse it in a solution that liquefies the tracheal tissue but leaves the mite intact, then smear the remaining matter on a glass plate and view it under a microscope. Tracheal mites also shorten a bee's life, curtail its flights, and can ultimately undermine the health of the entire colony. First detected in Texas in 1984, they spread rapidly across the country.

A couple of years later, Miller was in the bathroom of the Peacock Alley bar in the old Patterson Hotel in Bismarck, North Dakota, during a beekeeping conference, when he ran into a Florida beekeeper he knew. The Florida beekeeper was based in West Palm Beach. He hauled his bees up the East Coast to pollinate the blueberries of Maine, then headed west, arriving in Steele, North Dakota—about an hour from Miller's summer base in Gackle—around July 20. This late date coincided with the fading of the summer's major clover and alfalfa blooms, which didn't seem a viable business model to Miller—but the Florida beekeeper was nonetheless flush with cash and fast cars and big boats and airplanes. He would arrive at beekeeping conventions in beautiful sports cars with beautiful women, parking in front of the hotel so everyone could watch. "Bee guys," Miller says, "didn't know how to cope with this." It was perplexingly un-bee-guy-like behavior. The guy's riches, Miller later learned, derived not from his bees—of course not—but from bales of marijuana he would transport up and down the East Coast along with the bees. Garden-variety drug enforcement officers had neither the equipment nor the gumption to search among and inside active beehives for contraband. Someone finally caught him, though, and he ended up in the Dade County lockup. But before he did, he'd brought a truckload of bees infested with tracheal mites from Florida to North Dakota, where the mites had not yet been found.

When Miller ran into the Florida beekeeper in the bathroom of the Patterson Hotel, he didn't ask him about his cars or his women, although, since this was before the arrest, Miller certainly would have liked to learn how a man could live like a rock star off the fruit of his bees. Instead, he asked him about a rumor he'd heard in the halls. Was it true? Did his bees have tracheal mites? "He turned to me and said if I were you I'd get my bees the hell out of North Dakota," Miller recalls. The state of California had embarked on a campaign to stave off the mite, destroying outfits in which mites had been detected and closing state borders to hives from states where tracheal mites had been confirmed. The Florida beekeeper knew that North Dakota would soon be on that list. Miller called his father that day and convinced him to move the entire outfit to the company's then home base in Idaho, where tracheal mites had not yet been detected. Other beekeepers were not so lucky; California soon closed its border to North Dakota bees, forcing migratory beekeepers who usually overwintered in California to tough it out instead on the frigid northern plains. The harsh winters, combined with back-to-back droughts the following two summers, spelled the end of a number of once-thriving beekeeping businesses.

The frantic border closures and hive destruction did nothing to prevent the spread of the tracheal mites. They proliferated rapidly, hopping from hive to hive and state to state, eventually colonizing the entire continent. The mites killed colonies everywhere and wreaked havoc on the entire interstate beekeeping industry. And then they didn't anymore. Over the years, as the colonies that were most susceptible died off, American bees appeared to develop a genetic resistance. Today, beekeepers and bee inspectors rarely test for tracheal mites—there are so many worse things to worry about. But in the mid-1980s, the beekeeping industry was in a genuine panic as it struggled with a new pest that could gain purchase so quickly in a world of increasingly fluid natural borders. Migratory beekeepers had allowed a whole host of migratory problems to hitchhike along with their bees.

The dread would only escalate when, at 10:30 A.M. on September 25, 1987 (a time so precise it could only come from the memory of a beekeeper), an apiarist named Gary Oreskovic spotted a strange insect the color of dried blood riding on the back of one of his bees. He looked again to make sure, then called a neighbor, David Miksa, to come see whether it was, in fact, a varroa mite, as Oreskovic feared. Miksa was a queen-breeder of Croatian descent who had attended a beekeeping meeting in Budapest in 1983 and, while there, had toured central Europe to visit cousins and bee operations. In the 1970s, the varroa mite, which originated in Asia, had swept through the Soviet bloc countries, sequentially wiping out the bee industries in Romania, Bulgaria, and Yugoslavia before blowing through the rest of Europe. Miksa's cousins were among those who lost most of their hives, and it was in their apiaries that he saw his first varroa mites: "I counted twenty-one mites on one bee in Zagreb," he says. He realized instantly that they wouldn't be his last. If the Iron Curtain couldn't stop the parasite, there wasn't much that would. Four years later, on a September day in

Wisconsin, Miksa confirmed that Oreskovic's novel pests were, indeed, the first wave of varroa mites in North America. Oreskovic destroyed nineteen of his 1,800 hives and sent a sample to the U.S. Department of Agriculture laboratories in Beltsville, Maryland. The lab verified the infestation.

No one knows exactly how the varroa mite first arrived on U.S. shores. Mite-infested bees could not have flown on their own from varroa-affected areas, even those in South America, where the mite had been found in the 1970s. Those places were beyond the reach of even the most determined swarm. Most beekeepers and scientists believe the varroa mite entered the United States not through Wisconsin, but through Florida, where most of beekeeping's scourges seem to originate. Oreskovic and his neighbor Miksa both took their bees to Florida in the winter to pollinate citrus, bell pepper, and watermelon crops, and the hives on which Oreskovic first detected the mites had all been stocked with bees he had bought in central Florida.

Bee importation has been illegal in the United States since 1922, and the speculation is that the mite arrived either on a swarm that had taken refuge on a boat that docked in Florida or on an airplane. Miksa heard rumors that swarms had emerged from Drug Enforcement Administration planes flying between Florida and South America. Or perhaps they disembarked with beekeepers sneaking in queens from another country, a practice called "pocket importation," because the smuggler literally hides the queen in a cage in his pocket or carry-on luggage. Not that it mattered: the mite had arrived, by whatever means, and by the time it was detected in Wisconsin, it had already spread extensively through Florida. By January 14, 1988, the Florida Department of Agriculture reported eight thousand infested hives in the state.

Once the presence of the mites was confirmed, the Federal Animal and Plant Health Inspection Service swung into action, receiving emergency certification from the U.S. Environmental Protection Agency for beekeepers to use fluvalinate, an insecticide that had proven effective against varroa mite in Europe and had been rapidly approved for sale in the States under the trade name of Apistan. When Miller found his first varroa mite, he quickly ran out to buy several thousand Apistan strips, flexible plastic sticks coated with low doses of the miticide. He placed them in his hives, and "they worked like a charm," he recalls. At the same time, major beekeeping states like California moved to prevent varroa-infested hives from passing their borders. The Canadian government closed its borders to American bees and to queen breeders, who had previously done a booming business in Canada. Such quarantines did nothing to stop the spread of the pest, however. Swarms from infested hives had no regard for state lines or state laws, and worker bees plied the paths to their chosen blossoms from state to state. Many beekeepers, likewise, traveled their usual migration routes, evading quarantines by driving at night and on back roads.

It took two to three years from the time the first varroa mite was spotted until the nation's first bee colonies started to experience difficulty. It took another couple of years until the mite, aided by large-scale migratory operations, had blanketed the country, jumping from hive to hive with alarming rapidity. During the first wave of infestation, the varroa mite killed nearly every single one of the continent's feral colonies, obliterating the wild bees that once did much of the work pollinating the nation's crops and flowers. Today, only an estimated 2 percent of the pre-1987 feral bee population remains, and those hives are most likely recently escaped swarms from beekeeping operations, not survivors of the varroa apocalypse. Because of the varroa mite, wild honey bees are now, for all practical purposes, extinct in the United States. If a bee guy doesn't take care of his hive, it will be dead in less than two years; if a hive doesn't have a bee guy to look after it, the chances of its survival are close to nil. Well-kept colonies like Miller's escaped major damage only because of extreme vigilance and regular Apistan applications.

THE VARROA MITE WAS FIRST IDENTIFIED IN INDONESIA IN 1904, when a naturalist named Edward Jacobson found a smattering of reddish brown mites in a colony of indigenous Asian *Apis cerana* honey bees on the island of Java. He sent them to the Leiden museum in Holland, where the Dutch biologist A. C. Oudemans determined that the insect belonged to a previously unidentified arachnid species. Oudemans gave it the taxonomic name *Varroa jacobsoni*, after its discoverer. It turned out that the parasites were endemic throughout Asia and did little damage to Asian bees, having coevolved over millions of years. The Asian bees had developed a natural defense, detecting mites on adult bees and in capped cells and ejecting them. So for another century after Jacobson's discovery, no one bothered to take a deeper look.

Entomologists believe that European honey bees (*Apis mellifera*) and Asian honey bees (*Apis cerana*) branched from the same genetic forebear a few million years ago. Like European bees, Asian bees live in colonies, produce honey, and can be easily domesticated. Asian bees are smaller and less hairy, with more distinct stripes on the abdomen, and they tend to fly faster and more erratically. They are also more defensive. They swarm and spread more quickly, and their smaller colonies produce less honey. Thus it is the European bee that has accompanied humans, spreading from Europe to every temperate place where humans have settled. Scientists speculate that some one hundred years ago, the European bee completed its circumnavigation of the globe. They believe it moved from west to east via the Trans-Siberian Railroad and was reunited in Asia with its Eastern siblings, as well as the mites with which they coexisted.

Sometime in the early 1950s, the mite made its own fateful move. Some—perhaps only one—of those Asian mites jumped successfully from *Apis cerana* onto the Western honey bee. Scientists believe it happened somewhere in eastern Russia. In the 1960s, the mite spread through Russia and North Africa. By the 1970s, it had moved across Europe; mites were found in Paraguay in the 1970s, too. Someone also found a lone mite in Maryland in 1979. But until Gary Oreskovic spotted his bloodred tick on a September Wisconsin morning in 1987, the United States considered itself uninfested. No more: the mites blanketed the North American continent in the late 1980s and early 1990s, then jumped to South Africa. They reached New Zealand in 2000, where beekeepers lost more than thirty thousand hives; more than two thousand beekeepers "retired" soon after. In 2008, mites landed in Hawaii. To date, Australia is the only major beekeeping nation that has not hosted a mite. The varroa mite had once lived in the inconspicuous shadows where most creepy-crawly species reside, garnering little attention. But once it pitched the entire global bee supply into precipitous decline, this previously harmless parasite was, abruptly, the bee world's public enemy number one.

So the bee world embarked on a crash course in varroa mite physiology. For four decades now, entomologists have studied it intensely, learning about its life cycle, its sex life, its behavioral propensities, its chemical sensitivities. The more they've learned, the more complex they've found the mite's relationship with the honey bee to be. For instance, the mite's effects appeared to vary as it traveled the globe: bees in South America and eastern Russia were relatively resistant; those in Western Europe and North America suffered near-universal mortality. In addition, the varroa mites on European bees were noticeably larger than those on their Asian siblings; scientists first attributed this variation to the fact that European bees and colonies are larger, offering the mites more nutrients and hosts on which to thrive. But in 2000, an Australian bee pathologist named Denis Anderson reached another conclusion.

I first heard Denis Anderson speak about the varroa mite at a beekeeping conference I attended with John Miller. Anderson wore jeans and a collared shirt opened a couple of buttons farther than most insect geeks would dare; he looked more Steve Irwin swashbuckler than entomology nerd, and he made varroa mites sound as interesting—and menacing—as saltwater crocodiles or box jellyfish. Anderson smiles easily, almost compulsively. He's got quizzical arched eyebrows, a sharp nose, and a boyish face ringed by thick, shaggy brown hair and a beard. Although he is pushing sixty, his hair betrays barely a hint of gray. He travels the world studying bees and their diseases, spending six months a year at the entomology department of the Commonwealth Scientific and Industrial Research Organisation in Canberra, and the other six months in the field studying bee diseases and pests across Asia. He is the principal scientist working on bee populations and the varroa mite in Australia, which, as the last varroa-free bastion, has the luxury of devoting funds to more esoteric investigations than do afflicted nations, whose research dollars go mainly toward finding chemicals to kill it.

Anderson first began working with the varroa mite while doing field research in Papua New Guinea, Australia's closest neighbor to the north. It was a fascinating place for a bee pathologist. Thanks to the political and migratory forces that swept the island of New Guinea in the twentieth century, Asian and European bees intermingled there, providing an excellent laboratory for observing the behaviors of the pathogens they shared. Australian missionaries had brought European bees to New Guinea before World War I, while Asian honey bees arrived in the 1970s, after the Indonesian government relocated thousands of Javanese farmers to Irian Jaya, on the western side of the island. Those peasants brought their own domestic animals, such as chickens, pigs, and Asian bees. And they also brought the Asian bees' theretofore harmless co-rider, *Varroa jacobsoni*.

It was 1989, just a couple of years after the mite had arrived in the United States, and Anderson was well aware of the damage inflicted on European bees in the Northern Hemisphere. In New Guinea, the mite was everywhere, on both European and Asian bees. But Anderson quickly noticed that it seemed to behave differently on the European bees of New Guinea than on European bees elsewhere. The mites weren't able to reproduce inside the brood cells, and thus were unable to spawn populations large enough to endanger hives. "When I first saw this I was new to the varroa mite and I thought, 'What I'm looking at here is just an aberration,'" Anderson says. But it wasn't an aberration; it was the norm there. Varroa mites were not able to replicate in European hives. "I looked at it for four years and said, 'Look, this mite is not reproducing.'"

The question was why: were the European bees resistant to varroa mites in New Guinea, or were the mites themselves different? Anderson devised an experiment. He raised European queen bees in Perth, Australia, and he artificially inseminated them with semen from a single drone, so their offspring would come from a narrow genetic base. Then he moved twenty of those offspring to New Guinea and twenty to Germany, to see how they responded to the mites found in each location. In New Guinea, the hives did fine. In Germany, they collapsed. The mites found in Germany could readily reproduce in the Perth bee colonies. Those in New Guinea could not.

He then conducted the same experiment in Java, the densely populated island that is home to Indonesia's capital city, Jakarta, and found that the mites there could not reproduce in European colonies. But in 1994, soon after Anderson's experiment concluded, he began hearing reports that varroa mites in Java had suddenly begun to reproduce on European bees, killing colonies across the island. He examined samples of mites from collapsing hives and noticed that they were much larger than the ones he had studied in New Guinea and Java in previous years. And while the larger mites had overrun the hives, he could also find the smaller mites—which were still not reproducing. It was then, he says, that he had his own eureka moment: "I realized that there were two mites here," he says.

The new mites in Java were not only larger; they were also more oblong. By the mid-1990s, DNA technology had evolved to the point where it was possible to sequence segments of the genetic code from the mites. So Anderson studied the variation in sequence of a particular mitochondrial gene on both mites and found them to be different. He then traveled across Asia collecting additional samples, sequencing their genes as well. He discovered that there was not just one mite riding around on the world's Asian honey bees, but a complex of mites, comprising four entirely different species and eighteen separate regional genotypes. Of those eighteen, only two were found in European bee colonies globally—and neither belonged to the species that had long been blamed for causing the damage to global bee populations. *Varroa jacobsoni*, the mite Anderson found in New Guinea, was native to Indonesia and could not reproduce in the brood of the European bee. It was, University of Georgia entomologist Keith Delaplane wrote in a 2001 editorial in a bee science journal, a "benign homebody, still restricted essentially to its original host . . . and not the culprit to worldwide calamity that we had thought." The mites didn't behave differently in different regions because the host bees were different. No, the mites behaved differently because they were, in fact, different mites. For three decades, Anderson realized, entomologists had been studying the wrong mite.

The culprit was not *Varroa jacobsoni*, but the larger mite, one of the two genotypes that could reproduce in European bees. One of the offending genotypes had originated somewhere on the Korean peninsula; the other in Japan. The Japanese mite was the one that had found its way to South America in the 1970s via a shipment of varroa-infested bees from Japan to Paraguay. It had remained restricted in both the damage it caused and the scope of its spread. The far more pathogenic variant had evolved on the Korean peninsula. At some point it made the transspecies jump from *Apis cerana* onto Russian bees and spread to Europe and the United States. Those Korean mites showed little genetic variation in Anderson's studies, suggesting that there may have been only one single female mite that made the reproductive jump between hosts—a founding foundress, so to speak, that cloned herself around the world. Delaplane compared Anderson's discovery to a "scientific revolution," if not on par with the discovery of gravity and relativity, one that was nonetheless earth-shattering "for that fraction of the world's scientists who work on the parasitology of *Apis mellifera*." As discoverer of a new species, Anderson was entitled to naming rights. Rather than christening it *Varroa andersonii*—"I don't think I would like to be remembered as a parasitic mite"—or by reference to its homeland, he opted for a devastatingly apt, melodramatic, even comic-bookish moniker: *Varroa destructor*.

☙

AS AUSTRALIA'S PREEMINENT BEE PATHOLOGIST, ANDERSON is keenly involved in his nation's efforts to prevent that destruction from spreading to Australia's shores, striving to keep any foreign bee that could harbor the mite well away from the island continent. This is no easy task in an era of slapdash mobility. Bees have crossed all the great oceans. They arrive on all variety of conveyances: in the pockets of bee collectors looking for the next great queen; in the holds and spars of ships; in airplane baggage compartments. The problem is compounded by the fact that the world is no longer dealing with only one dangerous species of mite. Since Anderson observed and named *Varroa destructor*, another variant has jumped from Asian to European bees. As luck would have it, it has done so in the very population Anderson first became familiar with, in the very location where he first studied the mite.

In 2008, reports emerged from New Guinea about beekeepers losing *Apis mellifera* colonies at an alarming rate. Anderson went to look at the situation. "The first colony I opened," he says grimly, "there were reproducing mites in nearly every cell." He couldn't be certain, without access to sophisticated technology not available in New Guinea, which species of mite was causing the problems. So he improvised: he retrieved some *Varroa jacobsoni* from an Asian bee colony and compared them to the ones that had infested the European colonies, taking photos of both with his digital camera and uploading the images on a laptop. They were exactly the same size and shape. He shipped a sample to a lab in Australia for genetic testing. "Sure enough," he says, "it was a population of Java mites." The *jacobsoni* mites had, for the first time, begun reproducing in European colonies. The prospect is unsettling, because like *Varroa destructor*, these newly pathogenic *jacobsoni* mites could carry unfamiliar viruses that could cause even more problems for already-embattled bee populations across the world. In addition, Anderson doesn't know yet whether the *jacobsoni* mites that can now reproduce on European bees can still reproduce on Asian ones. If they can, it only hastens the inevitable moment when the varroa mite will reach Australia: "The way that mite will get out of New Guinea," Anderson says, "is on the Asian honey bee."

The European honey bee doesn't fare well in the tropical lowlands of New Guinea. It needs lots of care and tending to survive. The Asian honey bee has no such problems; it is considered an invasive species there. It swarms easily and travels long distances. Since its introduction in Irian Jaya, it has spread across the island to the former Australian territory of Papua New Guinea, and east to the island of New Britain, and 1,300 miles farther to the Solomon Islands. It has also made incursions onto Australian soil: in May 2007, a beekeeper from Cairns, in far northeastern Australia, was called to remove a swarm from the mast of a yacht in drydock. He realized that the bees were unusual and called officials from the local agriculture authority. The officials recognized the bees as *Apis cerana* and promptly declared an emergency. Queensland biosecurity officials restricted all movements of managed Australian bees and sent three surveillance teams racing through the continent's lightly populated north country in search of swarms. They put out a call for citizens to report any unusual bee sightings, combed the area with sweep nets, and tested the pellets of bee-eating birds for *Apis cerana* DNA. They also used a process called "beelining"—capturing and marking foraging Asian bees that had been lured to strategically placed sugar feeding stations, then releasing and tracking them back to their nests.

When the teams found and destroyed three colonies within a one-kilometer radius of the yacht harbor, it became clear that the bees had been living there long enough to swarm and spread. Authorities reckoned that they could have been onshore for as long as three months. The search widened, and by July 2010 they had found more than one hundred Asian beehives. It seemed unlikely that they could stop its spread: the Asian honey bee had probably become endemic to northern Queensland. Tests on the bees and comb from the nests showed that all the nests were related and had descended from a single colony—probably a swarm that hitched a ride on a boat from New Guinea, eluding quarantine inspection. The tests also confirmed that there were no mites on the bees. Although the risk remained that the Asian bees would rob and attack European bees or outcompete them for food, Australia had dodged the varroa bullet for the time being. Still, Anderson knows that it is only a matter of time before varroa mites arrive on Australian shores. It might be the newly destructive New Guinea variety, the Korean variant, or another damaging genotype newly cooked up in the global bee melting pot. "It's not a matter of if it will arrive," he says, "but when." Anderson's knowledge of varroa mite genetics will do little in the short term to stanch its spread or control the devastation.

For in addition to being a remarkably destructive creature, the varroa mite is also a tremendously adaptive one.

✽

THIS IS A LESSON JOHN MILLER LEARNED THE HARD WAY IN the winter of 2005. In the initial period after American beekeepers first encountered the varroa mite, treatment was easy. A beekeeper simply placed an Apistan strip in each hive in the fall and forgot about it. The Apistan killed the mites, which never grew numerous enough to overwhelm the hives. But after about ten years the medicine stopped working. Apistan, it turned out, killed most of the mites, but small numbers survived, and over the years the surviving mites reproduced, replicating the genetic capacity that resisted the miticide and growing in population until, finally, the resistant survivors' offspring made up the majority of mite populations. The medication had selected for stronger, more resistant mites. Fortunately, a second compound, called coumaphos, was in the process of EPA approval and was rushed to market. Coumaphos was also effective against mites, but it was much harder on bees. Soon after Miller began applying it, he noticed that his queens were less fertile, and that they failed, and died, sooner. Miller's friend Kevin Ward—who produces some of the best star thistle honey on the planet—likes to joke that coumaphos "killed everything but the mite."

Beekeepers had resorted to protecting their frail charges with the very thing they had been fighting against since the dawn of industrial agriculture: pesticides. Starting in the 1950s and '60s, lethal chemicals like methyl parathion and Furadan had been sprayed on crops nationwide and nearly indiscriminately, killing birds, wild insects, and managed bees. The effects were dramatic: when foragers were inadvertently caught in a spray of pesticides, they would fall out of the air as they were flying. If bees survived the initial dusting or visited a flower that had recently been sprayed, they might bring back contaminated nectar that would doom the whole hive. For weeks after chemicals were applied, fields remained lethal, their fences pasted with placards warning "Peligro"—danger.

For beekeepers, the danger was more than hypothetical: their livelihood could be destroyed with one poorly timed spray or wrongly placed pass of a crop duster. Miller remembers being "popped" by a stray plume of Furadan that drifted over his hives from alfalfa fields near Tracy, California. Dead bees piled up not only in the "customary puddle o' death" outside the hives, but also, more disturbingly, inside the hives. "I was fighting tears," he says, "bagging up bees." When he sent them to a state lab for analysis, the techs told him they had never measured Furadan levels that high in bees. In California and some other states, farmers are required to inform beekeepers when they treat crops with insecticides; in others, the onus falls on the beekeeper to keep abreast of farmers' pesticide plans. That was next to impossible. Treatments applied miles away could kill entire bee yards when a drift traveled unexpectedly on the prevailing breeze.

Beekeepers hated everything about insecticides. Before the onslaught of the varroa mite, the strongest thing any self-respecting beekeeper would put in his hive was an antibiotic called Terramycin to treat American foulbrood. Now they were forced to dose their own hives with chemicals. "It ran counter to everything we believed about good husbandry," Miller says. But the only other choice was not to treat for varroa mites— and guarantee the loss of 80 to 90 percent of their operation. Few beekeepers were willing to do that. So Miller swallowed his pride and continued to use the coumaphos. For three or four years, it did the trick.

But in the late summer of 2004, he realized, too late, that it was no longer working. He was in a bee yard in rural Lehr, North Dakota, on the farm of Wilbur Hauff, a "cool old bachelor" in his eighties, a gifted gardener with a soft spot for honey. Hauff's yard was on sandy soil, and Miller's hives sat in an area that was relatively free of grass, making it easier to work the hives (no hidden badger holes) and to see what was going on at the base of them. The colonies were not doing well, and Miller couldn't understand why the bees weren't making honey. Then he examined the base of the hives. "I looked down, onto the sand," he writes, "and there they were ... ANTS!"

Ants are what Miller and Ryan Elison, his right-hand man, call worker bees that have been parasitized by varroa mites. They are undersized bees with deformed wings—infants, barely hours old but already ejected by the housekeeping bees. Exiled, they crawled in front of the hive entrances, confused and underweight, riddled with deformed wing virus, a destructive pathogen that mites carry with them into a hive. Miller got down on the ground to observe the ants more closely—just, perhaps, as young Lorenzo Langstroth had, wearing out the knees of his pants in pursuit of insect knowledge—and experienced a distinctly unpleasant flash of recognition. "Eureka, Jeeves, I've got it!" The mites were adapting. The coumaphos was failing. So were his hives. "The outfit was crashing, right before my very eyes." It was too late to stop the conflagration. The hives were too heavily infested, and the last bees of the summer harvest were too sick to forage. They would not produce enough honey for the winter. It was too late to restock with healthier bees; there was nothing to be done. Miller put his hives away for the

winter sick and hungry, and hoped against all his years of accrued wisdom that they would recover.

They wouldn't. The varroa mite, once a frightening but
manageable problem, had become a wily adversary, a daunting
foe, a small, red great white whale. The next January, Miller saw
the fruits of its handiwork. He unloaded an early semi of bees
in a large orchard in Los Banos, California, in preparation for
the almond bloom and discerned immediately that they were
"garbage." Most had only two frames of healthy bees instead
of the usual eight; whole semitruck loads were dead. The honey
crop had been bad that year, so his hives had headed into winter
light. He had less honey, fewer bees, ineffective coumaphos, a
high mite load, and a high virus load. It was, he says, a "darn
near perfect storm." By spring Miller had lost four thousand
hives; his life's work had diminished by more than a third. The
same was true for many of his colleagues. "In the old days we
were shouting and spitting and swearing if we had an eight percent dud rate. Now people would be happy with that," he says.
"We hauled semi loads of dead bees and equipment from the
orchards."

It was a lesson Miller didn't need to learn twice. From then
on, he took no chances with the varroa mite. As is typical
of beekeepers, Miller blamed himself. He didn't see it coming, he wrote, "because I wasn't doing the work INSIDE the
hive, taking sticky board samples, opening brood, LOOKING,
LOOKING, LOOKING . . . I was neglecting about the most
important thing a beekeeper can do; to monitor hive health is-
sues." After the "dope slap" of 2004, he began inspecting his bee
yards far more frequently and monitoring the gossip grapevine
among bee guys and bug guys to learn what could kill mites
without killing hives. He began spending nearly every free mo-

ment in his "Frankenstein yard"—an apiary stocked with non-
honey-producing colonies where he performs daily counts of
mites and treats different hives with different EPA-approved
and not-so-approved medicines.

In his Frankenstein yard, Miller tinkers with materials like
formic acid, which, he learned, is reasonably effective at killing mites, but only if temperatures stay between 60 and 80
degrees for two weeks. At colder temperatures it doesn't emit
sufficient fumes to kill the mites; at warmer temperatures it becomes volatile, and although it doesn't appear to harm bees, it
can harm humans, who must wear a respirator while applying
it. The grapevine conveyed stories of beekeepers who neglected
the respirator and ended up puking blood in their bee yards.
Thymol, a plant extract that is the main component of thyme
oil, is also approved for use in beehives and effective against varroa mites, but the bees don't like it, and if there's a firestorm of
varroa mites in a hive, a beekeeper can't count on thymol to put
it out. Oxalic acid is a natural wood-bleaching compound that
can, with regular, conscientious application every three days for
the varroa's twenty-one-day breeding cycle, disrupt the mite's
progress. It's less dangerous to humans than formic acid—it
only causes temporary blindness—and works better, nuking the
hemolymph of the mites without damaging the bees. But it is
not EPA-approved, and it doesn't work nearly as well as Apistan
and coumaphos once did.

It is difficult to find a material that will kill bugs on bugs.
Miller compares it to having a chimpanzee on your back, grab-
bing you by the throat and biting you on your neck. You are
bleeding profusely, and you have to find something in your
medicine cabinet, quick, to splash on the chimp that will kill
it but not you. In the case of the varroa mite, beekeepers need

materials that will kill acarids—ticks and mites—without harming bees or contaminating the honey. "We don't have a lot to work with," says Miller, "and by the way, I'm trying to protect honey's good name." Many of the approved natural miticides require a level of intervention that is not possible for large-scale beekeepers. Apistan and coumaphos were easy—plastic strips coated with low doses could be placed in the hives and forgotten. Other treatments require beekeepers to remove each frame from a hive and spray a light mist on the bees. This has to happen once or twice a week for three weeks during the brief time in late fall when there are few capped brood cells that can hide the mites and no surplus honey being produced for sale to humans. For hobbyists with a few backyard hives, it is possible, but for commercial beekeepers with a thousand or more colonies, it's not.

Instead, many beekeepers have turned to an off-label pesticide called amitraz, also known as Taktic, which is used to kill ticks on sheep, cows, and swine. Amitraz is said to work as well as coumaphos once did, with fewer toxic side effects. It is illegal to use on bees. But as long as beekeepers are careful that there are no residues on their colonies when their hives are producing honey for sale to the public, most agriculture inspectors won't ask too many questions. Critics of the practice argue that insecticides seep into honeycombs as water absorbs into a sponge, infiltrating the honey that is stored in it. But this was already the case with coumaphos and fluvalinate. And regardless, it is only a matter of time until the amitraz stops working. In the meantime, scientists are racing to find a more sustainable solution.

Research in the world's "few lonely bee labs," as Miller describes them, tends to follow two tracks: developing a better miticide, or breeding a stronger, more disease-resistant bee. So far, however, these efforts have been more successful at breeding a better mite through pesticide use than at breeding a better bee. Indeed, the varroa mite has proven far more adaptable than either the honey bee or its human protectors—every effort to control the mites has ultimately succeeded only in producing a more powerful and resistant creature. "Eventually," says Miller, "we could breed a mite that was resistant to a hammer." This dynamic isn't helped by the fact that the process of developing miticides for approval by the EPA takes at least three years, often longer, and that the research requires considerable time and money. There's rarely sufficient profit motive for a chemical company to do the research needed to get a new varroacide approved—in case it's not abundantly clear by now, there's not a lot of money in beekeeping. Were several effective miticides on the market at a time, beekeepers could engage in a rotational scheme of "integrated pest management," using materials for limited periods, switching before the mites developed resistance. As it is, by the time a new miticide is approved, the old ones have failed. So beekeepers either follow the rules and risk losing everything or try nonsanctioned home remedies to keep their hives alive.

There are other, more palatable options on the horizon. Mites live in what Denis Anderson, the Australian entomologist, describes as a "chemical world." They don't have eyes; they have hairs and sensory organs that respond to chemical signals that tell them where they are. "It's quite a complicated world, a huge city of bees, and they've got to get around that city and get to a particular spot in that city where they are able to reproduce and then spread out into the bigger world," he says. "A bat sees with sound. A varroa mite sees with chemicals."

Scientists studying the varroa mite are looking into the possibility of developing traps that mimic the chemical smells that attract mites and tell them when to reproduce. Genetic research has also yielded incremental progress. The Asian bees did, after all, learn grooming and hygienic behavior to detect and expel varroa mites from their midst. Researchers have, with limited success, sought to breed European bees with similar survival mechanisms. Others are designing hives with holes in the bottom that the mites fall through when they leave their hosts for a new brood cell. Some beekeepers claim that mite loads disappear when bees are placed in "top-bar" hives that mimic a natural hive environment, though that does not explain the disappearance of so many feral colonies. Top-bar hives also are difficult to move and work with, for all the reasons that led the world's beekeepers to adopt the Langstroth box hive in the first place.

So beekeepers have had to learn to live with losses that, twenty years ago, were unthinkable. If a 10 percent loss was considered horrible then, a 20 percent loss isn't so bad today. Beekeepers now realize they had it easy before the varroa mite. Their bees still suffered from bacterial invasions, fungal infections, moths, mice, skunks, and bears—it was still difficult to make a profit—but really, beekeeping provided a pleasant lifestyle. You could leave your hives in a meadow and do other things—go on long vacations, run a marathon, go fishing, hunting, watch TV. The honey bee would take care of itself. It would forage, build, swarm, run wild, go feral, survive. Today, thanks to the varroa mite, the European honey bee is, in most of the world, a purely domesticated creature, and one on life support, at that. Without beekeepers, Western honey bees would not survive.

"It used to be pretty simple," Miller wrote.

American foulbrood.

European foulbrood.

Chalkbrood.

Ants, predating ants that could be sent to ant heaven with a shovel, and a tablespoon of Cyanogas dust deep into the nest . . . great stuff; very lethal.

Then came this tracheal mite thing . . . and hard on its heels, came Ms.

Varroa.

All of a sudden, the world changed.

It was, and remains: Ms. Varroa, her children,

And

Everything else.

There are, however, some advantages to losing half the nation's bee herd in less than two decades. Miller likes to say that bee guys always knew they were important, but nobody else did. Now that bees are dying, almond guys—and cherry guys, apple guys, watermelon guys, canola guys, blueberry guys, cantaloupe guys, and all the other pollination-dependent farm guys—have also come to realize that bee guys are important.

Chapter Four

....

Faustian Bargains

VARROA MITES ARE TERRIBLE FOR BEES. SO ARE ANY NUMBER of other pests and diseases. The first European honey bees arrived in America in the 1620s; the first widespread European bee losses were reported in 1670—around the time that honey bees themselves became widespread. Historians now suspect that this early North American die-off was caused by American foulbrood, the same pestilence that afflicted Miller's dad and Miller's granddad and at one time seemed like just about the worst thing that could happen to a beekeeper. Foulbrood is a bacterial contagion that grows like a mold within brood cells and gives the normally pearlescent white bee larvae a stringy yellow hue. The larvae turn a macabre brownish black tint as they die, emitting what Lorenzo Langstroth described as a sour, "noisome stench." Langstroth believed the disease could be regarded "as the greatest possible calamity to beekeeping." Even today it is, if left untreated, a calamity. When worker bees discover contaminated larvae and clean out a hive, they spread the disease spores throughout it. The spores can remain inactive for as long as forty years and emerge to spark another epidemic. In Langstroth's day, the only way to control the disease was to burn an infected hive with all of its inhabitants. This scorched-hive strategy offered only temporary respite: outbreaks in the 1930s and '40s brought losses as large as anything wrought by varroa mites or CCD. Until the advent of sulfa-based antibiotics during World War II, foulbrood's mass carnage was a regular feature of the beekeeping life.

Foulbrood wasn't beekeeping's only problem. It was an invasion of wax moths that prompted Langstroth to declare the years before he invented his hive in 1851 "some of the worst seasons ever known for bees." The moth, a dreary-looking creature about the size of a nickel, thrived in "discouraged populations" and seemed particularly well adapted to life in the confinements of the hive. It could "crawl backwards or forwards, and as well one way as another"; it could "twist round on itself, curl up almost into a knot, and flatten itself out like a pancake." It could employ, in short, all manner of "stratagems and cunning devices" to make a beekeeper's life miserable. The wax moth was nothing new in Europe: Langstroth recalled that Virgil, Columella, and other "ancient authors" described the insect as a "plague of their Apiaries"; Swammerdam dubbed it the "bee-wolf." The "ravages of the bee-moth" halved the number of colonies in the "Northern and Middle States" in the 1830s and '40s, Langstroth wrote, and as for beekeepers, "multitudes have abandoned the pursuit in disgust."

In his 1853 treatise, Langstroth also described nosema, a diarrheal disease associated with muddy black excrement on hive entrances and floors. It had an "intolerably offensive smell" and tended to occur during winter, when northern bees were confined in poorly ventilated environments: "Is it not under precisely such circumstances that cholera and dysentery prove most fatal to human beings? The filthy, damp, and unventilated abodes of the abject poor, becoming perfect lazar-houses to their wretched inmates." He also lamented the incursions of mice, wasps, ants, spiders, "gallinaceous birds," even amphibians: "The toad," he noted, "is a well-known devourer of bees."

Langstroth's new hive helped detect and destroy many of these pathogens and predators by allowing beekeepers to examine their colonies. But even with improved hive technology, the world's apiarists remained subject to recurrent losses. In 1904, nine years after Langstroth's death, a mysterious ailment devastated hives on the Isle of Wight, a British island in the middle of the English Channel. The disease wiped out nearly all the hives on the island, then jumped to the British mainland, where it also wreaked havoc. Not until 1921 did a Dr. J. Rennie identify the tracheal mite as the culprit responsible for the losses. It was the world's first known mite infestation—though not the last. In 1922, the United States prohibited the importation of honey bees, managing to forestall the arrival of the mite for more than sixty years—but also isolating the gene pool of American bees and making them more vulnerable to those pathogens that inevitably did arrive.

And arrive they did. They came in trickles; they came in waves; they came in tsunamis; they came and kept coming. There came the imported red fire ants, which are native to South Africa and arrived in Mobile, Alabama, sometime in the 1930s aboard a Brazilian cargo ship. The ants now infest most of the southern and southwestern United States, overrunning colonies, driving bees away, and eating everything in the hive, then moving on to destroy nearby crops. There came chalkbrood, a fungal disease that leapt from Europe to the States in the mid-1960s. Chalkbrood preys on the brood in weakened hives, leaving behind chalky white discarded "mummies" scattered at the entrance. There came tracheal mites and varroa mites, the twin parasitic curses from the 1980s onward. There came Africanized bees, bred in Brazil by accident in 1953. In 1990 they crossed the U.S. border, invading hives, interbreeding with European bees, and creating more aggressive offspring. There came small hive beetles, which aren't all that small. Little black pellet-like insects, they arrived in the United States from South Africa in 1998. They eat their way through a colony's larvae, pollen, and honey, defecating every inch of the way, leaving in their wake a foul, gelatinous goo—a "violent ooze," as one of Miller's friends once described it.

There came "crazy Rasberry ants," named after Tom Rasberry, the exterminator who figured out how to kill them—not an easy task because the ants, which eschew typical regimental ant columns, pile the dead over areas where pesticides have been applied and march to safe haven. Crazy Rasberry ants first debarked at a Houston port in 2002 and by 2008 had doubled their range, gumming up fire alarms, sewage pumps, computers, and gas meters and inflicting grave damage on beehives, where the ants dine on larvae and move into the collapsed hives to lay eggs. There came sinister-sounding pathogens like Kashmir bee virus and Israeli acute paralysis virus and black queen cell virus and deformed wing virus and Kakugo virus, which infests bee brains and makes them unusually aggressive. All were identified only recently. Bad things have been invading beehives for a long, long time. But in the last thirty years, they have come faster and faster, in wave after breathless wave. For that, we have the almond to thank.

JOHN MILLER FIRST TOOK HIS DAD'S BEES TO A CALIFORNIA almond orchard in 1974. Before then, the family had overwintered its colonies in Idaho, lining the hives up on a gentle south slope, clustering them together six hives per stand, enrobing them in straw, tarpaper, and chicken wire to protect them from north and west winds, and hoping for snow to further bury and insulate the bees. In late March, after winter's worst months had passed, the Millers would remove the packing, "discover 10,000 mice also enjoy the straw insulation; occasionally discover a skunk," John Miller wrote. In a normal year, they could expect a 2 to 4 percent loss over the winter; to replace dead colonies, they'd drive their GMC 5500 flatbed through Nevada to Live Oak, California, where they'd pick up five hundred three-pound packages of bees and queens from a guy named Eugene Walker.

John's grandfather Earl had stopped migrating when he set up his beekeeping operation in Idaho in 1919. He wasn't peripatetic like his father, N.E., or his brother Woodrow. Earl was, says John, "content to do business, buy property, run bees, be the mayor of little Blackfoot, Idaho, and play cards at the Elks Club." Rather than lay off his summer beekeepers after the harvest and move the bees to California, he kept employees busy building houses to sell.

Earl handed over the business in 1957 to John's father, Neil, who would have been content to follow suit, but in the late 1960s he found himself in a predicament. The alfalfa growers whose fields surrounded the Millers' bees had begun using dieldrin and heptachlor, new insecticides that proved remarkably efficient at killing both alfalfa weevil and bees. Neil's losses were horrific. In addition, he began to notice that the small farms and dairies in southeastern Idaho were getting bigger and more mechanized.

Farmers were now, with the help of modern chemical fertilizers, planting more potatoes and less alfalfa, and when they did plant alfalfa, they were replacing their old ten-foot mowing machines, the kind that hung off the back of a tractor on a three-point hitch, with platoons of freestanding twenty-four-foot, six-mower conditioners that could knock down a field of alfalfa in two hours and empty the valley of hay in three days, before it began to bloom. That was when the hay was most "bovine nutritious," says John, but not, alas, at all apis nutritious.

This did not bode well for a business that needed lots of flowers to feed lots of bees, and Neil began to consider getting out of beekeeping. He just couldn't see a way to make a good living at it anymore. But in 1968, a guy named James Powers— a mercurial, "hulking brute of a man" who tended not to play well with others but happened to be a good friend of Neil's— rolled through Blackfoot from his home base three hundred miles west in Parma, Idaho. He was on his way to North Dakota, where the climate was ill-suited to large-scale cultivation of grain and cattle, and clover and alfalfa still reigned. Powers had begun keeping some of his twenty thousand bees there. It had been a year of crop failure in southeast Idaho. Not so in North Dakota. "Jim said, 'Come up to North Dakota, there are lots of flowers,'" Neil Miller, who is now retired, recalls. And then Powers issued an ultimatum. "He said, 'I'm telling you if you don't come look at this country I'll never speak to you again and I mean it.'"

Well, Neil liked Jim Powers, and he wanted to stay his friend, and he was also curious and a little bit desperate, so he got in the car and drove north and east to see the flowers that bloomed from horizon to horizon and to witness the tremendous crop those flowers were producing for Jim Powers. Powers mentioned that there was a small town named Gackle about halfway between Oaks, where Powers had his operation, and Bismarck, the state capital, that appeared to have all the necessities for a successful beekeeping operation: decent roads, available land, a small Ford dealership, a hardware and grocery store, and sweet clover as far as the eye could see. When Neil visited Gackle, a patron sat next to him at the local café and said, "You're new here, aren't you?" He asked Neil what he needed, and Neil said he was looking for a warehouse building to start a honey production business. By the next morning, the Gackle Improvement Association had offered to purchase a piece of land for Neil on the south side of town and to let him occupy it property-tax-free for five years until he got the business off the ground.

The next year, the Millers moved into Gackle, where the flowers bloomed unmolested, as promised. But the winters there were much tougher than in Idaho. Beekeepers who over-wintered in North Dakota could expect annual losses of more than 20 percent. The necessary evil of a northern operation, it seemed, was a southern operation. Neil had to find a place to put his bees in the winter, preferably one where they could make lots of honey. He consulted with Jim Powers, who was winter-ing his bees in Parker, Arizona, and appeared to be prospering. Neil found a spot just across the Colorado River from Powers in Blythe, California. But it was 1973, and bee turf was hard to find in warm climes: "Like anyone that comes-lately, all the good spots were taken," says Neil. John, who was a teenager at the time, remembers the experience with little nostalgia.

The Colorado, at the time, replenished willows and scrub brush; and each spring, the desert sang with hardy plants in bloom.

The abundance also blushed large numbers of scorpions, snakes, and spiders, who love to escape the sun beneath a beehive.

As spring wanes and summer waxes, more critters hide below more beehives.

Recall, this was also Before Pallets; so everything was hand-loaded, as in, pick the beehive up; discover what is coiled between your legs; in a bad way . . . and by the way, you have a BEEHIVE in your arms; don't you DARE drop it!

Blythe was not my best experience.

Nor was it Miller Honey Farms' best experience. "The bees came up fine, but we were all pretty well insane and sun-damaged by the time Blythe was in the rearview mirror," John Miller says. Looking for a better place to park his bees in the cold months, Neil conferred with Eugene Walker, the queen-breeder who provided bees to restock the Miller hives each spring. Walker had begun pollinating bees for a Tracy, California, farmer named Ed Thoming, who had, in 1959, gotten sick of the work involved in planting sugar beets and beans every year and instead put in one of the largest blocks of almonds in the Central Valley—about five hundred acres of trees. The recent pesticide kills across the country meant Walker needed more of his hives than usual for breeding queens, and the Thomings needed more bees to pollinate their trees than Walker could supply. The contracts were modest at the time, about eight dollars a hive, which barely covered costs. But they did provide a place to keep and feed bees for six weeks in the dead of winter.

Almonds seemed more appealing than another winter among the rattlesnakes. So the Millers started delivering bees to the

Thoming orchards in the spring of 1974, and signed on with a few other farmers in the Tracy area. The timing was propitious: the interstate highway system was close to completion, allowing the Millers to move large numbers of bees on trucks. Improved forklift technology allowed the Millers to use pallets to load and unload multiple hives at a time, requiring less backbreaking labor—Miller Honey Farms' first forklift, a skid-steer 610 Bobcat with a Clark mast, dates to 1973. And more and more farmers were planting almonds, which meant there were more and more people who needed to pay beekeepers for a service that used to be free! As almond demand chased bee supply, pollination prices climbed to around twelve dollars a hive, which even promised a little profit for beekeepers willing to haul their hives to California each spring. It seemed as good a way as any for a beekeeper to spend the last months of winter, and in 1976, Neil bought the family's current property in Newcastle, east of Sacramento, to serve as a base of operations during the winter months. John moved from Blackfoot to California with his new bride, Jan, in 1978.

SO NOW FEBRUARY IS, IF NOT THE HIGHLIGHT OF JOHN Miller's beekeeping season, certainly the crux of it. He brings every hive he owns to California; so does almost every commercial beekeeper in the country. It is a spectacle: the miles of unbroken blossom, the panoply of bee rigs jamming the roads, flatbeds and hives and netting and ropes and helpers—rush hour for beekeepers. Miller enjoys a spectacle, so every year during the almond bloom he hosts what he calls the "native migrant tour" to introduce newcomers to the wonders of the bee and the bloom. It's a simple concept, a bee tourism marketing pitch, of sorts:

I hunt up a couple of gullible naifs for a tour of the almond orchards, and the overall agriculture miracle . . . emphasis on the role of the honey bee.

The first time I joined him on the tour was in February 2006, a week or so after Valentine's Day, when the bloom begins, and a week or so before the bloom's peak in late February. Miller picked me up in his red Corvette, transferred me to a large red pickup with a Miller Honey Farms logo on the side, and headed seventy miles south from Sacramento to Modesto—holding forth the entire way, of course. We pulled into a sparse but clean motel just outside Modesto that was humming with beekeepers, bee brokers, and a lot of hired help. In 1983 the Millers had moved their bees from the Thomings', a half hour west of Modesto, to the east and south side of the valley, where the blocks of almond acreage are larger and more contiguous, thus easier to service. Modesto lies at the center of California's Central Valley, which lies at the center of California, which lies at the center of the agricultural universe. The area is the most productive farming region in the nation—on earth, in fact. But there is little rural romance here. The valley smells like a brew of fertilizer, chemicals, and manure, and it hosts an eternal ebb and flow of mostly Hispanic migrant workers. Venture along Crows Landing Road, Modesto's gritty main agricultural strip, and you'll find taco stands, chicken farms, El Tio Auto Sales, and more tractor dealerships per square mile than anywhere else on the planet, along with flea markets ("You can buy anything you want," said Miller: "a wet umbrella, a dry umbrella, a dead policeman's badge"), and of course, acres beyond acres of almond trees. There is no better place to grow almonds. "When God was thinking about almonds," says Miller, "this was the dirt he made."

God was selective when he was thinking about almonds: the four-hundred-mile stretch of the Central Valley between Bakersfield in the south and Red Bluff in the north remains the only North American location where almonds can be cultivated for bulk commercial sale. The sandy loam and Mediterranean conditions there are perfect for the mass production of almonds—fifteen to twenty inches of rain a year; dry, hot summers; six hundred annual chilling hours during November and December; mild Januaries and Februaries; well-drained soil; flood irrigation. Farmers here have made a science of the ostensibly natural process of growing the nuts: the trees are planted in an orderly, perfectly spaced, nineteen-by-twenty-foot diamond grid, each tree leaning ever so slightly to the northwest, whence come the most damaging winds. Thanks to extensive research into almond productivity, the grid has grown tighter over the years: in 1985, the standard almond grid was 95 trees per acre; now it's 135, even 150 trees per acre in some spots. To enhance their survival and output, growers graft cuttings from almond trees—which are, in nature, reedy, delicate flora—onto hardier peach rootstock. Pruning techniques vary among planters—German Baptists, Miller says, prune very vertically. But these days most growers just let the trees grow—the more tree, the more almonds, the more money. The soil is tilled with nitrogen and phosphate fertilizers. The ground under the trees is soaked in herbicides to keep the area beneath the canopies clear. The trees are sprayed with fungicides to combat nasty diseases like jacket rot and ground rot, and with pesticides to combat worm infestations. Then they are soaked in ample water to keep them alive and growing. They begin producing nuts in about five years, reaching peak yield in about ten, and tapering off in about twenty-five.

Almonds are a stone fruit related to cherries, plums, and peaches. The nut meat is the pit; the fuzzy green hull is the fruit. They were served to Egypt's pharaohs; they receive prominent mention in the Old Testament; their English name derives from the Latin *amygdala*—"tonsil plum." They have been so widely eaten and traded for so many years that no one knows where they originated. They may have once grown wild on the mountain slopes of central Asia and been dispersed via traders along the Silk Road from China to the Mediterranean region and northern Africa, where the nuts flourished in the hot, arid climate—though some food historians place their origins in the Middle East. Their New World provenance can be situated more precisely—the almond tree traveled to the California coast with Franciscan missionaries in the 1760s, and for two hundred years they fared poorly in the moist weather. Then in the nineteenth century, someone planted an almond orchard in the Central Valley. The trees thrived in the hot, dry climate. By the turn of the twentieth century, almonds had become an important California crop; by the 1950s, they were an industry; by the 1970s, a movement; by the 1990s, a global market force.

Almond season is bracketed by holidays. The bloom begins around Valentine's Day and the harvest winds down at Halloween. In between, buds form and open into pale whitish pink flowers and then fall, petals covering the orchard floors like snow. Nuts begin to grow in the flowers' place. As the almonds ripen on the tree, their outer greenish hulls harden and then, in July, crack open, the fissure widening through late summer and early fall to reveal a pale inner shell. Inside the shell sits the oblong brown-skinned kernel—the nut that launched three-quarters of a million acres. The preparation for the harvest begins in early August, when "shakers" come through, knocking the nuts to the orchard floor, where they lie in the sun for a week or two to dry. Before the early 1960s, workers tapped trees with tall mallets to shake the fruit down onto a canvas; now they drive hundred-thousand-dollar trapezoidal tractors with air-conditioned cabs and names like "Shock Wave" that use rubber-coated hydraulic pincers to grip the trunks and jiggle them with a force that has been compared to an earthquake or an electric chair. The machines can strip a tree of nearly every nut in less than a minute.

Next, "sweepers"—low-slung contraptions that look like a cross between a street sweeper and a tank—pass through, using brushes and wheels to push and blow the nuts, leaves, and workers' discarded lunch wrappers into neat rows between the trees. Then comes the pickup machine, whose belt looks like a vacuum-cleaner rotary. It sucks up the almonds, dirt, leaves, and lunch wrappers, leaving the ground utterly bare but for enormous pluming clouds of dust. By this time, all the trees, grass, fences, irrigation pipes, and roads in the vicinity are covered in a fine loam that hangs in the air for days. The pickup machine deposits its load onto a screen that sifts the dirt and blows off the leaves and lunch wrappers. From there the nuts travel to a processing plant, where they are sorted, piled, fumigated, hulled, shelled, packed, and shipped with the help of a series of elevators, under-rollers, conveyors, perforated sorting trays, nets, blasters, and vacuums. The machines pull off the soft hulls, crack off the shells, and siphon off the remaining dust. Then they grade, size, and weigh the nuts for shipment in one-ton wood containers. Throughout their mechanized odyssey, the nuts are handled with great delicacy—unsullied nuts fetch top dollar at market, while chipped nuts are sold at a discount for baking and product manufacture.

California supplies the vast majority of the world's almonds, both a pleasant accident of geography—the valley's superlative climate and soil—and a purposeful result of the industry's remarkable productivity. Almonds are California's leading agricultural export—ahead of raisins, lettuce, avocados, strawberries, and cattle. They book more than twice the revenues of the state's wine exports. In recent years, the nut has become ludicrously profitable. Almond ranchers break even if their almonds sell for more than a dollar a pound wholesale. In 2005 they sold for three times that price, grossing California growers somewhere around $3 billion. Since then the price has fluctuated at around $2.50 a pound. The last decade has produced for the industry what almond farmer Dan Cummings, who manages several thousand acres of almonds and walnuts in the Sacramento Valley and serves on the Almond Board of California, has called a "perfect storm"—the good kind, this time. Almonds grew in popularity, especially in Europe; the euro appreciated; and competing nut prices stayed high.

It's no surprise, then, that record almond profits, combined with depressed prices for other crops that also grow on land suited for almonds, have enticed a lot of Central Valley farmers to plow over their cotton, wine grapes, peaches, and apricots and plant more almonds. Growing almonds makes perfect sense for a farmer seeking to maximize his profit and minimize his labor costs and headaches. Nut crops command high value at market. They are less perishable than most fruits and vegetables. They can be harvested mechanically, unlike such stone fruits as peaches, which must be handpicked. Almond acreage has increased from 400,000 acres in the 1990s to 800,000 today (with around 740,000 actually producing nuts), pushing harvest totals from 236 million pounds twenty years ago to nearly 1.4 billion in 2009. Those observing the frenzy have taken to calling it the "almond rush," as every sane and sensible farmer in the region has planted himself a diamond grid. "We make our determinations on what we plant by the highest and best use of the land," Cummings told me. "And it's almonds."

When I traveled with Miller to Modesto that first time, we drove to a high point in the middle of an almond orchard. From there we could see nothing but almonds. Mile after monocropped mile of pale pink petals extended from the western horizon to the eastern mountains—a monumental reshaping of the landscape—grass- and shrubland eclipsed by a bloom so enormous you could certainly glimpse it from space. Along the superhighways, new almond trees abounded, foot-tall, diamond-gridded grafts stretching cheerfully toward the three-dollar-a-pound future, staking out roadside real estate in intense competition with the equally rootless strip malls and stucco-encrusted housing developments that had sprouted across the landscape in the previous decade. The almond boom, like the real estate boom, had created its own sprawl; it had also generated remarkable wealth. On the back roads near Modesto, it was easy to spot an almond rancher's home amid the tin roofs, tired siding, and dusty driveways that pass for typical farm structures in that part of the world. The almond-funded homes were hand-plastered and mansard-roofed, their paver-laid driveways invariably lined with palm trees. Miller likes to draw a graph of the rise of "cabins owned by almond guys" at Lake Tahoe from 1970 to the present—a soaring diagonal, approaching infinity. Meanwhile, says Miller, "bee guys don't even have timeshares." Miller regularly gets calls from almond farmers on their yachts in the Sea of Cortez and at backcountry heli-ski lodges in British Columbia. Miller went on a Caribbean cruise once ten years ago; "about every other year we'll go to some Jed Clampett time-share." That's about all the adventure travel he can cop to. "If you enjoy playing golf," LeRoy Brant, a bee broker and friend of Miller's, told me as we ate breakfast in Modesto, "don't become a beekeeper." Better, by a long shot, to be an almond grower.

In 1950, a consortium of almond farmers formed the Almond Board of California to combine grower resources for marketing and research. At the time, U.S. growers produced 50 million pounds of almonds and claimed 17 percent of the world market; Spain commanded 75 percent of global almond sales. Today California boasts an 80 percent market share. Almond economics have defied the laws of gravity. Typically, a large supply of a product will mean a drop in prices for farmers who sell it—hence the regular price supports for staples like corn, cotton, and soybeans, of which we often produce too much. But not just anyone can grow an almond—you need a specific climate and soil, a large investment to get the trees growing, and five years of patience and funding before they begin to bear. Those who can do it are amply rewarded, because in the almond world these days, there is no such thing as too much. Thus far, more nuts has simply meant more money. Even at the trough of the global recession of 2008 and 2009, almond sales set a record. Growers shipped 10 percent more in 2009 than they had the previous year. The almond was one of the few products, agricultural or otherwise, that continued to boom as the rest of the economy went bust. It was, apparently, the bulletproof nut.

The Almond Board has displayed remarkable marketing savvy in its campaign to increase demand. It has commissioned and advertised a number of studies touting the health benefits of almonds. Such campaigns have been credited for much of the increase in domestic demand, though the majority of Central Valley almonds today are still shipped overseas. The largest market is in Europe, but almond sales have also soared in India and China, where the Almond Board once deliberated over whether to rename the nut. The Chinese call it *xingren*—"apricot kernel"—and the board felt a less bitter-sounding moniker might boost sales. It toyed with names like "vitality nut," "good fortune nut," and "big California *xingren*" before deciding that continuing sales growth in China didn't warrant a name change. Exports to China had more than doubled from 2008 to 2009. And "apricot kernel" is, after all, a discernible linguistic improvement over "tonsil plum."

The board has also plowed profits into agricultural research, developing state-of-the-art fertility management, irrigation practices, planting strategies, and optimal grid patterns to increase the chance of a successful crop set. In Spain, hilly terrain and antiquated planting and harvest practices keep farmers from retrieving more than about 100 pounds per acre. Growers in the Central Valley, by contrast, can expect up to 3,000 pounds an acre. But for all their sophisticated strategies to increase yield and profitability, almond growers still have one major problem—pollination. Unless a bird or insect brings the pollen from flower to flower, even the most state-of-the-art orchard won't grow enough nuts. An almond grower who depends on the wind and a few volunteer pollinators in this desert of cultivated fields can expect only 40 pounds of almonds per acre. If he imports honey bees, the average yield is 2,400 pounds per acre, as much as 3,000 in more densely planted orchards. To build an almond, it takes a bee.

No one knows exactly when the honey bee began doing the reproductive work of the flowering plant. Paleobotanists place the development somewhere around 100 million years ago, during the Cretaceous period, when the number of plant species grew more than sevenfold and flowers learned that visiting bugs or birds could make their procreative task much easier. Some flowering plants pollinate themselves. But many make seeds and reproduce only when pollen—the sticky powder in the flowers—moves from one plant to the next. Although some types of pollen travel on the wind, many fruiting plants require outside help from insects and birds. Some pollinators are attracted by bright colors; others, like honey bees, by the fragrant nectar the blossoms emit. The nectar lies deep at the base of the petals, and when the insects retrieve it, they get covered in dusty pollen, the male product of the bloom. When they fly to the next flower, some of that pollen rubs off and—voilà—fertilizes the seeds in the stigma, the female part of the blossom. Thus flowers evolved to emit more nectar for the insects—and developed sweet smells and bright colors to attract them. Bees began bringing that nectar home to evaporate into honey, storing it in wax cells for feeding the young and surviving fallow periods. Honey supplies, in turn, allowed the bees to develop larger, better-organized communities, the better to collect nectar and pollen. Bees and flowers adapted to help each other.

There are other insects that are more efficient than honey bees. Blue orchard bees, for instance, can pollinate fifty times the flowers that honey bees can. But they are solitary insects, and their populations increase by a factor of only three to eight a year; honey bees can expand from a queen and a few dozen attendants to tens of thousands of bees in just a few weeks. And honey bees live in naturally portable communities that are easy to move from bloom to bloom. That appeals to the almond farmer, who has a lot of flowers to pollinate—twenty-five thousand blossoms per tree, 135 or so trees per acre—about three and a half million flowers per acre. That's a lot—an inconceivably large number—of flowers, and for that, solitary bees won't do; you need a mob. Unlike most fruit and nut crops, which must be thinned to reduce competition for resources among fruit, an almond tree can't have too many flowers. (Those that don't "set"—that aren't successfully pollinated and fall off—have been given the apt nickname "old maids.") The more almond blossoms that set, the more almonds, the more pounds, the more sales, the more dollars. Which means, for the almond farmer, the more bees the better. Most agricultural extension agents recommend that growers place two colonies for every acre of almond trees. Some growers, seeking to maximize their yield per tree, will use more than three colonies per acre.

The quantity of bees can't guarantee the quality of the crop, however. Bees won't forage if it's under 50 degrees, or if it rains (when it does, they hunker down: "You can see them fighting over the clicker," Miller says). If it doesn't rain and there's not sufficient supplemental irrigation, the pollinated nuts won't grow. If there's a hard freeze at the wrong time, the blossoms won't survive. (Growers have been known to hire helicopters to hover over their crops during a freeze so that the rotors move warmer air down from the valley's inversion layer.) If it's too warm in December and the tree doesn't spend enough time in a dormant state, it will store fewer nutrients and produce fewer flowers and hence fewer nuts. These are matters that are beyond the ken of the honey bee. It just does its one job, and does it well. But without it, none of the rest matters: one thing every almond grower knows is that if there are no bees, there is no crop. And to get a bee these days, you need a traveling beekeeper.

Pause to think about it: bee guys pull off a remarkable feat—one that, like pollination itself, is so invisible as to be almost mundane, and so complicated as to be almost inconceivable. Every January, 1.5 million hives—somewhere in the vicinity of two thirds of the nation's bees—are imported to California to fulfill the almond farmers' pollination demands. Miller takes his bees to California in late January, waking them prematurely from their winter's rest in the cellars of Idaho. They arrive at his headquarters in large semi loads, around five hundred hives per truck, four double-deep hives per pallet. The pallets are unloaded and stacked in a holding yard down the hill from Miller's house. A smaller truck delivers the hives to one of Miller's many nearby bee yards. Miller is lucky. Because he has run this territory since 1976, he has access to fifty-five or sixty bee yards in the vicinity of Newcastle, an old Gold Rush community with a historical-society-precious main street lined with log-and-blond-brick buildings. He knows every back road, meadow, and field better even than the pot growers and the police, although he sometimes has to tie a T-shirt to a tree to remind himself where to turn off the road for a particularly well-concealed yard. He is always on the lookout for new apiaries—in this countryside where prospectors once panned the rivers and excavated the hills for veins of gold, he prowls for perfect meadows. He calls it "mining yards." Like gold deposits, there are fewer and fewer.

His apiaries are located mostly in the hilly country nearby, fields dotted with farms and ranches, and, increasingly, with the cedar-and-stone McMansion ranchettes of what Miller likes to call the "wine barrel literati." Many of these property owners do not look kindly upon strange beekeepers visiting their upscale redoubts. When one of the properties on which he keeps his bees gets sold, Miller offers the axiom that the nicer the remodel, the sooner his bees will get kicked off the land. Miller had kept bees at his friend Eddie Ferrera's place, for instance, for twenty-five years. Ferrera loved honey, and his sweet tooth didn't appear to inconvenience him. He died at age ninety-two with a mouthful of perfect teeth. "He had the most amazing set of teeth I've ever seen in my life," Miller says. His hilltop home was sold, and soon after, the new owner razed it, built a demi-castle, sued the long-established cattle ranch next door because of the noise and smell, and kicked Miller's bees off the property.

Still, Miller counts himself luckier than many beekeepers who travel to California for the almonds. Many of them must keep their bees in massive holding yards without a flower in sight, feeding them syrup and waiting for the almonds to come into bloom. Miller's still got plenty of good yards. In January, when the brown fields have turned unearthly green with the winter's rain, some of Miller's bee yards could be mistaken for paradise. There are fields the color of jade, bordered with live oaks, valley oaks, blackberry, and belly-high flowering yellow mustard, dotted with round granite "earth eggs" and quartz outcroppings, scattered with ponds and big red heifers and cawing geese. There are needle-strewn, bear-scratched clearings among the ponderosa and twisted digger pines of the Sierra foothills, manzanita and madrone and ceanothus and even poison oak thrusting into bloom. There are stark ravines with sunburnt grass and bleached clay buttes. Bees, of course, don't care about the view; they will happily set up housekeeping near a quarry or a sawmill or a landfill, just so long as there is ample water, nectar, and pollen.

At the end of January and early February, Miller and his

crews work three straight weeks of ten-hour days, taking only Sunday off. They receive semis, place bees, feed them, examine the hives to see how they fared over the winter, and remove the "duds" that didn't make it. Then they begin transferring the bees to orchards in the Central Valley, piling hives back onto semis for the trip to Modesto. The same precision that drives every step of growing an almond also applies to the placing of bees. Miller and his crews move the hives at night, when the bees are dormant. Whether the grower has forty acres or two thousand, the hives must be placed where they will best penetrate the canopy of the orchard. They always sit at the ends of rows where they are easy to move with a forklift and not likely to get in the way of mowers that shear vegetation on the orchard floors close to the ground. A beekeeper must be aware of the location of irrigation systems—if the hives are placed too close to a Rain Bird, the bees won't fly. If the grower uses flood irrigation, the hives must be off the orchard floor, on an irrigation berm or row end. If there's a school near the orchard, the hives should be placed far away. If the location is muddy and has heavy clay soil, the trucks will invariably get stuck; there's not much Miller can do about that.

With so many acres of almonds, the months preceding the almond bloom are, for Miller, a virtual bazaar, a flurry of phone calls, emails, inspections, haggling, wheeling and dealing, matching hives to acres, tinkering with contracts, signing them, and hoping really hard that the bees arrive healthy enough to keep his promises. The negotiations and logistics surrounding the renting of honey bees have become so complex that many beekeepers and growers rely on "bee brokers" to bring the two parties—pollinator and pollinatee—together, to inspect the hives and grade them according to their health, to oversee their

placement, to see that beekeepers get paid, and generally to ensure that the almond farmers who pay their bills will not end up
with what Miller calls a "superabundance of lumber"—a lot of
wooden beekeeping equipment without healthy bees. Miller has
longtime relationships with growers and works directly with
them. He prefers not to use brokers, but "if I know the grower's
a sonuvabitch and doesn't pay—or if he's a cherry grower—I'll
use a broker."

Almonds didn't always require this degree of intervention—
nor did all the other insect-pollinated crops that farmers grow
and we eat. When farms were smaller and crops were varied,
growers could rely on native pollinators and local beehives to
get the work done. But large farms have replaced small ones,
and farmers now plant larger crops with less variety—rows and
rows and rows of crops like corn and grain, which provide little
to no nutrients for bees to survive on, or almonds, which bloom
for twenty-two days a year and then, after the petals fall, leave
behind a desert—not a hedgerow, not a weed. Furthermore, the
land is plied with pesticides that kill insects and herbicides that
kill the plants that insects rely on for year-round survival. Huge
swaths of land are thus custom-designed to sustain no living
thing except one designated crop.

So just like that, something that used to happen freely now
requires three layers of management—keeper, broker, and
grower—to unite flower and bee. It is a very American story:
creating a market where once there were just bugs and plants
and unfettered visitation. But for what the bee-and-agriculture
crowd has come to call the "largest managed pollination event
in the world," that degree of middlemannery is necessary. The
almond now occupies vast stretches of land—the Central Valley
floor—that were once covered in oaks, California poppies, and

native grasses. Because there are so many almond trees planted so closely together, and because there are so few local bugs anymore, insects from, say, North Dakota, Minnesota, and Florida—in 2004, the USDA for the first time allowed almond ranchers to import hives from Australia as well—must now be trucked or flown to California to pollinate a tree that originally came from across the world. Such are the wages of modern agriculture. The first known bee rental for pollination was recorded in a New Jersey apple orchard in 1909, but it wasn't until the 1960s that farmers began paying for pollination on a systematic basis, and it wasn't until the late 1990s that beekeepers began making real money from pollination fees, rather than just supplementing their earnings from honey production. In the 1960s, hives rented for as low as $6; in the 1970s, a beekeeper could expect to earn $12 a hive from an almond grower; even as recently as 2004, hives were renting for only $48. In 2010, those willing to wait until the very brink of the bloom earned as much as $210 a hive. Miller, who says he is "not brave enough to play that game," is happy to settle at a guaranteed $140 or $150 a hive earlier in the season.

These almond-fueled superpaydays may be fleeting, however. Almond acreage continues to grow. So does demand—so far. "There probably is a saturation point there somewhere," almond farmer John Thoming, whose father was the Millers' first pollination client, told me. "We thought that when we got to a billion-pound harvest we'd have problems, but then we got to a billion, and now a billion and a half, and we haven't reached that saturation point yet."

Someday, certainly, they will. Australia has beefed up its almond plantings. And in western China, the purported birthplace of the almond, authorities have embarked on a forced-labor

campaign, enlisting ethnic Uighurs of the northwestern Xin-
giang region—one person and donkey cart per household, at
risk of a hefty fine—to plant almond trees. Eventually China's
massive state expansion may put a dent in growers' sky-high
profits.

The prospect of struggling almond growers is a troubling
one for bee guys, because without the almonds, most commercial beekeepers would not be able to make a living. Like bees and
blossoms, bee guys and almond guys are engaged in a symbiotic
relationship: neither could survive, much less prosper, without
the other. We know that what is bad for the bee guy is bad for
the almond guy—without bees, there are no almonds. But the
reverse is also true: starting in the mid-1990s, when the price for
a pound of honey fell below what it cost to produce it—a victim,
like many homegrown industries, of cheaper Chinese competitors with names like Wuhan Bee Healthy Co.—almond guys
were the only thing keeping most bee guys afloat. Other crops,
like cherries and apples and melons, provided a place to park
bees with ample nectar and pollen between seasons, but those
crops didn't fetch enough on the commodities markets, and
thus couldn't pay enough, to net beekeepers much of a profit.
So what's good for the almond industry is, at least in the short
term, good for the beekeeping industry. "Thank goodness for
the almonds," Miller says. "I want those guys all driving new
Escalades."

Still, Miller and his bee guy friends also know that in the
long term, the almond rush is not so good for the beekeeper.
Indeed, the success of the almond and the survival of the honey
bee appear to have an inverse relationship—the higher the price
of almonds rises, the harder time beekeepers have keeping their
charges alive. There are plenty of explanations for this sorry

state of affairs. Bees didn't evolve to work so hard in the dead of winter. Spring comes early in the almond orchards. It's a chilly and rainy time of year, when any northern honey bee in her right mind should be huddled up with her companions in the bowels of the hive, keeping still and quiet. To build up summerlike numbers for large-scale pollination during winterlike conditions, beekeepers must convince their bees that spring has arrived. So they move them to warmer climes, then pour corn or beet or sugar syrup into plastic feeder troughs or drip bottles and place pollen patties—granular cakes of human-harvested pollen, brewer's yeast, and sucrose—across the tops of the hive frames to provide a protein boost. That's how commercial bees get pumped up for their orchard acrobatics. "It's not a natural thing to have big booming hives in February," Miller says. Bees are adapted to cold climates—"but we bring them down here to make money."

Scientists also suspect that this unnatural life cycle— the double-time migration pioneered by John Miller's great-grandfather—may disrupt the rhythm of the hive. The bees work all summer, get loaded onto semis, take a brief nap, then start summer again in February, going from complete dormancy to white-hot stimulation in the almonds, then to a nectarless postbloom desert and, after a brief ride in the back of a huge truck, to the apple bloom, and then to the windswept northern prairies to wait for the clover flow to begin. This is a lot of stimulation and dearth, and at some point all of those conflicting signals may be disruptive to the superorganism of the hive. The colony is manhandled, jostled, exposed to pesticides and parasites and to lots of feast and famine, and it does not come out of the process stronger. Farmers expect bees to function like yet another farm machine—like shakers, sweepers, tillers, and combines. But bees are living things, with short life spans to begin with—about six weeks from larva to winged maturity to senescence. Riding in trucks and eating fake flowers and living in a constant state of natural or artificial peak bloom can take it out of a bee. There are too many crops to pollinate, too many miles between them.

In the wild, one would expect to find three to four colonies per square mile; in the prelude to the almond bloom, apiarists must often stack thousands of hives in tenement-like holding yards. In North Dakota, Miller keeps only 40 hives per yard; in California, he places around 240 hives per yard. Some bee-keepers must keep 2,000 hives in one spot, their bees competing with millions of others for what meager wild forage exists, subsisting on syrup and pollen patties and engaging in periodic interhive death matches. If the bloom comes late, the situation is even more precarious—a delayed bloom in 2007 coincided with the initial onslaught of CCD deaths. And even when the trees finally flower, it is crowded. A healthy hive can typically pollinate about an acre; but with two or even three hives per acre in the orchards, these arrangements bear far less resemblance to wild meadows than to feedlots for cattle or swine.

And then of course there's the danger of contagion—the fact that, for that six-week period when nearly every commercial hive in the country has been shipped to California, the Central Valley is essentially a single four-hundred-mile-long bee yard, with bees from Florida "swapping spit," as Miller says, with others shipped from North Dakota, Arkansas, Pennsylvania, Texas, and Florida. Each winter, pests and pathogens from one region hop with ease onto still-untainted bees from the rest of the country. Miller tries to rent his hives close together during almond season to limit their exposure to other beekeepers' misfortunes. But the laws of supply and demand aren't always so accommodating. He currently has bees with three large growers, but a few years ago his hives were scattered across three hundred miles and twelve growers, exposing them to that many more threats. "You may be applying best management practices" to stave off varroa mites or nosema or hive beetles or foulbrood, Miller notes, "but if your neighbor is not, the mites vector from his hives into your hives." And when beekeepers return home from the almond fields, they infect bees that have stayed at home with smaller-scale beekeepers, as well as whatever feral bees may have survived the previous season's contagions.

The almond orchards have been compared to a brothel for their remarkable capacity to transmit disease across the country; another apt metaphor might be a wartime military barracks, or a slave ship. Bees have been favorably compared in their work ethic to "volunteer pollinators," so logic would suggest that commercial honey bees are in fact conscripts—and the conditions of conscription are rarely conducive to health. The age of mass production has not been kind to bees.

Bees were always mobile, but the almond industry has made them almost blithely global: they are hauled across the country or across the Pacific to pollinate trees that produce merchandise—nuts—that is hauled to a port and placed in a shipping container and hauled back across the globe. The almond tree, though less obviously peripatetic, has made a similarly far-flung journey that began, perhaps, in China, and from there moved to Spain, and from there to the California coast, and from there to the Central Valley, where it found a home so hospitable that it became a global icon of health and prosperity, which brought it back to China, which has conscripted its own slaves to produce the nut. The almond has come full circle—and as it has risen, billions of bees have fallen. But while it has consumed legions of bees, it has kept their keepers in business—and without those keepers, there might not be a European honey bee alive any-where. It is, says Miller's friend and bee broker Pat Heitkam, a "Faustian bargain." Almonds pay the bills "but they are also what brought us all of these problems."

Many of the writers of old found occasion to write about bees. In *Paradise Lost*, John Milton compared the zealous indus-try of bees to the labors of angels.

> *As bees in spring time, when the sun with Taurus rides,*
> *Pour forth their populous youth about the hive*
> *In clusters; they among fresh dews and flowers*
> *Fly to and fro, or on the smoothed plank,*
> *The suburb of their straw-built citadel.*

The angels he described were fallen; they were building hell. So too today's honey bees pour forth into the almonds, unstint-ing, diligent, forbearing; they are assembling their own demise. The almond industry is killing John Miller's bees. But it allows him to do what he loves, which is to keep bees—so all in all, it is a pretty good deal with the devil. And on a sunny morn-ing sometime after Valentine's Day when the valley floor turns white-pink with almond blossoms, he can drive into an orchard and park his truck. He can turn down his Pink Floyd CD and open the windows. He can sit still among the pale pink blos-soms for a time. Sitting still, recall, does not come easily to him. But for this, he can sit still. So he does. He sits and listens to his bees hum in the almond trees, making nuts and money. "Bee guys like that," he says. And in that first flourishing of spring, Miller's bills get paid.

Chapter Five

....

Trespasses

WHEN JOHN MILLER WAS A BUDDING BEEKEEPER, HIS FATHER gave him a painful task. The year was 1976 or so, the early days of almond pollination. It was just on the cusp of the bloom, and the Miller bees had been distributed on Ed Thoming's farm at the intersection of State Route 132 and Bird Road in Tracy, California—a place where occasional farmhouses and migrant dorms marked the thin edge of civilization. A few days after the bees were placed, Neil received a call from Ed Thoming, who had received a call from his pesticide consultant. The guy had been visiting an almond orchard in Newman, California, about forty-five minutes away from Tracy, and he'd happened to see 136 hives with a suspiciously fresh, thin veneer of white paint sprayed over still-legible one-inch stenciled black letters: MILLER HONEY FARMS, BLACKFOOT, IDAHO. It seemed weird to the pesticide guy, because he knew the Millers' bees were already spoken for in Tracy, and he probably also knew that the Millers were meticulous in the care and branding of their bee hardware and would never brook a sloppy paint job.

The Millers checked on their hives, found them missing, and alerted the sheriff. The sheriff looked into the situation and ascertained that the bees had in fact been stolen from the Millers. The villain was a bee guy named Allred—try as he may, Miller can't remember the first name—who had entered into a pollination contract with the farmer in Newman for more hives than he possessed. To make up the deficit, Allred had used a (stolen) forklift to remove the Millers' hives from their pallets in Tracy and put them in his own (stolen) truck, then tossed the pallets into the nearby California Aqueduct.

Allred was, in his way, a "clever bugger," John Miller says. He had given some thought to his caper. Each of the hives Allred stole had been stacked two boxes high—the lower box holding the brood chamber with the queen and nurse bees, the upper harvest box holding worker bees and honey. Allred brought his own empty bee boxes—no frames, no bees, just empty white boxes—and placed them on the bottom layer of his own pallets. Then he divided the Miller hives in two and stuck the full Miller boxes on top of the empty Allred ones—thus "doubling" his hive count and also doubling his rental fee from the duped almond farmer. Split this way, only half of the new hives were "queen-right," with a resident matron to calm and organize the workers. The other hives were full of bewildered, pissed-off, queenless bees, far more interested in stinging hapless passersby than in pollinating almond flowers. Such an arrangement wasn't a great way to establish a long-term relationship with an almond grower, once he found out that most of his trees would not be pollinated. But it did hold the promise of a quick buck.

Now Allred had been found out. Everyone agreed that he had done a bad thing. His tactics were unsavory, his beekeeping mores abysmal. There was no question he'd stolen the bees. But he had signed a contract with the farmer, and a contract was a contract. Regardless of whom they belonged to, the bees could not be moved until the farmer released them from their duties. This didn't seem fair to the Millers, who had the bees under contract to pollinate an orchard forty-five miles away. So the next night—sheriff be damned—Neil went to get his bees back. He drove to Newman, dressed up bee-commando style (that is to say, in a white suit and veil), and, in the darkest hours of night, stole back his hives. He hauled them to a secluded spot in the Sierra foothills near Penryn, California, which lies somewhere between Ophir and Loomis, Auburn and Roseville. It was a place Allred, the sheriff, and the duped almond farmer were unlikely to find, and where, more importantly, the still-angry bees were unlikely to find human flesh to punish for Allred's trespasses. John was given the job of recombining the hives. The bees were furious, and it was not fun. Nor was it painless. "I can still remember *that* day's work," John Miller says. "Vividly."

Allred's misadventures with the Millers' bees did not dissuade him from a life of bee crime, however. He proclaimed himself the "Jesse James of Beekeeping" and continued to steal from apiaries across the Central Valley. He must have had some aptitude around bees, because he managed to get away with it for quite a while. His spree ended only when, Miller vaguely recalls, he was caught in the act by a bee guy named Knoeffler, "shotgunned in a bee yard," and held until the police arrived. Allred did time as "a guest of the state" in some prison or another. And that was the last Miller heard of him. For the life of him, Miller can't understand why Allred decided to make a career of stealing bees—why not take something valuable, like almonds? Stealing bees is like—it's hard to find the right metaphor for such feckless decision making—"like stealing a two-year-old. You're just making more work for yourself," Miller says. Nonetheless, bees get stolen all the time.

The "robbing" of hives is surely as old as the profession of beekeeping itself: "All agreed on this one point, at least," wrote Lorenzo Langstroth, "that stolen honey is much sweeter than the slow accumulations of patient industry." Bears and skunks and honey badgers grab handfuls of honey, bees, and larvae to stuff into their mouths. Human "honey hunters" have long stalked the woods searching for wild "bee trees" from which to extract a sweet reward. Beekeepers, as a matter of course, deprive colonies of their hard-earned provisions. Bees too steal from other hives—it is much easier than gathering nectar, snoutful by snoutful. Typically, stronger stocks assail weaker ones, especially in times of low honey flows. But sometimes bees steal honey from other hives just because they can. "There is," Langstroth wrote, "an air of roguery about a thieving bee which, to the expert, is as characteristic as are the motions of a pickpocket to a skillful policeman. Its sneaking look, and nervous, guilty agitation, once seen, can never be mistaken." Bees that learn to plunder the honey of others rarely return to "honest courses," Langstroth continued. The marauders become "so infatuated with it as to neglect their own brood." They sally out with "the first peep of light" and continue their depredations until so late that they sometimes can't find the entrance to their own hives in the dark.

Honest bees leave the hive light and return laden with heavy burdens of nectar and pollen. Their plundering kin reverse the process, losing all moderation. They enter "as hungry-looking as Pharaoh's lean kine" and exit with the "burly looks" of an alderman who has "dined at the expense of the city," stuffed to utmost capacity. Human bee thieves are, by contrast, more dif-

ficult to spot. Because all beekeepers wear white suits and veils;
because most hive boxes are nearly identical; because there are a
million and a half beehives being moved on thousands of trucks
up and down the Central Valley during almond season; because
almond acreage is vast and resources to enforce bee crime are
small—for all these reasons, it is difficult for law enforcement
and almond growers to tell who is moving his own bees in the
dark of night and who is stealing someone else's.

Beehives are not the easiest things to steal. Thieves must
have a working knowledge of beekeeping in order to emerge
unscathed. They must have equipment—a truck, a bee suit, a
smoker, perhaps a forklift. That's why most bee thieves come
from within. They are renegade beekeepers looking to pocket a
quick payday in an orchard or to expand their businesses or to
make up their losses without purchasing new bees and equipment. Bees are worth a lot of money before almond pollination;
they're worth less after, when a beekeeper is faced with the prospect of keeping them alive for another year. When the almonds
are in bloom and bees are in hot demand, almond ranchers must
do anything and everything to pollinate their trees or risk losing their crop. Most pay what they feel are extortive prices for
a sufficient supply of hives. Or, if they are desperate, they may
resort to renting bees from shady amateurs at bargain-basement
prices. As pollination prices have risen, Miller and other beekeepers across California have seen increasing losses to theft in
the weeks before the bloom. Each almond season, around one
percent of Miller's hives "evaporate," he says, and the only time
he's recovered any bees was the time he and his dad stole those
136 hives back from the notorious Allred.

Here's how the thieving works: You see a batch of hives—a
stack of money, if you are crazy enough to associate bees with

income—sitting on the side of a desolate stretch of rural road, away from the shaded interior of an orchard. If you have a flat-bed and a forklift, it can take all of ten minutes to load up ten thousand dollars' worth of hives. All you have to do is watch the semis roll through and wait until just after the bees are placed. The beekeeper probably won't be back for a few days while he tends to other hives. You pull your truck off the road just a tinch so you don't block traffic—and the bees are yours. You drop them off with a grower, who generally pays half the pollination fee when the bees are delivered and half when they are removed. Many bee snatchers are happy to collect the first payment (for two hundred hives, it would have hovered around fifteen thousand dollars in recent years) and abandon the bees in the orchard.

For big operations the loss of a hundred hives is a costly nuisance; for smaller beekeepers it can be ruinous. To deter thieves, beekeepers brand their boxes, pallets, and frames (Miller is registered as beekeeper number 42 in county number 31, thus all his frames are branded 3142). "We strive to get behind locked gates at all times," Miller says, "and if there's a mean dog there, all the better." For many years, Miller staged his syrup tanks and other beekeeping equipment in an open-air shed belonging to Gary Thompson, a Modesto fire chief who also paid the Millers to pollinate his almonds. Thompson had lots of guns and liked to shoot. His son also had lots of guns and liked to shoot. But Miller's brother Jay inherited that contract when they split the business recently, and now John stages his equipment in an orchard that is sadly deficient in firearms enthusiasts—too bad, because a few years later, thieves stole all the diesel from Miller's trucks there.

Beekeepers also enlist local agricultural cops to run periodic "sting operations" (pun very much intended) to deter thieves. During almond season, ag cops will pull over beekeeping rigs for traffic stops to make sure the operations are legitimate, and sometimes, they run night patrols with aircraft and chase-cars. Some beekeepers have even installed radio frequency and GPS tracking devices in hives, though the technology is too expensive for widespread use. So really, the main idea is to discourage thieves by convincing them that there's some remote likelihood they could get caught.

Unfortunately, that likelihood is slim. Prosecuting agricultural offenses is never easy—produce doesn't carry serial numbers; heifers aren't much use in a lineup; almonds look the same no matter who grew them—but bee detective work is particularly thankless. For police who lack the proper gear and training, patrolling bee yards can be dangerous. It's no surprise, then, that most perpetrators get away with their buzzing booty and that beekeepers rarely bother to report thefts. "You see people working on beehives in the middle of the night with white outfits and netting, you assume it's their bees," says Frank Swiggart, who was a deputy sheriff with the Modesto County Agricultural Crimes Unit until he was promoted to sergeant in 2009. Swiggart had been a cop for going on fifteen years, working patrol, street level narcotics, sheriff's tactical and recon. Then he became a deputy on the rural crime unit—but he had never prosecuted a big-time bee rustler until 2003. That's when he nabbed an amateur beekeeper and state firefighter named Daniel Suarez. Swiggart is the first to admit that he only caught him because Suarez was spectacularly inept.

Suarez worked for the California forestry department overseeing fire crews. Each day on his way to work, he'd drive along the rural roads of the Central Valley, passing the hundreds upon thousands of hives that migrated to his neighborhood every winter. Each night, on his way home, he'd load a few into his truck and stash them in a holding yard in Merced County. In late November 2002, Orin Johnson, the white-haired, wide-faced, second-generation beekeeper from Hughson, California, set out to visit a bee yard near Sonora, in the foothills above the fog line. Johnson kept seven hundred hives altogether, and he'd left sixty-four on an isolated ranch behind locked gates. But when he got there, he found the lock on the gate cut and the bees gone. He had no cell phone service, so he drove to a high spot in the almonds where he could get a signal. He called the police, waited a few hours until a deputy could get there, and gave his report. The deputy dutifully took down the information: "I'll keep my eyes out for 'em," he assured Johnson. Johnson was not assured. There were twenty thousand hives wintered in a ten-mile radius, and it wasn't likely the deputy was going to recover the bees simply by keeping his eyes out.

It was the first time Johnson had lost so many bees, and he was stinging mad. He knew they were nearby; you don't steal hives in that part of the country shortly before almond pollination and move them somewhere else. So he went over his options. He could hire a plane and do flyovers of orchards, looking for suspicious caches of beehives. But it was wintertime, the valley was fogged over, and there were so many caches of beehives that it would be hard to spot suspicious ones. Or he could roam the region's back roads looking for a lucky break. It was his idle season before pollination began, and he spent more time than he should admit driving his pickup through areas of the valley where he had heard there might be some "known renegades or lowlife beekeepers" and looking at other people's hives with binoculars. He took out an ad in the newspaper, offering a reward.

The paper's staff initially wouldn't print it—"How do we know they're stolen?" they asked. He gave them the police report, and they finally agreed. He got a few calls from readers who said they'd seen a beehive sitting off a rural road somewhere, but they had no concept of how many beehives were sitting off rural roads in that ten-mile radius.

Finally, Johnson contacted Merced County's agriculture department, which in the spring sends inspectors to keep beekeepers from bilking almond growers with empty hives or bad bees. He sent a description of his missing hives (wood, rectangular, painted white, branded JOHNSON APIARIES on the side) and the department faxed it to six or seven counties. Lo and behold, a couple of months later Johnson got a call from a county inspection agent who had come across his bees, along with those of seven or eight different outfits, in an almond orchard. The hives had come from Merced, Fresno, Madera, Stanislaus, and Tuolumne counties, and from Oregon, Washington, and Montana. They had all been stolen by Suarez, who had signed pollination contracts to place three hundred hives in the orchard. Of those, perhaps a dozen belonged to him. That's when Swiggart got called in—and as sheriff's deputies began matching brands in Suarez's collection to hives that had been reported missing, they solved thefts up and down the valley.

Here was where Suarez had made his mistake. Every beekeeper has his own way of building and painting boxes. A smart bee rustler is aware of that and obliterates identifying brands, or, better yet, places the stolen honeycombs in different boxes. But Suarez was only half smart. He reused the same pilfered boxes, as Allred had, and though Suarez did a more thorough job of painting over the previous owners' stenciled or burned-on brands, he did so while they were still on the truck with which he had stolen them, using a paint roller to go over the boxes. But the brands that had faced inside remained. The police also reported that when they arrested Suarez, they found dead bees in his vehicle (though if that were the threshold for crimes against bees, every beekeeper in the country would be found guilty). Still, the evidence was overwhelming. Suarez was sentenced to nine months in jail, though because of prison overcrowding and the relatively inconsequential threat that a bee thief poses to society at large, he never served a day. Johnson asked the judge to ban Suarez from beekeeping for life, but the judge would not agree. Suarez is, as far as Johnson knows, still keeping bees.

Even a few years before, Johnson's hives wouldn't have proved such a tempting target. As with all crime waves, the targets of agricultural transgressions tend to ebb and flow with commodity values. Bee thefts rose in tandem with pollination prices, which rose in tandem with almond prices and bee deaths. Almond thefts rose, too. When the wholesale price of the nuts skyrocketed from one to three dollars a pound, thieves made off with a number of semis containing hundreds of thousands of dollars' worth of almonds. When diesel prices went up a few years ago, tractors across the Central Valley mysteriously ran out of fuel. When metal prices rose—to where a four-inch brass valve was worth twenty-five dollars in a recycling yard— nearly every brass irrigation valve disappeared from the region; they are all plastic now. Someone even made off with a thirty-foot-tall, thousand-pound windmill, presumably to recycle for metal. The same fate befell agricultural chemicals, all-terrain vehicles, heifers: when demand went up, commodities went missing. People who steal in the agriculture industry do so only when they can find ready buyers; in theft, as with everything in agriculture, the laws of supply and demand very much apply.

On a perfect late March day a few years after Suarez almost went to jail, and a couple of weeks after the waning bloom had blanketed the Central Valley with petals deep as snow, Detective Roy Tighe of the Modesto County Agricultural Crimes Unit took me for a drive in his government-issue pickup. Tighe is the clean-cut, broad-set, forty-six-year-old cop who succeeded Frank Swiggart in his rural crimes job after Swiggart was promoted to sergeant. He was dressed like a farmer—jeans, work boots, a green serge shirt, cropped graying hair, and a neatly trimmed mustache. He had worked narcotics and fugitive apprehension before taking on farm crime, but his father was an almond grower, so Tighe was comfortable in the rural realm. He liked it: instead of wearing a uniform and chasing urban thugs, he could drive around in farmer's mufti searching for siphoned diesel, kidnapped calves, illicit cockfights, methamphetamine labs, stolen tractors, stolen almonds, and stolen hives.

A few weeks before I visited, Tighe had recovered his very first batch of stolen hives. A farmer had placed an order through an almond-hauling organization for thirty-two hives. But the farmer's son had offered to find him bees for less money and had gone ahead and dropped some hives off at the back of his orchard. The dad hadn't canceled the contract with the bee broker, however. When the bee guy went to deliver the hives, he noticed the bees in the orchard. He noticed, furthermore, that the hives belonged to people who didn't know their bees were there. Tighe wasn't surprised to learn that the people on this particular farm were up to no good. They lived just a few farms down from his father's house. Although they were Mennonites—the father had a long beard; the wife wore a bonnet—the son who had stolen the bees was a known meth addict and a longtime problem in the community. ("I'm always trying to nail that kid,"

Tighe said, although the "kid" was probably fifty years old.)
The son lived in a trailer near his father's blond-brick ranch, and
before his alleged foray into bee theft he had most recently been
linked to a scheme to grow marijuana between cornstalks in a
nearby field, stealing a neighbor's irrigation water to keep the
product green.

Ultimately, though, it wasn't the theft of bees that nailed
the kid. The county's drug task force was after him, and they
ended up making an arrest because, Tighe told me, they "had
put together a better case." That's not surprising. There are few
crimes that are harder to comprehend and apprehend than those
involved with bees: "How do you prove that that's my bee right
there?" Tighe asks. "Over there, that yellow bug with the little
black stripes on it, that's my bee." A bee, after all, can go any-
where it likes. You can't fence bees in; you can't keep them out;
you can't guarantee that they'll return to the hive each night;
you can't track their whereabouts. You can move the equipment
in which they live; you can transfer them in netted trucks; you
can smuggle queens inside ballpoint pens and little cages. But
once your bees are airborne, they no longer belong to you. The
law on bee possession is clear—once a bee is away from the hive
and out of sight of the owner, it's considered wild. "The phrase
I use," says John Miller, "is that honey bees are free-flying insects, and though a beekeeper may provide habitation, shelter,
or equipment to house them, the beekeeper owns the equipment
but not the bees. They can elect to live in the equipment I provide but the door is open and they may come and go as they
please."

Even without malign human intervention, bees change owners without so much as a permission slip. Studies indicate that
apiaries miles apart can interchange 3 percent of their bees over

the course of just a few weeks. Worker bees lose their way and end up in different hives; bearing nectar and pollen, they are usually accepted by the guard bees at the entrance (though if it is late autumn, when the hive is winnowing its numbers, the newcomer might instead find herself set upon and torn apart, wings and legs shredded, body bits discarded outside the hive). Bees from failing hives abscond en masse to find better homes. Drones, especially, are prone to drifting between hives. ("They're like men," says Miller.) Queen-breeder David Miksa participated in a Cornell University study back in 1961 in which researchers painted the drones of seven different bee yards, each a mile apart, a different color. By the end of the summer, the yards boasted a veritable rainbow of different-colored drones. Bees have a great sense of smell, and if they detect honey and pheromones from a big bee yard, they may find the lure hard to resist. Miksa recalls that Horace Bell, who was once Florida's biggest beekeeper, was hugely unpopular with beekeepers who lived near his home territory because his apiaries were so large that nearby bees would regularly succumb to the Bell colonies' overpowering pheromonal lure and abandon their hives. Bell could grow his colonies just by being the biggest bee guy around. It was not fair, but it was not theft.

BEES WILL HURT YOU THAT WAY. THEY DON'T CARE WHO owns them. They don't care who loves them. They do what they do. They forage; they build; they leave; they rob; they kill; they die; they sting. Oh, do they sting. This may be the proper—if belated—occasion to confess that before I met John Miller I had never been stung by a bee. I was once nailed on the eyelid by a yellow jacket, which hurt a lot, and while riding a bike I'd had a

few things fly down my shirt that caused some burning discom-
fort. But I hadn't, to my knowledge, ever experienced a bona
fide bee sting, and I wasn't all that keen on doing so. Miller is a
persuasive spokesman for the honey bee, however, and he is well
accustomed to comforting the uninitiated: he assured me that
I would be well protected in a bee suit and promised he would
lend me one, along with thick leather gloves and a veil to protect
my face and head. "I provide the bee suits," he wrote in an email
as my first visit approached. "If you are 52XX I need to honestly
know, so I have the right equipment."

I knew both from hearsay and research that a bee left alone
will not sting, because the sting kills the bee, and it is then of no
use to the hive. When a bee is incited to sting, the twin barbed
shafts of its stinger dig into the skin and pump poison into the
puncture—but the shafts can't withdraw without ripping the
center from the bee's abdomen, so it dies to protect its kin, and
in so doing emits a banana-like odor that attracts other bees to
finish its work. Langstroth believed the honey bee's sting was
proof if any that God intended bees to be domesticated: "If it
had been able to sting a number of times, its thorough domestication would have been well nigh impossible," he wrote. He
also noted a number of popular remedies to salve the pain of
a sting. Tobacco juice was one; the "ripe berry of the common
coral honeysuckle" another. Others swore by the milky nectar
of the white poppy, plantain leaves, "spirits of hartshorn," and
even getting another bee to sting you in the same spot. Langstroth preferred a simpler cure: "In my own case, I have found
cold water to be the best remedy," he wrote.

Bees are resourceful when it comes to stinging: they like the
face best, but they'll go for any flesh they can find—a hole in a
glove, a minuscule gap in the zipper of a bee suit. For a budding

beekeeper, the first sting is something of a crucible—it deter-
mines whether you are cut out for beekeeping or whether you
should find some other line of work, like selling insurance or
writing software. Miller had explained to me that there are two
types of people: the kind who shy away when the hive is first
opened, and the kind who lean in. Miller gets so excited when
he opens a hive, he nearly jumps in, so eager is he to see how the
bees are faring. And when he takes someone new to visit a hive,
he observes them as carefully as he does his bees. He informed
me—flattered me—that the first time I opened a hive with him,
I leaned in, too.

Then one day, while visiting an operation run by a friend
of Miller's, I leaned in too far and a bee flew up—like that!—
and stung me fast on the face. I hadn't put on a veil, because
we hadn't planned on bothering the bees. It turns out that *most*
bees won't sting when left to their own devices; occasionally,
though, an ornery one decides you're annoying her and goes out
in a blaze of glory. Mine was one of those. The ancient Roman
writer Columella cautioned that bee-going folk "must avoid
such things as offend" bees, like being "unchaste or uncleanly;
for impurity and sluttiness . . . they utterly abhor"; along with
"smelling of sweat, or having a stinking breath, caused either through eating of leeks, onions, garlick, and the like" (he
suggested quaffing a cup of beer to make it go away); or being "given to surfeiting or drunkenness"; or being too loud or
sudden in one's movements. "In a word, thou must be chaste,
cleanly, sweet, sober, quiet, and familiar; so they will love thee,
and know thee from all others," he wrote. Maybe I wasn't. Bees
tend to go for dark spots, for eyes and ears and nostrils. This one
aimed for my eye, and she stung me unprovoked on the brow,
and it hurt. It really hurt. I had assumed that bee stings would

be less painful than those of more aggressive insects like yellow jackets and wasps, but I was wrong. My first bee sting did not resemble the mild spreading burn of the things that had flown down my shirt. It hit like a wallop, a tiny but powerful battering ram, a deep, pounding pain. I jumped up and back, and then I bellowed. My eye swelled shut, my face swelled around it, and it stayed that way for two days.

In 1984, an Arizona entomologist named Justin Schmidt invented a "sting pain index" that rates the relative pain caused by various insect stings, ranging from zero for stings that cause no sensation to four for those that cause "absolutely debilitating" pain. Schmidt is the author of the holiest text of the insect-sting field: *Insect Defenses: Adaptive Mechanisms and Strategies of Prey and Predators*, a 482-page tome on "defensive ensembles" and "predatory strategies." But he's better known for his simple index, which dissects, in the evocative language you might associate more with a wine-besotted sommelier than an entomologist, the sensation of getting stung. The index was derived from personal observation: Schmidt became interested in social insects and how they defend themselves and their communities, and because of the nature of his research on venomous insects and arthropods, got stung a lot. At present count, he has sampled the venom of more than 150 species of insects. He rarely does it on purpose—such contrived encounters might not produce normal amounts of venom—but, he says, if you hang around with stinging insects, "sooner or later you're going to goof up and get stung." When it happens, Schmidt pays meticulous attention to the type, intensity, and longevity of the pain, describing it in vivid personal detail.

There are two ways that insects defend themselves, Schmidt explains. The first is simply to kill or impair the attacker: four to five bee stings, for instance, provide enough toxin to murder a mouse. It would take more than a thousand stings to kill a healthy adult human, unless that adult happens to be allergic, in which case he could die from circulatory or respiratory collapse in minutes from only one sting. No insect can kill a nonallergic human with one sting, although Schmidt has described stings that made him lie down and scream for a few minutes before the pain subsided, and stings that left him quivering in peristaltic waves of agony for an entire day. The second, and arguably the most common, reason that insects sting defensively is to scare menacing creatures enough that they'll think twice before trying it again. Menacing creatures particularly like to bother bees, because their primary food source is so irresistible—and their larvae and adults are pretty tasty, too. Thus it is more than reasonable that bees have developed a way to defend their community that inflicts pain on creatures of both malign and innocent intent. As Miller says, "There's a reason it hurts."

The honey bee, by the way, ranks just a notch above dead center of Schmidt's index, which goes like this:

1.0   **Sweat bee:** Light, ephemeral, almost fruity. A tiny spark has singed a single hair on your arm.
1.2   **Fire ant:** Sharp, sudden, mildly alarming. Like walking across a shag carpet and reaching for the light switch.
1.8   **Bullhorn acacia ant:** A rare, piercing, elevated sort of pain. Someone has fired a staple into your cheek.
2.0   **Bald-faced hornet:** Rich, hearty, slightly crunchy. Similar to getting your hand mashed in a revolving door.
2.0   **Yellowjacket:** Hot and smoky, almost irreverent.

Imagine W. C. Fields extinguishing a cigar on your tongue.

2.x HONEY BEE AND EUROPEAN HORNET: Like a match-head that flips off and burns on your skin.

3.0 RED HARVESTER ANT: Bold and unrelenting. Somebody is using a drill to excavate your ingrown toenail.

3.0 PAPER WASP: Caustic and burning. Distinctly bitter aftertaste. Like spilling a beaker of hydrochloric acid on a paper cut.

4.0 TARANTULA HAWK: Blinding, fierce, shockingly electric. A running hair drier has been dropped into your bubble bath.

4.0+ BULLET ANT: Pure, intense, brilliant pain. Like firewalking over flaming charcoal with a 3-inch rusty nail in your heel.

If Miller had the time to create his own index, it would be specific to the honey bee, a "cowboy words index" that rates the number of curse words you're likely to say depending on where you're stung. He's gotten this far in his own formulation: If you're stung by the eyes, you use lots of cowboy words. If you're stung on the index finger, you might not use any. I called Schmidt and told him about Miller's idea. Schmidt liked it; he is a big fan of cowboy words where bee stings are concerned: "I prefer to swear up a blue storm when I get stung by a honey bee. It's very satisfying," he said. He likes to swear only when it's something "boring" like a honey bee, though. If it's a novel or interesting creature like, say, a tarantula hawk, he's usually concentrating so intensely on what the sting is doing to him that too much "oral activity" (such as swearing) makes it difficult to observe the physical effects of the sting. Since he's gotten plenty of bee stings, he feels there's little new for him to learn about the sensation—in which case, he agrees, swearing is an excellent coping mechanism.

Schmidt has opinions about which body parts hurt most. The under-eye, he notes, is "going to floor you," as is anywhere on the cartilaginous part of the nose. The upper lip, too, will engender "immense amounts of undue grief." The scalp, Schmidt says, is "weird. It makes a hard little knot which is very annoying for a while because the tissue up there can't expand." Miller swears that if you get stung on the scalp, you'll feel a phantom pain on the bottom of your foot.

I had opportunity to test that hypothesis. Two days after my first sting, my eye still swollen near shut, it happened again. Bees are angry when their hives are being divided; after I watched Miller's employees split some hives to create new profit centers for the coming summer, I drove a couple of hundred yards uphill to his office and took off my veil—safely removed, I thought, from the chaos of displaced bees. But when I got out of the car, a bee flew straight into my hair, struggled for a few seconds, and dug into my scalp. *Whabang!* I pulled on my veil, but another bee was inside it. That one got caught in my hair as well. And that was it. I threw my veil and gloves and notebook and pen and digital voice recorder to the ground and began flapping my arms and running in circles. This is, apparently, normal. "We have these innate reactions that are almost impossible to overcome," says Schmidt, especially when it hasn't happened to us often. Bees appear to know that: "They seem," wrote Langstroth, "to take malicious pleasure in stinging those upon whom their poison produces the most virulent effect." Experts, such as venomous insect specialists and beekeepers, react in a less frenzied manner, a response bred by long experience and peer pressure to prove that "you can get stung and don't show it," Schmidt says. "The only thing that sort of works is a whole lot of training. You know what you're supposed to do and do it."

"Ineffective flapping" and running in circles is, of course, not what you're supposed to do; it only attracts more bees. Better to run in a straight line away from the offending insects. "Most people like to flap and scream and duck and run, but that doesn't get the bee out of your hair," he says. The absolute dumbest thing you can do is jump in a body of water, because the bees just wait for you to emerge and then sting your nose and mouth, which makes it harder to hold your breath underwater. The smartest thing is to get inside, away from the bees. That's not what I did. I kept running in circles until one of Miller's employees led me inside to the office and removed the bees from my hair, along with a stinger and a three-inch-long string of bee intestine that was attached to my scalp. Perhaps I felt it on the bottom of my foot; I was too sweaty and agitated to notice. What is certain is that I felt on my scalp a tight, not remotely fruity pain that throbbed down my forehead and sinuses. From my description of this experience over the telephone, Schmidt correctly conjectured that my hair must be dark—bees go for dark-colored things because their main predators, such as bears, skunks, and honey badgers, are also dark. "Anemic" light-haired people from northern Europe, like him, have that advantage over their darker brethren. He also deduced that my hair was curly—bees get stuck more easily, and even if they hadn't planned to sting initially, they often end up doing so. He assured me that the main problem with having bees in your hair is the anticipation of what those bees are going to do to you. I thought the sting was pretty unpleasant, too. And humiliating: I had shrieked like a toddler. Perhaps I *wasn't* cut out for beekeeping.

Bees make honey. They pollinate one third of our fruits and vegetables. And they will happily give their lives to cause you pain. I once read a particularly memorable newspaper account of two French horses that were attacked by bees left behind when their hives were moved. The three-year-old gelding and eighteen-month-old filly were covered in a thick layer of bees—witnesses estimated there were more than sixty thousand bees swarming their paddocks. The horses received thousands of stings all over their bodies. The veterinarian tasked with saving them put on a beekeeper's suit and soaked the horses with fly spray to kill and repel the bees that continued to attack. Both horses were administered "massive doses" of cortisone along with fifteen different antihistamines, sedatives, and morphine. Nonetheless, the filly died of asphyxiation eighteen hours later; the gelding of intestinal necrosis ten hours after that. (The bees that had stung them died, too, of course.) Starry-eyed bee worshippers can say what they will; honey bees are not always forces of beneficence.

SOMETIMES BEES GO WHERE YOU DON'T WANT THEM TO GO. For all the talk of how important pollination is to the survival of humankind and the agriculture industry, there are some plants people would prefer that bees not pollinate. Blackberry and star thistle, for instance, make fabulous honey but aggressively send out creepers or windblown spores. They invade farms, destroy pasture, and spread across the landscape like . . . well, like weeds.

Farmers would also rather that bees not visit certain citrus groves. This is a recent development. Oranges and bees were once a symbiotic dream team. The bees made the oranges taste and look better: sweet and juicy and big and symmetrical. The nectar kept the bees alive in early spring and helped them create what many in the industry consider some of the best honey around. But in April 2006, beekeepers in the southern San Joaquin Valley received a disturbing letter from a lawyer representing a huge agricultural firm called Paramount Citrus. Paramount is the largest citrus producer in California, a subsidiary of Los Angeles–based Roll International Corporation, which is run by Stewart and Lynda Resnick. The Resnicks made their estimated $1.5 billion fortune with the Teleflora flower-delivery service and the Franklin Mint collectibles company. They own the cleverly marketed Fiji Water and POM Wonderful brands; they control the Kern Water Bank, one of the largest underground reservoirs in the nation. They have mansions in Beverly Hills and Aspen and serve on the boards of prominent museums across the country. They are generous philanthropists, well-known liberal donors, and Hollywood favorites, perhaps the most formidable couple in California.

In the 1980s and '90s, flush with cash from Teleflora and Franklin Mint, they purchased large almond, pistachio, pomegranate, and citrus holdings in the Central Valley. They did so at exactly the right time, acquiring 120,000 quality acres at bargain prices from oil and insurance companies hit by a downturn in the 1980s. The acreage included that of a company called Paramount Citrus, a name they used for all the citrus acreage they subsequently acquired. In 2000, Paramount replaced many of its navels and Valencias with seedless tangerines, also known as clementine mandarins. Paramount was not alone: as consumer tastes shifted toward less messy seedless fruit, California mandarin plantings grew from 10,000 acres in 1998 to 31,000 in 2008. Seedless varieties, with their intense flavor and ease of peeling, typically fetch three to four times the market price of other varieties.

But only if they don't have seeds. Until recently, clementines wouldn't grow unless they were cross-pollinated with another tree, and the process of cross-pollination created seeds. But in the 1980s and '90s Spanish orchards developed a technique to simulate the growth hormones secreted by seeds. Farmers using the hormones could obtain an excellent harvest without relying on pollination. The seedless fruit that resulted quickly captured a large share of the high-end citrus market, commanding huge premiums and producing jaw-dropping profits. It seems that Americans will pay lots of extra money to avoid having to spit out the seeds in their fruit.

People in the business of selling things enjoy jaw-dropping profits, and California citrus growers rushed to plant their orchards with similar varieties. The two most popular were the seedless *Clementine nules*—the classic thin-skinned clementine—and W. Murcott Afourer, another seedless, flavorful, and easy-to-peel mandarin that ripened later than clementines and thus extended the growing season for California producers. But the trees had a bee problem. If bees made a trip to a clementine or Murcott blossom while brushed with the pollen of another citrus variety, the fruit would explode in a riot of seeds, ruining the farmer's crop. To prevent cross-pollination, growers consulted with South African citrus experts, who recommended that they plant the varieties at least ten rows—or about a third of a mile—away from other types of citrus. On their advice, growers invested millions of dollars to plant thousands of trees on orchards across the southern swath of the Central Valley, carefully isolating the clementines and Murcotts ten rows away from other citrus trees.

Unfortunately, that wasn't enough. In 2003, Sun Pacific—one of the earliest growers to plant mandarins in the Central Valley and a partner, with Paramount, in a joint venture to sell and market clementines and Murcotts under the California "Cuties" brand—found significant seeds in some of its plantings. The fruit had to be sold for juice at a deeply discounted price. The buffer zone, it turned out, was about six times too small. The South African experts had believed that the ten-row buffer was sufficient because bees tend to return to the same small area each time they leave the hive. It's true, bees stay "constant" to one plant in one area. But bees also transfer pollen from worker to worker inside the hives. And if a bee that had visited a clementine tree rubbed against a bee that had visited a different type of citrus blossom, then returned to the clementines for another nip, it would effectively poison the flower, creating a seedy fruit that was worthless on the premium citrus market. So the proper buffer was in fact two miles. This presented a problem for growers who had staked big money on seedless fruit trees. Either the trees or the bees had to move. Because bees are easier to move than trees, Sun Pacific asked beekeepers in Maricopa, where most of the company's seedless mandarin trees had been planted, to clear the area of bees within two miles of their plantings. As recompense, the company found the beekeepers new locations on Sun Pacific's holdings in the main citrus-growing area farther north. They effectively emptied the area of bees in what Joe Traynor, a Bakersfield-based bee broker who represented some of the beekeepers in their dealings with Sun Pacific, came to call a honey bee "cleansing."

In 2006, Paramount Citrus encountered the same problem and attempted a similar cleansing. They sent beekeepers near Paramount's mandarin groves a letter explaining that their bees were "trespassing" on Paramount's clementine crop and should move their hives a minimum of two miles away. Should the beekeepers resist, Paramount threatened to seek compensation for "any and all damages caused to its crops as well as punitive damages." Paramount offered alternative bee yards, as Sun Pacific had, but there simply weren't enough good locations to absorb all the displaced bees. Creating a two-mile bee-free zone around the eight sites Paramount sought to protect meant clearing about seventy thousand acres of prime citrus-belt territory of bees. Pollination had become a crime, as had the mere existence of bees in a large swath of the Central Valley.

Unlike almonds, most orange trees do not need bees—they can pollinate themselves, and for that reason, bee guys who place their hives in citrus orchards typically pay the growers a couple of dollars a colony (or a few cases of highly coveted orange blossom honey) for the privilege. Now some beekeepers who had kept their bees on nearby properties for decades were being kicked off their longtime yards, lest the landowners feel the wrath of Paramount's considerable—paramount—power.

The California citrus belt, the very place where N. E. Miller first wintered his bees, was no longer a friendly place for beekeepers. Paramount began pushing a "Seedless Mandarin Protection Act" in the state legislature, seeking to establish "no-fly zones" of two miles for hives around designated orchards. Rowdy public meetings ensued. Beekeeping advocates began speaking of a twenty-first-century range war. Finally, when Paramount's legislative efforts sputtered and it became clear their legal efforts would do the same, the company backed down. They began netting their trees to keep bees from pollinating the blossoms. But the beekeepers who had already relocated from their "homeland," as Traynor calls it, are unlikely to reclaim their prime citrus yards, because mandarin demand continues to grow and "additional mandarin settlements have been planted in the occupied territory." In large swaths of California citrus country, the orange varieties that bees once visited are now forbidden fruit. It is an uneasy peace.

John Miller actually grows mandarins on his property. They are, besides the bees and his trucks and his grandchildren, his pride and joy. They are called Owari Satsuma mandarins, and they are delicious.

> What you buy at Whole Foods is a rank amateur; a rotting, half-globe-trotted waste.
>
> Gassed, and waxed, it's a sad excuse for Mandarins!
>
> I know!

The mandarin crop coincides with Miller's quiet time of year. The oranges are ready to pick just before the bees go into the cellars. That gives him plenty of time to "help" with the harvest.

> The bald fat guy eats his way across the orchard.
>
> You can spend a splendid afternoon, with your gimpy knees, and broad butt towards the sun; oblivious; completely oblivious to everything. . . .
>
> You are set beyond what a normal mortal should expect of life.

It is ironic that Miller has chosen to grow a fruit that doesn't need bees at the epicenter of his California operation, but he considers himself a savvy businessman, and sterile mandarins are a savvy investment. Other citrus growers have reached the same conclusion: in recent years, they have rearranged some

Murcott chromosomes to create a sterile hybrid called the Tango, which is identical to the original but averages only one seed in five fruits regardless of how many bees hover nearby. Millions of the new trees have been planted. But for those who made early investments in trees that can't tolerate bees, the new hybrids arrived too late. It is easier to interdict bees than replace trees.

Unless, of course, you are a beekeeper. Unless you need billions of flowers to feed billions of insects that you can't truly possess, that you can't control, that can't read NO TRESPASSING signs or understand the concepts of no-fly zones or hybridization or changing consumer preference. Unless you love something that can't love you back, that is just as happy to hurt you, that lives without concern for its keeper or his profit margins or his pride, and that dies with astonishing indiscretion—that simply does what it was born to do.

Chapter Six

Charismatic Mini-Fauna

WHEN THE ALMOND BLOOM APPROACHED IN LATE 2006, BEE-keepers hoped—as they always do—for a better year than the previous ones, when varroa mite had wreaked havoc across the industry. But then Colony Collapse Disorder came along, and people's bees went missing, and Miller began getting lots of phone calls from journalists on the hunt for loquacious bee-keepers. Before CCD, Miller received calls once or twice every year or two from some eager apiary neophyte—like me, or a food writer for the *New York Times*, or a reporter from *North Dakota Horizons* magazine—and he'd invite us along on his native migrant tour and make us a T-shirt and wow us with his quick wit and endless enthusiasm for the wonders of bee-assisted modern agriculture.

By the spring of 2007, though, as the CCD toll mounted, Miller began getting calls more frequently, from daily newspa-pers and German magazines and British filmmakers and Cali-fornia food writers seeking to explain this new contemporary woe. Mass die-offs, apian or human, are always intriguing to those in the line of work that involves informing the public—especially when they may presage the end of the world or at the

very least one third of our food supply, including the really good
stuff like blueberries and cranberries and melons and almonds.
This particular die-off was sexier yet for its inexplicability, and
so the calls began coming fast and furious. A few weeks into the
CCD hubbub, Miller sent me an email: "Hey!" he began:

> Tomorrow, NBC will be shooting and interviewing
>
> Gene Brandi on this whole damn thing. . . .
>
> it was supposed to be me . . .
>
> but NOOOOOOOOOOOOOOOOOOOO;
>
> I'm on a plane to Bismarck.
>
> America's Loss.
>
> Stock market collapsed upon the news that my 15 min. were
> now yet to come another time. . . .
>
> Gene will do extremely well.
>
> It's his 15 minutes, he has to.

Brandi, a longtime fixture on the California beekeeping
scene, did just fine. But Brandi's fifteen minutes, and Miller's,
and those of all the nation's beekeeper-sages, were nothing
compared to the fifteen minutes of David Hackenberg. He's the
Pennsylvania-based beekeeper who in November 2006 visited
his hitherto healthy Florida apiaries and discovered them virtu-
ally vacant, though still containing a full complement of honey
and brood. Hackenberg had been seeing some weird things for
a couple of years, but he couldn't quite put a finger on what was
wrong. In 2005 he had lost 40 percent of the bees he had placed
in apple orchards in upstate New York: "They swarmed out of

the boxes and just flew away," he says, leaving their honey behind. He'd restocked those hives with new bees, but they'd disappeared, too, and on a couple of occasions, he'd noticed bees hanging on the side of the hives but not occupying the interior. In January 2006 he'd tried again, stacking the honey boxes from the disappeared colonies on top of unaffected hives. Those colonies vanished, too.

And then, in November 2006, he pulled into a bee yard in the late afternoon, around three-thirty or four, and noticed there weren't many bees flying. He didn't think much of it at first and went about his business, lighting up smokers to calm the bees and preparing his forklift to move the hives. Then it hit him. "All of a sudden I realized there's nothing home," he told me. "I started jerking lids off, and there's nothing there, like someone took a sweeper and cleaned the hives out." Nor were there any dead bees on the ground, as there should have been. The surface underfoot was gravel, so it was easy to see that there was nothing to see—"The dead bees wouldn't have filled the bottom of a five-gallon bucket." There were some more beehives across the field, and when he sent one of his employees to look at them, he reported seeing good-looking hives with plenty of bees. "Here's three fifty, four hundred beehives, and those bees aren't even *attempting* to rob this stuff, they aren't even sticking a head in," Hackenberg said. Under normal circumstances, rival hives would have marauded the dead colony's honey stores, but there was no sign of that. He had seen lots of bees die in lots of ways, but he had never seen this before.

Hackenberg dresses like a ranch hand, with a leather vest and jeans that extend somewhere close to his armpits. Like John Miller, Hackenberg is a talker. The first time I spoke with him, he had two or three phone conversations going on at the same

time, and even so, his call-waiting was clicking in every few minutes. He talks loudly, with the wound-up patter of a horse-race
announcer; a constant crescendo. So when his bees disappeared,
he did what comes naturally to him: he started making phone
calls. He called Jerry Hayes, Florida's assistant chief of apiary
inspection, and described the bee yard scene. Hayes told him
that a Georgia beekeeper had just lost six hundred of his nine
hundred hives in a similarly disconcerting manner. Hackenberg
kept calling around and kept hearing about hives collapsing in
the same way across the country—in Florida, Georgia, Texas,
New York, California, Pennsylvania, and the Dakotas; thirty-
six states eventually. All had remarkably similar symptoms:
adult bees abruptly vanishing from the hive, leaving few bodies
inside or nearby; a queen, a healthy store of brood, a few young
adults left behind; and little to none of the typical pillaging that
would be expected of a collapsed hive's honey and pollen stockpiles.

Hackenberg also shared his weird findings with scientists,
including Dennis vanEngelsdorp, who was acting state apiarist
in Pennsylvania. He and vanEngelsdorp had seen each other
only a month before, in early November, at the annual Pennsylvania State Beekeepers Association meeting. Hackenberg
spends summers in central Pennsylvania when he's not on the
road pollinating blueberries, apples, cantaloupes, pumpkins,
cranberries, and almonds. He had just transported his hives
down to his winter base in Florida, and he announced at the
meeting that he was pleased with his bees—they were, he told
vanEngelsdorp, "fantastic." Perhaps that should have been the
first sign—John Miller can attest that it's the rare season that
ends as it begins. Because sure enough, only a month later,
Hackenberg called vanEngelsdorp to describe the woeful scene

in his apiaries. VanEngelsdorp immediately assumed the problem was varroa mites—"we blame everything on varroa mite," he says—but nonetheless asked Hackenberg to send him some dead colonies. When he examined the scattering of corpses that remained, says vanEngelsdorp, "we found the bees didn't have varroa mite—but they did have every other condition going."

VanEngelsdorp, who was in his late thirties at the time, was a senior extension associate and Ph.D. candidate in Penn State University's entomology department. A stocky, vaguely Norse-looking Canadian with a prow-like forehead and a thin covering of blond hair, vanEngelsdorp holds a master's degree in entomology from Cornell and intends to finish his Ph.D., if ever he escapes the maw of permanent apiarian crisis. His work originally included a combination of research on bee epidemiology and outreach to local beekeepers to help them minimize the spread of disease. But after he autopsied Hackenberg's bees, his job description changed. Typically, when a bee is sliced open, its viscera appear a creamy white. These bees were different. Their internal organs were blackened, their sting glands and intestinal tracts swollen, discolored, and full of melanized scar tissue, as if their insides had been incendiary-bombed.

Hackenberg had also contacted vanEngelsdorp's colleague Diana Cox-Foster, another Penn State entomologist who specializes in bee viruses and other pathogens. Cox-Foster conducted a molecular analysis on the afflicted bees. The results were mystifying: they had multiple viral, bacterial, parasitic, and fungal infections, but none seemed to suffer from the exact same infection. Some had deformed wing virus; some had sacbrood virus; some had black queen cell virus; some had chalkbrood; some had nosema; some had other viruses that hadn't yet been identified. None had the same exact combination of pathogens. Nor did they have large loads of mites, as nearly everyone had expected. Had mites been responsible, the scientists would have found large numbers in surviving colonies or sealed up with the brood yet to hatch. They didn't.

What all this confounding evidence suggested wasn't entirely clear. The affected bees' immune systems—fragile under any circumstances—simply weren't functioning as intended. Much as an AIDS patient suffers from a variety of exotic and typically rare infections, so did Hackenberg's bee populations. The Penn State entomologists gave it an appropriately apocalyptic yet vague name, Colony Collapse Disorder, and set out to determine what it was.

Among their first moves was to put together a collaborative "working group" representing a variety of disciplines and including USDA Research Service scientists, university entomologists, agricultural extension educators, and geneticists. To understand the distribution of the disorder, they conducted winter loss surveys, contacting bee inspectors who in turn contacted beekeepers across all fifty states, to find out where and how bees had died that year. The team also took samples from both healthy and afflicted hives in Florida, Georgia, California, and Pennsylvania. They put them on dry ice and sent them to various labs for analysis. Wax samples and bee corpses went to the pesticides group at Penn State, whose scientists examined the chemicals found in CCD hives and unaffected hives. Honey and pollen samples went to entomologists at North Carolina State University, who conducted a nutritional analysis of the food in the abandoned hives. The team shipped frozen bees to the Greene Infectious Disease Laboratory at Columbia University. Scientists there typically work with human tissue, but they agreed to employ a recently developed technique for reading short DNA sequences to create quick genetic profiles of the viruses, fungi, and parasites found in the CCD survivors. They sent samples to entomologists at the University of Illinois, who would compare the genomes of the affected bees to those of healthy colonies sequenced a few years earlier. They sent Hackenberg's empty bee boxes to be irradiated by a company that uses gamma rays to kill bacteria on fruit and medical equipment. Then they repopulated the boxes with new bees to see whether they fared better in the sanitized equipment.

In doing so, the team aimed to answer three fundamental questions. First: Was there a pathogen involved in the disorder—a new or reemerging strain of virus, bacteria, fungus, parasite, or amoeba? Second: Was there some type of nutritional or genetic stress, such as poor forage or a new genetic defect, that was present in CCD-afflicted bees but absent in healthy ones? And finally: Had the bees been exposed to pesticides or other environmental chemicals that might have compromised their immunity or affected their behaviors? The working group believed that those three hypotheses offered the most likely culprits in the mystery.

Out in the general public, however, plenty of other theories floated about. Among the most outlandish were suppositions that the disappearing bees prefigured the coming Judgment Day, and the oft-repeated hypothesis that signals from cell phones led foragers astray. ("You should never let the bees have them," joked a visitor to a beekeeper chat room. "They get distracted talking and never get any work done.") Given how frequently beekeepers complained about poor cell signals in their bee yards, however, the argument never gained much traction.

Beekeepers had their own, generally more plausible, ideas. Every so often, I'd get an email from Miller describing the latest theory waggling through the migratory hive. "The suspected pathogen is a new strain of nosema," he'd write.

> Nosema is common in insects; you can inoculate
> grasshoppers with nosema spores,
>
> and watch them die

A few days later, I'd receive another:

> psst.
>
> it's BT Corn that's killing the bees.
>
> you got it here,
>
> first.

Hackenberg, for his part, blamed the bloodbath (or rather, the hemolymph-bath) on a class of pesticides called neonicotinoids, which are chemical forms of nicotine used to treat a wide variety of crops. Neonicotinoids are among the world's best-selling insecticides. They are used on more than 140 different crops and in home gardens and flea collars, and they generate billions of dollars of sales a year. Developed by Bayer CropScience, Inc., they were first approved for use in the United States in the 1990s; fifty other companies have since jumped into the market, selling them under catchy names like Gaucho, Poncho, Flagship, Assail, and Calypso. Neonicotinoids are sprayed on leaves, but also soaked onto seeds before they are planted. Because they are "systemic" pesticides, which are absorbed into every part of the plant, passing from the coated seeds through the plant's circulatory system to the flowers, they remain in the plant—and its pollen and nectar—longer than many other insecticides. The neonicotinoid theory had a compelling logic, and lots of people in the environmental community quickly leapt to the same conclusion as Hackenberg—but it was, at that point, simply a theory. The CCD working group had a lot of methodical scrutiny—a lot of autopsies and surveys and studies and assays—ahead of them before they could declare the matter resolved.

Their efforts posed some thorny problems. First and foremost, the disappearing bees had, well, disappeared and were thus difficult to examine. Researchers were left with a few immature adults and brood and the smattering of foragers that still remained in affected hives. And the problem was so widespread—more than a third of cultivated bees had died across at least thirty-six states—that it was difficult to ascertain which deaths were truly the result of the new disorder and which were due to the litany of other pathogens and environmental insults bombarding bee colonies. Entomologists needed access to control groups that had not been exposed to the same environment. But bees are uncontrollable; it was nearly impossible to find any that scientists could be certain had not been exposed to the same influences as the diseased ones. So vanEngelsdorp and entomologists across the country began to sift through the clues, applying a Sherlock Holmes–style process of elimination. They surveyed scores of beekeepers whose stocks had suffered from CCD, and scores whose bees hadn't. They talked to beekeepers who moved their bees and those who didn't, to small-scale organic beekeepers and large-scale industrial operations. No obvious pattern emerged; the disorder had been found across all groups.

They looked for specific ailments. They found high mite loads in some CCD bees, not others. They found fungi in the guts of many, but not all. They found contamination from past varroacide use, legal and unauthorized, in many CCD hives, but also in many non-CCD hives. They found contamination from crop-applied pesticides, but no clear pattern. They combed through climate and satellite data to look for weather-related problems, but found nothing to explain the nationwide distribution of the problem. They considered bad corn syrup, fructose, and pollen substitutes that beekeepers might have fed their bees, but nothing immediately stood out. They contemplated the issue of beekeeper neglect. Some of the worst cases showed telltale signs of bad beekeeping, but some of the nation's most diligent beekeepers also had the disorder.

The scientists looked and looked. They found no easy answer. For all the advanced science available to them, it was almost as if they were back in the era before Langstroth invented his hive, blind to the mysteries that went on inside a colony's walls. They admitted that they were as bewildered as the beekeeper next door, and certainly more so than the armchair apiarists on the Internet who had already decided the problem was neonicotinoids or genetically modified corn or cell phone transmissions: "Lots of guesses, and I have my own, but I've also changed opinion since I've seen so many cases in so many areas," Montana State University entomologist Jerry Bromenshenk, one of the scientists in the CCD working group, wrote in an Internet beekeeping chat room. "Funny, the CSI teams on TV do this in an hour." It would take much longer than an hour, a month, or even a year to tease out an answer to this mystery.

THE FACT IS, YOU DON'T ALWAYS KNOW WHY BEES DIE. Sometimes, they just do. On a perfect January day with just a hint of winter's chill and the first yellow blooms of spring mustard beginning to unfurl, John Miller and I visited a bee yard that he kept for two friends from North Dakota—beekeeping brothers, one a retired crop extension specialist and the other a plant pathologist who got to know Miller when they both served as officers in the North Dakota Beekeepers Association in the early 1980s. They ran their bees in North Dakota in the summer and Miller took the brothers' hives south with his own bees for the winter pollination circuit. I couldn't say the brothers' yard was quite as pleasant as those Miller reserved for his own bees—he's only human—but there was nothing wrong with it. The hives lay in a sunny flat spot along a bleached clay road surrounded by cut-off buttes that had been carved away to provide terra-cotta for a nearby quarry. The spot wasn't idyllic, but there was ample forage, water, and sunshine, and a bee doesn't ask for more than that.

Still, the brothers' colonies weren't doing well. There were mites. Some of the hives were infested with mouse-turd-sized small hive beetles—the relatively new honey bee hitchhiker that eats, poops, oozes, and wreaks general havoc in an apiary. I had visited lots of bee yards with Miller by then, but these were the first hive beetles I had seen, and the hives in which they were found were underweight and understrength. There were also real mouse turds, from real mice that had eaten their way into one of the hives. When a colony is weakened, mice are able to nest in a hive without meeting the usual deadly reception. Miller doesn't like to see bees die, but his compassion doesn't extend to all creatures. He has no remorse about smashing a mouse with his hive tool, which he did with one efficient stroke that left a little beast with its diminutive paws splayed upward and a tiny trickle of blood pooling below its smashed head. Most of Miller's hives had come into spring with six to eight frames each, teeming with bees and stocked with honey, pollen, or brood, but the hives in this yard were only three to four frames strong, even without mice and beetles. "They got fed and medicated; they don't have many ticks," Miller said. "I can't tell why they're crappy bees."

Bees have experienced mysterious die-offs from time immemorial. Long before CCD came along, they even disappeared without a trace. Langstroth, for instance, described hives that were "found, on being examined one morning, to be utterly deserted. The comb was empty, and the only symptom of life was the poor queen herself, 'unfriended, melancholy, slow,' crawling over the honeyless cells." In the case of CCD, though, honey is left behind. But Langstroth described that condition, too. "Occasionally," he wrote, "after the death of the bees, large stores of honey are found in their hives." Since Langstroth's time, such happenings have been documented regularly. An 1869 issue of *Bee Culture* magazine described mysterious departures in which hives were left with ample honey stores. In Colorado in 1891 and 1896, in a case known as "May Disease," large clusters of bees vanished—queens still there. There were the epidemics between 1905 and 1919 that killed 90 percent of the bee colonies on Britain's Isle of Wight; for many years, the term "Isle of Wight disease" was the common name for losses for which beekeepers could find no obvious explanation. There were nebulous tales of large-scale dead-outs, as dead hives are sometimes called, across the United States, from Florida to California to Oregon, in 1915; more were reported in 1917 in New Jersey, New York, Ohio, and Canada. In the 1960s bees disappeared mysteriously in Texas, Louisiana, and California— no bacteria, mite, fungus, virus, or parasite appeared to explain it; those bees that remained in the abandoned colonies appeared healthy and had plenty of honey. In 1975 Australia suffered a bout of "disappearing syndrome"; that same year a similar epidemic of "disappearing disease" cropped up in Mexico and then spread to twenty-seven U.S. states. Neither bore obvious explanation. There were also heavy losses in France from 1998 to 2000. And now there was CCD.

So the symptoms of CCD were distinct—disappearing foragers, a healthy queen left behind, ample honey stores, no signs of excessive mite or fungal infection—but not unprecedented. Bees often die away from the hive. When confronted with high virus levels, they seem to know they are sick and leave on purpose, so as not to infect others, sacrificing themselves the same way our ancestors must have done. Miller likes that idea. It makes the ruthlessly indiscriminate way that bees die seem somehow almost meaningful.

Think about that . . .

Grandpa walked out of the igloo, and fed himself to the polar bear when he knew his time had come. . . .

Is it so, that the 900,000 neuron bee-brain has,

in a secret chamber,

the altruistic knowing to go? . . .

Bees die. Bees disappear, and sometimes in droves. They have done the same in the past, and not infrequently. "What's unique about this situation," says vanEngelsdorp, "is that we've never had it to this extent." Such massive, inexplicable losses have never been reported so widely.

In September 2007, a few months after the disorder was first identified, the CCD team led by Penn State's Cox-Foster, who did the first genetic analysis on Hackenberg's bees, conducted a cutting-edge "metagenomic" analysis and found that a little-known pathogen called Israeli acute paralysis virus (IAPV) was present in 96 percent of the hives stricken with CCD. Furthermore, all the infected samples had come from operations that had imported bees from Australia after the varroa die-off in 2005. This suggested that the virus was imported from Australia along with the bees. The disease, which was first identified in Israel in 2004 and has since been found in many locations across the world, causes bees to suffer paralytic seizures. They are typically found trembling, twitching, and flailing dramatically just outside the hive. ("They're suffering," Miller whispered to me as we watched a video of a bee dying from IAPV at a beekeeping conference.) Though the symptoms of CCD were nothing like those of IAPV, the report concluded that IAPV was "strongly correlated with CCD."

Although the researchers were careful to say that IAPV was not necessarily the cause of CCD—and could in fact be merely a symptom, or its presence merely a coincidence, and that far more study was needed—the media was less fastidious in reporting what appeared to be the first big break in the case. A spate of articles trumpeted the solution to the CCD mystery and the link to Australian imports. A Pennsylvania senator urged the USDA to suspend all Australian bee imports, and the Australian beekeeping industry erupted in protest. A team led by Denis Anderson, the Australian scientist at the forefront of the varroa battles, quickly issued a rebuttal, calling links between CCD and IAPV "tenuous" at best. Anderson and a colleague noted that there had been no occurrences of CCD in Australia; that IAPV had been found in hives not suffering from CCD as well; and that other countries reporting CCD, such as Spain, Greece, and Poland, had not imported bees from Australia.

Anderson also pointed out that IAPV had now been linked to bee deaths in the United States as far back as 2002—three years before Australian bees arrived on American shores. The "problem solved" headlines trailed off, a victim of uncertainty.

Other scientists had also begun researching the CCD mystery, and the next diagnosis was *Nosema ceranae*, a new strain of a long-known fungal infection that had recently jumped from Asian bees to European ones. *Nosema apis*—an infection found in European bees—had been present in both the United States and Europe for many years. The disease is often associated with extreme diarrhea in bees but is easily treated with an application of antibiotics just before the bees hunker down for the winter. (A disease of confinement, *Nosema apis* is usually only a problem during the cold months.) The new Asian strain, however, caused symptoms at strange times of year when beekeepers weren't accustomed to treating it, symptoms that were in some cases suspiciously similar to those of CCD—bees died suddenly, often while away from the hive. Miller, blindsided by a summer epidemic of the new strain, lost 25 percent of his hives to it in 2008. After a particularly bad epidemic of deaths in Spain, a Spanish team declared nosema the main factor in the CCD epidemic: "We've no doubt at all it's *Nosema ceranae*," the lead scientist on the team told a Reuters journalist. There were some troubling incongruities, however: nosema had not been detected at levels considered high enough to cause collapse in many CCD colonies, and genetic tests revealed that the "new" nosema had been present in the United States since at least 1995 and was widespread across the country, both in locations affected by CCD and in those unaffected.

Probably the most common and persistent explanation for the disappearances placed the blame on pesticides—specifically the neonicotinoids that Hackenberg faulted for his own losses. France banned the products in 1999 after they were linked to major losses in sunflower fields and a disorder that local bee-keepers took to calling "mad bee disease." Sales had also been suspended in Germany, Italy, and Slovenia. The theory was a persuasive one. For as long as pesticides have existed, they have been responsible for massive bee losses. The chemicals are, after all, designed specifically to kill bugs, and honey bees are, de-spite their comic-book fuzzy reputations and close human con-nections, bugs—and thus tremendously vulnerable to chemicals designed to kill their exoskeletal brethren.

Hackenberg wasn't a natural ally of the antipesticide crowd. His father was a farmer, and his livelihood in the pollination business depended on the agriculture industry. When he first started poking into what caused his bees to go missing, he emailed some friends in France, who sent him "all this propa-ganda about Gaucho and so on and so forth," claiming that the problem was systemic pesticides. Systemics, he learned, work not by killing outright but by breaking down the immune sys-tem of the target insect.

He wasn't persuaded at first, but, he says, "as time went on and I started digging, the pesticide thing kept coming back and kept coming back and kept coming back." He recalled that some of his bees had disappeared after pollinating apples in New York and called the grower, and then the grower's pesticide applica-tor, to find out what pesticides they had been spraying in 2005. He learned that it was Calypso, a popular neonicotinoid. He then set his wife to searching the Internet, and she found a Uni-versity of Florida study that explained how systemic pesticides broke down termites' immune systems—"they go out to feed, and they won't come home," Hackenberg says.

Studies have established that chemicals can often work in sublethal ways. Massive worldwide frog declines, for instance, have been linked to the commonly used weed killer atrazine. One theory is that the herbicide kills frogs in indirect and insidious ways by destroying floating mats of algae but allowing algae on pond bottoms to thrive on the increased sunlight. This in turn provides more food for underwater snails, which explode in population, as does a parasitic flatworm carried by the snails. The flatworm then parasitizes and kills the frogs. Scientists believe that atrazine may also damage the frogs' immune systems, rendering them more vulnerable to various parasites that flourish in atrazine-affected environments. In complex ecosystems like freshwater ponds and beehives, balances can be tipped by unexpected factors, creating what amounts to ecological chain reactions.

Perhaps the accumulation of weeks or months of pesticide exposure from pollen collected from fields sprayed with neonicotinoids had finally tipped the balance in the nation's beehives. Perhaps, Hackenberg concluded, because residues remain in the plants at low levels for weeks after application, the poisons could accumulate in honey and pollen all summer. As bees turned to their stockpiles to survive the fall and winter, the neonicotinoids might degrade their nervous systems, causing disorientation, reduced immunity to disease—and perhaps mass die-offs like those seen in the cases of CCD.

There was plenty of circumstantial evidence to support these theories, and like Hackenberg, a number of respected beekeepers believed their losses correlated with exposures to the pesticides. Gene Brandi, Miller's television replacement on the NBC story about CCD, lost half his hives in the winter of 2007–2008 after he rented them to a watermelon farmer in the San Joaquin

Valley. Only later did he learn that the farmer had treated his watermelon crop with neonicotinoids; the hives that Brandi sent elsewhere survived. Initial studies seemed to indicate that pesticides could certainly be a factor: researchers found extraordinarily high levels of various pesticides in the wax, pollen, and bees that they extracted from CCD-affected hives. In studies led by Maryann Frazier, another Penn State entomologist, forty-six different pesticides were found in 108 pollen samples analyzed, and seventeen different chemicals were discovered in one single colony. Some were approved for use in hives to kill varroa mites. Some were garden-variety pesticides; some were systemic chemicals such as neonicotinoids. They even found insecticides that were no longer in use, like DDT, which was banned more than twenty-five years ago.

Farm chemicals clearly stick around in hives in greater numbers and for longer times than had previously been believed. This was true for neonicotinoids as well. There was also new evidence that neonicotinoids were more potent than previously believed: in December 2007, Bayer CropScience released a study that found that test trees given the same neonicotinoid doses regularly used on citrus and almond groves contained residual amounts high enough to kill bees, and that it persisted in the leaves of the trees for more than a year. With prodding from industry leaders like Brandi and Hackenberg, the National Honey Bee Advisory Board asked the EPA to ban the product. Instead the EPA called for further testing, allowing the products to remain on the market until the studies' conclusion in 2014.

Despite mounting evidence that neonicotinoids can harm bees in smaller doses than previously understood, there are major problems with the hypothesis that pesticides alone cause

CCD. There is, first of all, the fact that while the latest round of bee disappearances began in the fall of 2006, neonicotinoids have been on the market in the United States since 1994. That said, their use has increased dramatically in the last decade. Says Hackenberg, the products are now used on "everything—I mean literally everything, from your dog and cat to corn, soybeans, cotton, vegetables, lawns, and golf courses." Still, bees have settled in fields of sunflowers, canola, corn, and melons treated with the chemicals for years, to little obvious ill effect. Spokesmen for Bayer are quick to point out that there have been zero reports of CCD losses in Australia, which has also used neonicotinoids for many years. In addition, the prohibition of the chemicals in France has done little to restore healthy bee populations. French bee colonies never quite rebounded from the die-offs of the late 1990s, suggesting that there may be some other factor responsible for their continued malaise.

Most researchers now agree that pesticides don't appear to be the sole cause of CCD losses. A 2009 study at the French National Institute for Agricultural Research found pesticides in troubling numbers in all the hives tested, CCD or no, but found no evidence that any individual pesticide occurred more frequently in CCD apiaries than in control ones. (In fact, healthier hives often had higher levels of some pesticides, especially the varroa-killing chemical coumaphos.) Perhaps, though, chronic exposure to low doses of poisons weakened bees sufficiently so that another pathogen—one that would under normal circumstances cause only limited mortality—was able to finish them off. The French study showed that bees that did not succumb to pesticides or nosema alone often did succumb when exposed to both nosema and nonlethal doses of pesticides.

Other theories rose and fell. In the fall of 2009, a spate of newspaper articles trumpeted a British team's conjecture that the problem was a lack of variety among queen-bee mates—queens were not promiscuous enough, in effect. They were mating with fewer drones, creating a less genetically diverse population that was more vulnerable to disease and other biological insults. This may be one factor in the honey bee's difficulties in recent years, but the British study had not even gotten under way before press releases issued forth. Every scientist, it seemed, looked at the disorder through the prism of his or her own particular specialty and circumstances; every advocate favored his own particular cause or worldview. The disorder was so poorly defined that it was easy to shape to fit one's own conclusions. "A lot of people are jumping on everything dead and saying it's CCD," vanEngelsdorp told me. "It's like saying anyone who dies is dying of cancer."

Plenty of bees have died since CCD was identified, but not all perished from CCD. Mortality studies conducted by vanEngelsdorp found that beekeepers had been experiencing losses of about a third of the nation's bee herd each year since 2007, much higher than the 15 percent loss they considered "acceptable." But CCD was not always the main factor. In 2008, beekeepers reported symptoms of CCD in 60 percent of colonies that died; in 2010, however, they reported the same symptoms in only about a third of the dead colonies, and only 5 percent of beekeepers believed CCD was the main cause of their losses. The leading cause that year was starvation. "If anything, it's shown us that bees are dying in a lot of different ways," vanEngelsdorp said.

Many unaffected beekeepers, meanwhile, still placed the blame on the old standby, PPB (piss-poor beekeeping). Because the case definition of CCD was rather loose and open to interpretation, it is indeed likely that losses from any number of less glamorous causes were dumped into the large bucket of CCD, and that many beekeepers weren't able to check their hives often enough, especially in winter, to know whether their lost bees vanished quickly and en masse, as they do in CCD, or simply died from some other cause. Still, many of the same beekeepers who blamed the first year's losses on bad beekeeping ate their words in the second year, when they too lost huge proportions of their colonies. Richard Adee, the nation's largest beekeeper, was an outspoken proponent of the PPB theory in 2007. In 2008 he lost 40 percent of his outfit to the disorder. Even Miller will admit, under duress, that though he didn't have the unique experience of finding an entirely deserted bee yard, he did sometimes open a hive to find lots of honey and just a handful of bees. Though he continued to blame such problems on varroa mites or *Nosema ceranae*, he admitted, "I'm sure half of what we were seeing was probably related to symptoms described as CCD."

It is hard for a prideful beekeeper to cede control of his narrative. But tarring beekeepers who have suffered from the disorder with the broad brush of incompetence, says vanEngelsdorp, is like accusing someone who catches the flu of not washing her hands enough—perhaps she didn't, but plenty of conscientious people get the flu, too. Sometimes bad things happen to good beekeepers. "I don't think there are any beekeepers who survived the last twenty years, who survived the varroa mite, who aren't good beekeepers," vanEngelsdorp says. "We've lost them already."

※

SCIENTISTS HAVE BEGUN TO COME TO A VAGUE CONSENSUS about the CCD deaths, though it's not a particularly satisfying one. A 2009 study from the CCD working group concluded that the distribution of CCD apiaries suggested either a contagious condition or exposure to a common risk factor—neighboring colonies tended to die together—and that CCD colonies generally had higher viral loads and were coinfected with a greater number of pathogens than were the control colonies. A later study confirmed that CCD bees carried increased viral loads, particularly from a suite of picorna-like retroviruses that hijack cellular production of important proteins and work much like another retrovirus, HIV, which leaves humans vulnerable to opportunistic diseases that someone with a healthy immune system would easily ward off. A 2010 study found that in colonies with *Nosema ceranae* infection, the retroviruses were at levels two to three times higher than in healthy colonies—the presence of both nosema and the viruses together appeared to be a strong predictor of a colony's collapse. Later that year, a Montana team, using military technology developed to test for bioterrorism attacks, discovered that a pathogen called insect iridescent virus, which had not previously been found in honey bees, was strongly correlated with CCD losses in conjunction with nosema infection. The study received a lot of attention, with headlines again declaring the case closed, but in fact it only reinforced the notion that there is more than one pathogen affecting the nation's bees—and that we don't know why that is the case.

Most scientists working on unraveling the CCD mystery have concluded that no single factor can be blamed for the malady. Instead, a combination of factors is probably responsible—some sort of interaction between pathogens and variables such as nutrition, weather, varroa mites, pesticides, and the modern insults of long-distance beekeeping. "I still go back to the death-by-a-thousand-paper-cuts theory," says Miller. "That it's some combination of stress, accumulated pathogens, chemical materials, overstimulation, near starvation—an accumulation of what we do." Hives are stressed, and stressed hives appear to be susceptible to all variety of insults. This is not, of course, rocket science; Lorenzo Langstroth's tenth axiom of beekeeping said as much back in the 1850s: "The essence of all profitable bee-keeping is contained in [nineteenth-century beekeeping sage Johann Nepomuk] Oettl's Golden Rule: KEEP YOUR STOCKS STRONG. If you cannot succeed in doing this, the more money you invest in bees, the heavier will be your losses." But beekeepers aren't sure anymore how to follow even the simplest rules of beekeeping. In the five years since CCD first was given a name, the only thing that is obvious, says vanEngelsdorp, is that "bees dying from CCD are just sicker than the ones that aren't dying."

SICK BEES DO PROVIDE SOME BENEFITS. SICK BEES ELEVATE pollination prices for healthy bees. Sick bees—especially those that die by baffling means and in large numbers—pique the interest of the media and thus recruit new converts to the cause of the honey bee: city people and environmental people and foodie people who never thought much about bees. Now they do; they read about bees and worry about them and plant flower gardens and buy local honeys and put hives on their roofs. Beekeepers, after years of losing bee-yard locations to sprawl, are now suddenly receiving phone calls from strangers offering prime locations to help the bees.

Sick bees get folks like John Miller lots of airtime: "Attention is easy; recognition is difficult," Miller once told me. "I gravitated towards attention." The recent carnage has garnered

Miller and his colleagues a lot of it. In February 2007, when the CCD story first broke, Dave Hackenberg woke up one morning to a phone call from his son, telling him he was on the front page of the *Philadelphia Inquirer*. "Over the next two days," says Hackenberg, "a friend of mine tells me that I was in four hundred and eighty-something newspapers around the world." He tore through more than five thousand airtime minutes on his cell phone in that first month. He wore out his phone in three months. After receiving an enormous bill, he called up his provider. "I told them what my story was, and the guy said, 'Oh yeah, I read about you,'" and gave Hackenberg unlimited minutes. Sometimes it's hard to be a media darling. Hackenberg estimates he spends 20 to 25 percent of his time in his role as the face of the CCD-stricken beekeeper, time that he's not spending figuring out how to keep his beekeeping business—which has suffered crippling losses four years in a row—afloat. "I didn't ask to be the guy that discovered anything," he says.

But the attention to beekeepers has also wrought some long-overdue recognition—of the hard work required to keep bees alive these days; of the superhuman sacrifices required to make their living; of the quixotic delight beekeepers take in pursuing a difficult professional path. Perhaps that's why I was drawn to Miller. Though I had long been exceedingly fond of honey, I had no particular affection for bees. Beekeepers, though, are a different story. They are heroic characters, tragic characters, anomalous characters. They do the hard thing. I could appreciate that. I had alit on a profession that's even less commonsensical, even more economically obtuse, even lonelier than being a writer. Beekeepers deserve a little recognition for that.

The onset of CCD had fortuitous timing. Just a few months before, the honey bee genome had been decoded, providing new information on the insect's constitution, its strengths and vulnerabilities. A group of scientists had then met in Washington, D.C., and released a report on the decline of pollinators as a whole—honey bees, bumblebees, native bees, birds. The state of Pennsylvania, for instance, has been surveying bee populations for the last 150 years, according to vanEngelsdorp, identifying more than four hundred species of bees found there. Thirty-two of them have not been seen since 1950. Bats have also disappeared in droves thanks to a mysterious ailment called "white nose syndrome." Bats may have their backers, passionate as any other, but so far, the public has found their plight far less appealing. "I'm glad I'm a bee man and not a bat man," vanEngelsdorp confessed in a 2008 speech. There's less public sympathy for bats. Which means there's less research money for bats, too.

There is money—more of it anyhow—in bee research these days, because the public now cares about bees. With pollination prices at an all-time high during the CCD years, the almond industry, which always cared about bees to the extent that it needed them alive to pollinate crops, now cares about bees even more and has poured more money than ever into bee research. And that new research money—and the compelling mystery of CCD—has attracted new scientists. They have brought with them new technologies, such as those originally developed to study human genetics and epidemiology, enlisting and adapting them in the cause of the bee. Perversely, CCD has been, in the words of bee broker Joe Traynor, a "multimillion dollar gift" for the U.S. bee industry. "If the bee industry hired a public relations firm to convince almond growers and others of the problems beekeepers are facing it would have cost millions," he wrote.

CCD has been bad to bees, but it has been good for their image. The honey bee has always had an advantage over other insects—it's fuzzy; it's striped; it looks cute on baby clothes; it makes honey. And now, in the wake of CCD, it has also acquired a patina of tragic charisma. It pulls at our heart- and purse-strings the same way that pandas and polar bears and other vulnerable wild creatures do. Our affection for the bee is all the more remarkable considering that it's a bug, for heaven's sakes—a stinging, droning, unpredictable insect that crunches when you step on it and was never actually wild here in the United States because it was never actually a native. But no matter: it's the honey bee's fifteen minutes, too. "It's about time people got hyped up for bees," says Marla Spivak, one of the field's most active scientists, who recently won a MacArthur "genius" grant for her work on honey bee genetics. "At first I was uncomfortable, I didn't want to capitalize on bees' problems, but then I realized: Hey, wait a minute, the public is *getting* this. People get how important bees are. They may never understand bee diseases, but they will understand that bees need flowers, and that there are not enough of them anymore, and many of them are contaminated with pesticides. If we encourage people to have gardens, plant flowers, and keep pesticides out, that's an amazing cultural change. We can't hype that up enough."

So bees have acquired yet another job. As if they didn't already have enough work to do pollinating flowers, providing for the queen and her offspring, and building and protecting the hive, they have been assigned extra metaphorical tasks as symbols—of industry, selflessness, community, and domesticity, and lately as exoskeletal canaries in a coal mine. The public is fascinated with Colony Collapse Disorder because many believe that bees are *Silent Spring*–like harbingers of retribution for our crimes against nature. Dying bees are symbols of environmental sin, of the synthetic crimes of the chemical industry.

People put a lot on bees, and they take it on, as they take on all the other tasks they perform, because they don't have a lot of choice in how they live or what they do with their short lives or how they die. Honey bees are small creatures, but they must carry an enormous burden of preconception.

Chapter Seven

....

Survivor Stock

AT JUST SHY OF 5 A.M. EVERY DAY IN EARLY APRIL, A BLEARY-eyed bee guy pulls his truck into a Chico, California, parking lot and places a medium-size foam cooler on the front seat of a white van. The cooler sits beside the driver as the North Valley Shuttle loads its passengers, then pulls onto the highway and makes for the Sacramento airport. The van can seat a maximum of fifteen passengers. But in the early spring after the almond petals have fallen, the 5 A.M. from Chico can predictably be expected to hold more than fifteenfold the lives it is licensed to carry—the driver, the paying human passengers, and 250 minuscule travelers crowded in the front seat.

At 6:10 A.M., one of John Miller's employees leaves Newcastle to meet the van at the Arco station inside the Sacramento airport boundaries, and, promptly at seven, or whenever the shuttle arrives, "scratches on the window three times to alert the driver to the prearranged secret action code," Miller says—although we all know that no such thing actually happens. The employee transfers the box to the passenger seat of one of Miller's bee-emblazoned pickups, hands the driver some empty foam coolers and a bottle of honey, and departs "without signaling right or left." There is no time to waste. It is day 15, and if it were day 16 or even day 15½ it might be too late. If too much time should elapse, carnage will ensue. No leisurely cups of coffee now. The truck stops just long enough to pick up some supplies, then drives the foam box to a recently assembled apiary, where bees roam in disgruntled unease amid the blooming mustard.

There, the crew takes the Styrofoam lid off the cooler, removes the eggshell-foam lining, some sixteen-ounce hot-water bottles, and a few damp T-shirts, and extracts a bullet-shaped plastic plug encased in beeswax. The workers pull the top off each hive, pry open a quarter-sized space between frames two and three, and gently, very gently, place the plug between the top bars of the two frames, then carefully replace the top, then patiently wait a few minutes or hours, until a set of tiny mandibles eats through each wax cap and a pair of tiny antennae, then a tiny head and elegant, tapered body, emerge. Then there is no more waiting and no more confusion: a young, and we do hope vigorous, virgin queen clambers out of her cell, and the bewildered leaderless bees in her newly formed hive have found a reason to seek nectar and pollen and order, and spring is in its glory, and the future beckons.

Timing is everything in beekeeping, but for most events— preparing for honey flows, winter-proofing the hive—a few days here or there don't truly matter. The dates on which a beekeeper splits and requeens his hives, however—those are truly inviolate. On those specific dates, the beekeeper divides one colony into two or three new "nucs": bare-bones "nucleus" hives stocked with a brand-new queen, a couple of frames of brood, a couple of frames of honey and pollen, and some empty frames for the bees to fill with more brood and honey and pollen. In late March, when the bees are released from the almonds, Miller sends half of them to Washington state to pollinate apples and brings half home to Newcastle to be split and "nuked" and re-queened. The language suggests atomic precision: the complete and indivisible hive unit is, by an act of human fission, divided into unstable parts. It is a sensitive transaction. If an egg is laid on March 17, the virgin will hatch April 2—no sooner, no later— and the hive must be nuked three days earlier to receive her. There is no margin of error. She will start her mating flights between April 6 and 13, conclude her flights by the 18th, wait five days for her ovaries to mature, and then start laying eggs. By April 22 the beekeeper should know, by observing the egg-laying patterns within the brood chamber, whether the queen has survived and been successful in her reproductive efforts.

Most beekeepers travel from yard to yard to split their hives, hauling the extra boxes, frames, and pallets to each apiary, opening each hive, and finding the queen. If she is especially productive, some beekeepers may let her remain for another year, although most beekeepers kill their old queens—with bees as with humans, the young are more fertile, and no one wants to risk a whole year with a queen who lays two hundred eggs a day instead of two thousand. The keepers take half the frames from the old hive and place them in two new hives (or sometimes three), filling the vacant slots in each with empty frames. Then they leave the new hives alone for three days so the workers get used to the idea that their old queen is not coming back. If a new queen and her unfamiliar pheromones are introduced too soon, the hive's bees may sting or rip or "ball" her to death, sur-rounding her en masse until she suffocates or overheats. Once the chemical memory of the old queen has faded, however, the nucs can be easily requeened with mail-order matriarchs. And through this act of partition and proliferation, one hive becomes many, the winter's losses are recouped, and hope begins anew that this year, unlike the last one, or five, or twenty, will be a good one.

This is the way most beekeepers split their hives, and it's the way John Miller would prefer to do it if his outfit were small, if he didn't have so many bee yards scattered across so many miles of the Sierra foothills, if he didn't have to haul his entire crew and all the necessary equipment from yard to yard, and if he weren't John Miller and thus obsessively concerned with making things more efficient in the world of beekeeping. But instead of dragging his crew from yard to yard for two and a half weeks in March and April, he drags 3,500 hives home to Newcastle. There, under a tent in a clearing below his headquarters, he has designed his own proprietary "nuking machine," a Y-shaped conveyor belt that mechanically conducts much of the labor-intensive business of taking apart a hive. First, an employee pries open the top of a hive box and places the hive on a moving belt, which rolls under an overhanging machine that scrapes the top bars free of wax and propolis. The hive then rolls onto a foot-powered thruster that rams the frames from below, releasing them from the body of the hive. Another employee removes the frames and sorts them into stacks: one for frames full of honey; another for pollen; another for brood frames (those are where the queen is usually found, and if employees spot her, they'll sometimes squash her so the new queen has no competition, though usually they ignore her—"If she survives the drama of nuking," says Miller, "she is good in my book"). The assembly line forks there, and an employee places two empty hive boxes on each fork of the Y and pushes them down the line, where other employees reassemble the hives with brood, honey, pollen, and filler frames, then stack them on pallets. When a pallet has received its full complement of four hives, it is forklifted to the edge of the clearing. The dislocated bees spend a fitful night of confusion and bereavement and the next morning they are moved into a yard to await their new queens.

Like most of John Miller's beekeeping innovations, his nuking line started with a vision. Unlike his Mormon fore-fathers, who tended to receive their visions on pillars of light and such, Miller gets most of his at the gym, often while do-ing leg lifts. That's how it happened this time, anyhow: there he was, doing five sets of ten leg lifts at fifty pounds, and there it was, "right in front of me"—the nuking machine. The idea wasn't completely his own: "I know a good idea when I steal one," he likes to say. This one he stole from the Cowens of Parowan, Utah, who'd invented a scraper that removes the wax comb from the top bars of frames. Few beekeepers seem in-clined to steal the nuker idea from Miller, however. Even he would prefer yard-by-yard nucs, because fewer bees drift and swarm and die; but what he loses in bees, he more than saves in labor costs. With his machine, he can split two hundred hives an hour; doing it the normal way, even the most efficient crew can split only eighty a day. Still, most of Miller's colleagues find the nuking machine disturbing. His invention has won few—to be honest, no—converts. "Every bee guy just stares," he says.

In fairness to other beekeepers, Miller's nuking line is truly appalling. He is the first to admit it. There is no approaching the tent without a full bee suit and veil, and double gloves, if you're smart. Angry, confused bees fill the air like a black hailstorm, alighting on any warm surface—the apex of the tent, the crowns of employees' heads, their temperate butt cracks. Bees swirl and dive-bomb, bouncing off veils like popcorn. The nearby trees droop with escaped swarms, which Miller will visit with an empty hive later in the evening, when the bees' ill tempers cool, and coax back to safety. Even up the hill at Miller's office, the air is filled with angry drifters (this is where I got my "scalp hit"); they blast through the air and cluster on coffee tins and honey pails and shrubs. They litter the carpet in his office. It is no fun for the bees; it is no party for the beekeepers, either. During nuking season, Miller's hands and gloves are speckled with stingers. He sees bees in his dreams. But he knows no better option. The survival of his bees, of his business, and indeed, of the honey bee in America, depends on this violent springtime ritual.

Here's a surprising fact: for all the carnage of recent years, the actual number of managed beehives in the country has held steady. Individual honey bees are unimaginably fragile, but as a community, as a species, they have an astonishing capacity to regenerate. They work hard, remember: a queen can lay thousands of eggs a day to repopulate a hive. That's the strategy honey bees use to recover from the misfortunes that befall them daily, and it's also the strategy beekeepers like John Miller use to recoup lost hives. Introduce a good, hardy new queen each spring, and much of the winter's carnage can be forgotten. Without new queens, around 20 percent of a keeper's bees might be nonproductive during the honey flow, even during good years. Without new queens, national hive numbers would have plummeted disastrously in the recent bad years. New queens are also the reason that predictions of imminent honey bee extinction are probably off the mark. Lucky for bees, they have beekeepers to keep them going. No one has ever doubted that honey bees, with their wee nine-hundred-thousand-neuron brains, are, as organisms, awfully savvy in their quest for survival: just look how they have enlisted these improvident humans to risk all manner of painful indignity each spring so that they can prosper. How smart is that?

🐝

THE QUEEN IS, AS ANY OBSERVER OF BEES OR CONSUMER OF metaphor knows, the focal point of the colony. She is long and lissome, with shorter wings than the worker bees and a slimmer body than the drones. She is, wrote Lorenzo Langstroth, the only "perfect female" in the hive—the only creature that is capable of laying both male and female eggs. Some worker bees can, in a pinch, lay drones, but only a queen, with her fully developed ovaries, can produce both males and the female workers who will form the backbone of the hive. And produce she does. At her reproductive peak, a queen can lay as many as three thousand eggs a day, dropping her tapered bottom into cell after cell and leaving behind an upright nearly-rice-grain-sized deposit that will develop, with time and care and tending and feeding, into a juvenile bee. She singlehandedly populates the hive with workers: newly hatched nurse bees who clean the hive and care for the brood and feed the queen and build the cells, and then after a couple of weeks grow up to be guard bees who protect the hive from intruders, and then finish their brief lives as foragers who wander out for honey and pollen and propolis. She also lays the drones, the males who sit around eating, "in gluttony and idleness," wrote Charles Butler, "living by the sweat of others' brows," in case their sperm should be needed for mating flights. Without her singular reproductive purpose and powerful pheromonal influence, the thousands of bees in her orbit are utterly bereft. "If she is taken from them," wrote Langstroth,

> the whole colony is thrown into a state of the most
> intense agitation as soon as they ascertain their loss;

all the labors of the hive are abandoned; the bees run
wildly over the combs, and frequently rush from the
hive in anxious search for their beloved mother. If they
cannot find her, they return to their desolate home,
and by their sorrowful tones reveal their deep sense
of so deplorable a calamity. Their note at such times,
more especially when they first realize their loss, is of a
peculiarly mournful character; it sounds somewhat like
a succession of wailings on the minor key.

The queen exerts a powerful pull on bees and their keepers alike. Beekeepers like nothing more than seeing a bustling,
queen-right hive, and they pride themselves on locating the
queen before anyone else can. She is always found in the double-
deep brood chamber at the bottom of the hive stack, usually in
one of the interior frames, and always at the center of a whorl of
attendants grooming and feeding her and spreading her pheromones throughout the colony, her influence radiating outward
like ripples in a pond. She is the star of the show; she rules the
roost. She can live one to five years; the average worker, by contrast, lives one to four months. The preservation of her life is
indispensable to the colony's survival. Queens are the last to
perish in any fatal incident, because without her, the other bees
die as well. When a colony becomes "hopelessly queenless,"
wrote Langstroth, its destruction is certain. "While the common bees are ready to sally forth and sacrifice their lives on
the slightest provocation, a queen-bee only buries herself more
deeply among the clustering thousands." She is the colony's
ruler and also its foremost prisoner, an egg-laying machine who,
after one brief period of loveless flight into the larger world, is
confined for the rest of her life to the lower reaches of the hive

where the eggs are laid and stored. That is, until her reproductive capacities wane; then she is unceremoniously tossed aside for a younger model.

In nature, queens are created in panic or in prosperity. When a queen dies or fails to lay sufficient eggs to keep the colony going, the bees feed royal jelly—a thick, creamy substance secreted by nurse bees—to multiple freshly hatched larvae who would otherwise develop into workers. Although all larvae are fed royal jelly mixed with honey for the first two or three days after they hatch, developing queens are fed royal jelly exclusively and in large amounts through the entire larval period, spurring the formation of the mature ovaries required for queens to lay fertilized eggs. In a failing hive, the bees feed the jelly to larvae in worker cells that they enlarge in the hopes of growing a new queen before the hive falls apart. That's the panic mode. Then there's the prosperity mode: if the colony is too successful and all the hive's cells fill with eggs and honey and pollen so there's nowhere to lay eggs or store food anymore, the nurse bees go on a royal-jelly binge, feeding the highly nutritious substance to worker-bee larvae in specially built peanut-shaped "swarm cells" to raise a new queen so that the old one can depart with a swarm of young workers in search of roomier digs. In both modes, the workers cap the cells and wait for the queens to hatch. The first to do so eats her way out, then promptly chews through every other queen cell and stings her rivals to death— the queen's stinger is not barbed like those of worker bees, so she has the capacity to sting multiple times without sacrificing her life. After she has dispatched her sisters, she goes after her mother if necessary ("only room for one mom," says Miller). She feeds for four or five days, then flies out to mate.

Back in Langstroth's days they called the queen's mating

flight her "wedding excursion"—though the wedding would re-semble nothing a traditionalist would find appealing. A more apt metaphor might be a bordello debut. Her journey into the larger world outside the hive is far less romantic than it is lust-ful and utilitarian. To find prospective mates, the queen flies from the hive to an area where hundreds or even thousands of drones congregate each day, waiting for a new queen to take wing nearby. Some come from her own colony, but most have traveled longer distances from various colonies, thus guaran-teeing a degree of genetic diversity so that the stocks don't, in Langstroth's words, "become enfeebled by 'close breeding.'" The queen copulates in the air with as many drones as she can find—typically, eight to twenty fired-up males, who will, if they are lucky enough to fulfill their reproductive purpose, die im-mediately. Then the queen must find her way home to the hive without becoming hopelessly lost, or getting dashed by a wind gust against a tree or into the water, or grounded by rain, or eaten by a bird or a dragonfly. The queen's large size and slow flying speed make her easy picking for predators, some of whom make a point of lingering in drone congregation areas.

She must also ensure that she does not return to the wrong hive. If she does, she will quickly be stung or ripped to pieces and discarded. More queens are lost through attempting to enter a strange hive after their mating flights than any other way. This, says Langstroth, "accounts for the notorious fact that ignorant beekeepers, with forlorn and rickety hives, no two of which look just alike, are often more successful than those whose hives are of the best construction"; more meticulous beekeepers "lose queens almost in exact proportion to the taste and skill which induced them to make hives of uniform size, shape and color." Such mass-produced uniformity, of course, is standard today, so beekeepers scatter nucs in yards with as many landmarks as possible, arranging them in serpentine patterns throughout the yard rather than in straight rows, in order to create better reference points for the queens, and facing the hive entrances in different directions to minimize a queen's confusion. If she returns successfully, her spermatheca, a pouch in her oviducts, will be filled with about seven million commingled sperm from her various partners, and she will, after five days, drop her first cream-colored ovoid into the bottom of a wax cell. Then she will lay, and lay, and lay. The mating flight is a queen's only chance to accrue the semen she will use to lay eggs for the rest of her life. When the sperm runs out, so too does her productive life span.

That's how queens are created in nature; in California, they have help from guys like Pat Heitkam. Heitkam is the genial, thrice-married bee guy who stumbles out to the North Valley Shuttle each morning in the first half of April to ship, for instance, exactly half of the queen cells that John Miller will use in his hives every spring. Heitkam once owned a bike shop in Santa Cruz. He let a friend convince him to trade a beehive for a new bike—and "that," he says, "was the end of the deal." He accrued more and more bees and finally gave up on the bike shop, which required a little more human contact than he found entirely comfortable. Heitkam preferred a business where he could "go away by myself." Eventually he got interested in queens, moved up north to apprentice himself to a queen-rearer, and bought a rural property in Orland, a few miles outside Chico. There he enhived himself in a ramshackle array of aluminum-sided buildings surrounded by piles of boxes, pallets, pickup trucks, and an aggregation of aging Porsches. Heitkam has thick gray-white hair, a broad nose, and large, ungainly hands. He is kind and romantic—hence the three marriages and life's work in the bee-matchmaking racket. He is so good with bees, despite his oversize hands, that he rarely wears a veil and almost never wears a bee suit or gloves. Some call him a bee whisperer. I can't disagree, and neither can Miller, who considers him to be a "superb" beekeeper. During the springtime, Heitkam produces 1,000 queens a day, which is by no means a record—C. F. Koehnen & Sons, his neighbors in Ord Bend, just down Highway 45, make 3,000 nucs a day; and another neighbor, Ray Olivarez, who is capitalized by an almond farmer, produces 5,000 queens a day in late March and early April.

Queens in nature are produced through the unpredictable processes of supersedure (replacing a failing or dead queen) and swarming (producing a second one to split the hive); at Heitkam's place, they're produced with the help of two nimble-fingered Hispanic women named Esmeralda and Georgina who sit in a shed behind Heitkam's house. The shed is warm, lined with wet towels to keep things intensely humidified—great for incubating creatures, not so comfortable for humans. Inside, the two women use wood-and-plastic tweezer-like devices to pluck freshly hatched larvae taken from a breeder hive—a colony containing an artificially inseminated queen typically purchased from a university lab. They then "graft" each larva into a plastic queen cell and place it upside down—the royal jelly that was transferred with the larva holds it in place—in a special frame along with forty-four other queen cells. The frame is marked with a date and the type of breeder bee who laid the eggs, then placed along with two other grafted frames into a "cell builder"—a hive that is generously stocked with honey, pollen, and nine pounds of young worker bees. In the absence of their own queen, the worker bees make royal jelly to feed to the developing larvae day in and day out, then cap the plastic cells so they look like little beeswax acorns. Heitkam has, in essence, created an emergency: the workers have no queen, and the hive is working frantically to raise a new one. This method emulates the situation of "panic" whereby hives create new queens. But Heitkam provides lots of supplies to help them do it, also reproducing the conditions of prosperity in which bees prepare to swarm.

The queen cells stay in the cell builder for eleven and a half days (fourteen days after the eggs were laid), and no longer. Should a queen hatch in the cell builder, she would sting all of her competitors to death, ruining all of Esmeralda and Georgina's painstaking work. So Heitkam must leave the cells in long enough to mature properly, but retrieve them before the queens begin to emerge. Once pulled, some of the unhatched pupae are sold as queen cells for four dollars apiece to people like Miller. Miller buys three thousand cells from Heitkam each year because he prefers to mate the queens with his own drones to ensure the genetic continuity of his stock. The rest are transferred unhatched to one of twelve nuc yards that Heitkam has selected both for their proximity to drone congregation areas and for sheltered, landmarked topography that give his queens a better chance of surviving their mating flight. They are lovely spots along riverbeds and among huge gnarled oaks, brambles, and hedgerows, alive with wild turkeys and bobcats, locations that Heitkam just loves to visit because they remind him that he's chosen a terribly agreeable way to make a living, even if it's not the easiest living to make, with twenty employees, six thousand hives, and a rigorous timetable that makes Mussolini's trains look laggard by comparison.

For about two weeks, Heitkam's fledgling queens enjoy the bucolic splendor, too, sharing their nuc yard with dozens of other queens, Italians on one end, Carniolans on the other. They mate, and after a few days a crew of Heitkam's workers returns, examines each hive, and "catches" those queens that have survived their mating flight and begun laying fertilized eggs. Heitkam, with his big hands, grabs queens by the thorax; his more dexterous workers capture them by the wings, which flutter and vibrate insistently, unhappily. Heitkam expects they will catch and sell about 70 percent of the queens placed in the nucs. They slip them into small, rectangular vented cages and ship them, for $15.50 a queen, to customers across California, Oregon, and Washington, and even as far away as France, Mexico, and Jordan. Then, after one to three days' wait, Heitkam puts new, ready-to-hatch queen cells in his now-leaderless nucs and starts all over again. And just like that, the honey bee perseveres.

PEOPLE BEGAN SELLING QUEENS EN MASSE AS A WAY TO REplace winter losses. To repopulate empty hives in time for the first spring flows, northern beekeepers would send away for three pounds of bees and a queen—a "package" of bees that had been "shaken" from a populous hive into a screened box. The first beekeeper to try shipping bees was the famed innovator A. I. Root, who in the 1880s conducted experiments showing that bees and queens could survive for a couple of weeks on such light, shippable honey substitutes as sugar syrups and soft candy. He convinced the postal service to handle live bees and developed a lightweight, ventilated cage in which to ship them—to this day, the U.S. Postal Service is required by postal code to deliver bees through the mail. He couldn't quite get the food supply right, however, and more often than not, his bees starved to death before they could reach their destination. It took until well into the next century for beekeepers to discover that bees could survive on a small, inverted pail of sugar syrup poked full of holes. The syrup drips for a few minutes and then forms a vacuum, flowing only when a bee sticks her proboscis into one of the punctured holes.

Not just anyone can raise queens for a living. Queen-breeders must live somewhere warm—southern states like Florida, Georgia, Texas, and California—where the pollen flows early enough that the hives are close to full strength when northern customers' bees are just waking up. Many northern beekeepers prefer to receive bees from as northerly a location as possible, seeking shorter travel times and more cold-adapted breeds. The upper tip of the Central Valley, around Chico, is the epicenter of queen-rearing in North America. At least sixty operations are based there, because it was, for many years, the farthest north a queen-rearing operation could be located and guarantee sufficient warm and dry weather during the early spring for successful mating flights. This is where Miller gets all of his new queens. Half come from Heitkam; the others are provided by C. F. Koehnen & Sons.

The Koehnens are an august outfit—C. F. Koehnen was a commercial catfisherman who moved into beekeeping in the early part of the last century, buying twenty acres along a bend in the Sacramento River. Along the way he acquired more land for forage, and, eventually, orange orchards, and then walnuts and almonds. His sons and grandsons now run the business. The family got out of the honey racket in the early 1970s when they discovered that they could make far more money raising queens and nuts. Now that's all they do. They do it well. For a hundred days in the early spring, the Koehnens and an assembly line of workers labor seven days a week to graft, cage, and package queens to ship all over the country. They sell a quarter of a million queens each year. The Koehnens' property is as orderly as Heitkam's and Miller's are not, with beautiful wood-

clad offices and a spic-and-span punchcard room for the dozens
of Hispanic workers who graft, nuc, and catch for them each
spring.

In 2007, one hundred years after Koehnen bought the first
twenty acres, the family held a party to celebrate the company's
longevity. John Miller was there, along with thirteen hundred
of the Koehnens' closest friends. "We walked to check-in tables,
where names were verified, and name tags were dispensed,"
Miller wrote.

> We were then confronted with three enormous tents with white
> tablecloths.
>
> After a few minutes of socializing,
>
> we were escorted to the serving lines,
>
> eight serving lines, and 1300 people were served in less than
> an hour.
>
> Prime rib, and chicken and all the fixings.
>
> Class act.

They ate on china; Miller's parties usually feature paper
plates. There were two bars and an Elvis impersonator band.
Tributes followed, with "mercifully short speeches."

> Bob and Bill, the padrones, were gifted side by side shotguns,
>
> engraved, and admonished to "go shoot them a lot."

Darkness settled. Fireworks erupted to the west. Miller took
Jan to see the grafting shed, where half of his new queens are
produced each spring.

We reviewed the 2007 work-sheet,

and totaled about 240,000 cells, not grafts, but cells that
actually took,

and marveled at the family's success.

What a deal.

Glad I went.

As with worker bees producing royal jelly, queen-rearers
today create queens in situations of prosperity or panic—panic
for most beekeepers, who are losing their bees at such alarming rates; prosperity for the queen-rearers, who are replacing
them. Half the hives in the United States now go through twice
the queens they used to, and varroa mites and CCD have created even more demand. But queen-rearers are beekeepers in the
end, and they aren't in it for the money—if they were, they'd go
into almonds. So they haven't raised prices to take advantage of
the increased demand; that would be mean. There are already
enough beekeepers going out of business.

IT TOOK ONLY A FEW MILLENNIA FOR HUMANS TO FIGURE
out how, exactly, bees reproduce. The ancients believed they
were born out of rotting meat—specifically, said Virgil, "from
the putrid blood of a slaughtered bullock" who is beaten to
death in a narrow shed until "his innards collapse," then laid on
beds of thyme and fresh rosemary, until

> . . . it ferments, and wonderful new creatures
> Come into view, footless at first, but soon

With humming wings; they swarm, and more and more
Try out their wings on the empty air, and then
Burst forth like a summer shower from summer clouds
Or like a shower of arrows from the bows ·
Of Parthian warriors entering the fray.

Until the seventeenth century, people believed that the hive's ruler was—naturally—a king. It was the British beekeeping authority Charles Butler who concluded that the large bee that controlled the hive was in fact a female—though he believed it was the worker bees who did the egg laying. Later in the seventeenth century, Dutch biologist Jan Swammerdam determined that the queen laid all the eggs in the hive. He postulated, however, that the queen was impregnated not by drones but by an "odoriferous effluvia" he named "aura seminalis"—in other words, by airborne sperm. Finally, in 1788, the blind French scientist François Huber, with the help of his sighted servant François Burnens, discovered a queen leaving a hive chased by a throng of lusty drones and returning filled with semen. He concluded that the queens were fertilized not inside the hive but on the wing, during a brief "virgin flight." (Slovenian beekeeper Anton Janscha had published the same findings fifteen years before, but his account had gone largely unnoticed.) In 1760 a German priest named Adam Gottlob Schirach had observed that queenless hives produced new queens by enlarging the cells of young worker larvae and feeding them a different diet; and in 1888 an American beekeeper named G. M. Doolittle commercialized artificial cell cups that allowed beekeepers to graft queens—and sell them—on a large scale.

Breeding bees is a science, but also an art. Unlike, say, cows, whose pedigrees and partners can be closely monitored, even the most methodical and Koehnen-like operations can't control a concupiscent queen once she takes flight. The queen is not discriminating; she'll mate with any drone wily enough to catch her. The best that most breeders can do to shape the genetics of their brood is to put the queen cell of their choice in a nuc, flood the area with drones of their choice, and hope the queen mates with the right ones (a process not all that different from raising a teenager, come to think of it). To shape brood genetics more deliberately, you must mate a queen in a lab. Way back in the eighteenth century, Huber attempted to paint drone semen onto a queen to encourage her to reproduce. That didn't work. In the late nineteenth century, an aptly christened German clockmaker and beekeeper, William Wankler, used his toolmaking skills to construct a silver, bee-sized "artificial penis" to deliver semen. That didn't work, either. Nor did efforts by USDA scientist Nelson McLain to hold the queen's sting chamber open with wooden clamps while using a hypodermic syringe to inject drops of semen into her vagina. In 1926, a bee guy named Lloyd Watson tried inseminating queens with a capillary syringe, forceps, a stereomicroscope, and a lamp; he achieved occasional success, but the method was not consistently reliable. Nor was a similar process developed by USDA scientist W. J. Nolan. Finally, in 1944, a USDA scientist named Harry Laidlaw—who is considered the father of modern queen-rearing ("He was the pope to anybody that raises queens. To have shaken his hand is an honor," says Heitkam)—discovered the valve fold, a tongue-like obstruction in the queen's oviduct, and designed an instrument that was able to bypass the fold and inject the sperm into anesthetized queens.

Successful insemination allowed bee scientists and queen-rearers, and ultimately beekeepers, to exercise more control over the types of bees they could produce. Bee guys had long been aware that certain bees behaved better—were gentler and produced more brood and honey—than others. Until the nineteenth century, for instance, most bees in the United States and northern Europe were descendants of the mean-tempered black bees brought over at the time of the nation's founding. But during the Napoleonic Wars, a Swiss army captain stationed in northern Italy noticed that the yellow-striped honey bees he saw there were not only a different color than the ones he'd grown up with but were also less easily riled, more prolific in their brood production, and less sensitive to cold. He had some brought to his home in Switzerland, and from there they quickly spread throughout Europe. Word of the Italians' superior behavior and temperament traveled to the United States, and Lorenzo Langstroth was an early convert: "Its introduction into this country will, it is confidently believed, constitute a new era in beekeeping," he wrote. In September 1859, after a number of failed efforts to ship Italian bees across the Atlantic, Langstroth succeeded in importing one Italian queen, which he found amid thousands of carcasses when he cut out the combs of a surviving hive. "I never handled anything in my life with such care," he wrote.

Italian bees were adopted quickly throughout the United States, and today the familiar yellow-and-black bees dominate the American beekeeping industry. Second in popularity is the dusky brown-and-gray-striped Carniolan, another European subspecies that originated in the Balkans and Eastern Europe. Miller keeps mostly Carniolans, which he prefers because of their extreme gentleness, their superior resistance to some insect pests (although not, unfortunately, the varroa mite), and their impressive wintering-over capacity in colder climates. The hives tend to expand rapidly in the spring as the nectar flows and cut off brood production just as quickly in the fall, thus producing more nectar in the summer and consuming less honey over the winter than Italian bees do. Breeders have also experimented with designer bees, such as the Buckfast, a hybrid bred and patented by a Benedictine monk named Brother Adam, who kept bees at Buckfast Abbey in Devon, England. After concluding that certain breeds of bees—Italians, for instance—survived a notorious 1915–'16 British bee die-off better than the native black bees, Brother Adam traveled the world searching for superior queens, developing a cross of French, Greek, Egyptian, Moroccan, and Turkish bees that combined the traits he was looking for: good honey and brood production, gentle behavior, and disease resistance. Brother Adam is credited with introducing the idea that careful breeding could be used to create bees that were more resistant to disease and pests. The Buckfast is still sold by queen-breeders today.

Typically, bee breeders mass-inseminate their queens, or mate them on the wing in isolation from other breeds, then sell them to queen-rearers, who open-mate them with their own stock in larger numbers. Breeders have always tried to tailor the gene pool to favor traits that make bees easy to manage; now they're striving just as hard to create bees that resist the varroa mite as well. Essentially they are seeking to mimic the process of natural evolution, in a hurry. Some populations have survived the onslaught of the mite in Brazil, South Africa, and isolated pockets in France, Sweden, New York state, and the American Southwest—though often, when those resistant populations are moved to locations where the mites are more active, they too crash. Bee guys hope that with careful breeding, European bees might be able to develop more successful mechanisms to resist the mites. In 1997, the Honey Bee Breeding Laboratory in Baton Rouge, Louisiana, imported Russian bees hailing from the Vladivostok area and supplied them to breeders. Because the varroa mites first made the jump from Asian to European honey bees in that region of the world, the bees there have, over the 150 years that they have been exposed to varroa mites, developed some resistance. Some beekeepers swear by the Russian bees, though they fare best—no surprise—in cold climates, and their resistant traits tend to be quickly diluted in the gene pool once they are exposed to nearby bees of other breeds.

Since 2001, the Baton Rouge lab has also distributed a line of queens bred specifically for "varroa-sensitive hygiene"—or VSH. VSH worker bees are able to detect and remove mite-infested brood. They do so at some cost, however. The bees are refined so specifically for their varroa-resistant properties—they are so deeply inbred—that they aren't as good at all the other things bees need to do, like producing lots of brood and collecting lots of honey. The Minnesota Hygienic bee, developed by University of Minnesota entomologist Marla Spivak, is another resistant breed. Spivak developed a line of varroa-resistant bees by freeze-killing brood with liquid nitrogen and raising queens only from productive colonies whose workers detected and cleaned out the abnormal brood within twenty-four hours. She has since worked with queen-breeders across the country, teaching them to test for hygienic behaviors among their open-mated bees. The hope is that as more breeders select for varroa resistance—Heitkam, for instance, has been doing it for years—the drone pool will improve and it will take longer for resistant traits to be diluted through open breeding.

Bee researchers and desperate beekeepers like John Miller hope that these efforts will get a boost from recent advances in the understanding of bee genetics. In 2006, a team of scientists from the USDA's Beltsville, Maryland, bee lab oversaw a collaboration to decode the honey bee genome. To create the genetic "essence" of honey bee, researchers pulverized a collection of drones from a single colony—all of whom had the same DNA, because drones, which are created from the queen's unfertilized eggs, are always genetically fatherless. The drones were frozen, mashed into a big soup, and spun in a series of centrifuges that pulled off proteins, fats, legs, wings, and other miscellaneous body parts. What remained were solid crystals of bee salt. These were then ground in pestles, mashed into little plastic tubes, spun again, and washed with various solvents, until all that was left were small pellets of DNA. Those were suspended in water and placed in a thermal cycler, which somehow, inconceivably, provided graphs of each gene and pathogen found in the pellet. When read by someone who understands these things—not, in all likelihood, a beekeeper or someone who writes about beekeepers—the graphs provide all sorts of information about what those bees are like: what they can and can't do, are good at and bad at.

The lab's genome group is led by Jay Evans, a lanky, soft-spoken social-insect specialist—his graduate work involved high-alpine ants. Evans and his team use the genome information to compare variations among bees, looking, for instance, at differences between European and Africanized bees and between healthy bees and those sickened by nosema or any of the dozens of ailments that have lately afflicted America's bee herd. The lab, a brick building set on a labyrinthine complex on the outskirts of Washington, D.C., looks more like an old insane asylum than a cutting-edge genetics facility. It hosts only a few test hives in its backyard; other than that, there's not much evidence of bugs in the building, just denatured remains. Still, the work that goes on there is anything but antiquated: Evans and his team are also decoding the varroa genome, dissecting varroa brains and extracting DNA samples to understand and, they hope, disrupt the genes that dictate their reproduction, or to find pathogens to which the mites could be vulnerable. Lately, though, they've spent most of their time chasing a genetic explanation for CCD: "The main things we have found is that a number of things can kill off honey bees—viruses, pesticides, nutrition," Evans says. "It's amazing that they survive as much as they do."

Someday, it is devoutly hoped, bee genomics—beenomics— will trickle down to the queen-rearing community. Easy tests might someday let any beekeeper create his or her own pest- and plague-resistant local hybrids. For now, however, new breeds of bees tend to be created at universities and in bee labs, not out in the field, and the resistant traits developed in those labs are all too quickly diluted when they enter the promiscuous open- mated world. But even if those lab-created traits were to become dominant, some wonder whether it would be a good thing. After all, "better" bees tend to create their own monoculture, as Italian bees did in the nineteenth century. The queen-rearing industry then reinforces that monoculture by requeening each year with the same uniform matrons from the same swath of land in California or Florida or Georgia. Productive, gentle, perhaps even mite-resistant, but nonetheless standardized, they may be especially vulnerable to new scourges as destructive as the varroa mite or CCD.

Human selection often has unintended consequences. Before the Langstroth hive came along, beekeepers used to destroy their heaviest colonies to extract honey, thus inadvertently selecting for less productive bees. Thanks to the queen-rearing industry, bees that adapt to their local microclimates are replaced each year with bees from somewhere else. Still, the greatest damage to the national herd's genetic diversity has been wreaked not by breeders like Pat Heitkam and the Koehnens, but by the varroa mite, which wiped out almost every feral colony in the country. Feral bees had broadened the gene pool by mating with managed queens. Now the vast majority of the nation's beekeepers rely almost completely on mail-order commercial queens to supply new blood.

✳

ALMOST COMPLETELY, BUT NOT ENTIRELY. BECAUSE THE NA-tion's bee herd has also acquired an infusion of new genes from another source: Africanized "killer" bees, whose marauding swarms so panicked the nation when news of their depreda-tions first hit the media in the 1970s and '80s. The Africanized bee is a hybrid between several subspecies of *Apis mellifera*. It was created inadvertently in 1956 after Brazilian biologist Warwick Kerr imported forty-seven queens from Tanzania to Brazil in hopes of combining the best traits of the European honey bee—gentleness and prolific breeding—with those of the scrappy African bee (*Apis mellifera adansonii*), which produced more honey in warm environments than did northern-adapted bees. But before Kerr had a chance to create his superior breed, twenty-six swarms of the Tanzanian bees escaped and mated with local European drones, creating a feral hybrid whose de-scendants produced ample honey and worked hard, even in the rain and the dark, but were also defensive and easily riled, and thus extremely difficult to manage. The new bees were indeed well suited to life in the tropics—spectacularly so: they mated fast, usurped other bees' hives, interbred with European bees, and passed all sorts of bad habits on to their spawn. They attacked keepers and family pets and hapless passersby in large numbers and for long distances. They robbed other hives of honey. They abandoned their colonies at the slightest provocation.

They spread quickly, too, moving north through South America at a rate of almost a mile a day, blasting through Central America and Mexico, and arriving in Hidalgo, Texas, in October 1990. The bees then swarmed from the Texas border through southern New Mexico and Arizona and into Southern California. They have also been found in Louisiana, Arkansas, southern Utah, Florida, and Georgia, and wherever they go, they easily outcompete and outbreed managed bees. They are almost impossible to tell apart from their European cousins. They have slightly shorter wings, but not enough to be visible to the naked eye or even with the help of a microscope—the subspecies can only be definitively identified through mitochondrial DNA analysis. Thus a beekeeper may not realize his formerly gentle bees have been infiltrated by the Africans until one day they set upon him or his dog or kids or wife or newspaper boy.

There have always been nasty bees—those "improvident or unfortunate" insects that are filled "with the bitterest hate against any one daring to meddle with them," Langstroth wrote. "If a whole colony on sallying forth possessed such a ferocious spirit, no one could hive them unless clad in a coat of mail, bee-proof; and not even then, until all the windows of his house were closed, his domestic animals bestowed in some place of safety, and sentinels posted at suitable stations to warn all comers to keep at a safe distance." Langstroth's hypothetical breed would be far more malicious than today's Africanized hybrid; even the German black bees that he worked with in his day were considerably nastier than almost any bee you'd encounter today. Nor are Africanized bees any more venomous than your standard European bee—their stings, in fact, deliver slightly less venom. Their victims to date have died not from the bees' venom but because of underlying heart conditions or allergic reactions. Still, Africanized bees are far more defensive and will, if disturbed—by lawn mowers, power tools, or unsuspecting beekeepers—come boiling out of a colony en masse and pursue the offender. They'll attack eyes, mouths, and ears, anything, stinging in greater numbers than European bees, for greater distances, with greater persistence.

That's what John Miller learned back in 2005—in the same fateful span of time when his brother Layne crashed his truck and the varroa mite crashed his operation. That year the family decided to expand the empire into Rockville, Texas. They did so on the advice of a Texas honey impresario who told Miller's brother Jay that Rockville offered plenty of winter territory for the taking. John was against the move, arguing that all prime bee turf in this country was spoken for thirty years ago: "I said to them, 'If it's so good, why isn't anybody else there?'" But away they went. They dropped the bees off in the spring, splitting their hives and allowing the virgins to soar off on mating flights with local drones. By summertime, the bees were "so damn mean you could barely work them." A forklift would touch a pallet of bees, and hundreds of guards would explode to the attack from all four hives. The pallet next to it would do the same and the one next to that one. They'd set each other off like a stadium wave, surge after surge of belligerent bees. They'd do it any time of day, even in the coolest part of the morning. Within weeks, Miller's formerly gentle and industrious citadels had transformed into cantankerous mobs that attacked with little provocation. He got out of there, fast: cantankerous honey bees aren't for him. He doesn't like to describe them as "Africanized," though. He prefers to be politically correct about it. He calls them "behavior challenged honey bees," or BCHs for short:

> For 400 years, the scourge of the planet, the European White Guy
>
> selected nice, big, gentle honey bees.
>
> Italians, Carniolans.
>
> Over the past 400 years, while we were selecting for meaty, beaty, big and bouncy bees,
>
> and parenthetically, their equally robust drones;
>
> the Behavior Challenged Honey bee has fought its way through the jungle, taking on all foes,
>
> mating with the wily virgin, and staying light on their collective feet. . . .
>
> It Appears To Me
>
> that the BCH drone is slightly more nimble than the European drone.
>
> [I have heard the Euros have better cigarettes, however.]
>
> When our bees left CA after the almonds, they were just fine, normal behavior.
>
> When I delivered the same hives to honey-production bee yards in North Dakota

three months later;

They Had Changed.

Pissed Off All The Time.

Not Very Good Honey Producers . . .

Now, what was the question?

The European queens get hooked up with the African drone.

The African drone is a hot-headed devil,

and her children become more like their dad,

than their mom.

It took seven or eight generations—two or three years, countless stings, and lots of packages from Pat Heitkam and the Koehnens—to restore Miller's bloodlines to something close to their original benevolent state. For Miller the Africanized bee was a thorough inconvenience. But for those who seek to build a better bee, the nasty interloper may provide some guidance for navigating our brave new mite- and disease-ridden world of beekeeping. In Brazil, where the Africanized bee originated, honey production has skyrocketed, going from 6,500 tons a year before the arrival of African bees to 36,000 tons in 2008. During the half century in which they've coexisted, Brazilian beekeepers have learned how to interact with the bees; during the three decades that the varroa mite has been present in the Western Hemisphere, the bees also appear to have learned to interact with it. They recover far more quickly from its incursions than do bees of pure European descent. The same is true in the United States. Frank Eischen, an entomologist with the

USDA's Agricultural Research Service in Weslaco, Texas, works extensively with Africanized bees. He told me a few years ago that some colonies in his lab had survived for seven or eight years without any varroa treatment. Perhaps Warwick Kerr's mad experiment wasn't so disastrous after all. The suspicion is that because Africanized bees swarm more quickly, they also abandon a hive and its infected brood more quickly when confronted with collapse. Their mobility, the very aspect of their behavior that is so frightening, appears to provide a useful tool in fighting the varroa mite. European bee colonies collapse; Africanized ones abscond.

They are, in short, "survivor stock," and there is very little of that to be found these days. Beekeepers are harnessed by their own survival instinct to the treadmill of medication, resistance, carnage, and requeening—and honey bees are harnessed to those beekeepers. But until entomologists can pinpoint and target the exact mechanism of resistance and create a magic bee that fights off modern pests and still does all the other things a modern bee must do, there is only one surefire way to create a better bee: "You just choose survivors and breed those," says Eischen. Let the rest die. It would be best, says the Beltsville lab's Jay Evans, if they passed a law that prohibited the application of chemicals for varroa mites. Were American honey bees left to their own devices, some very small percentage of them would surely evolve a defense against the varroa mite, as *Apis cerana* did in Asia with its grooming behavior and as the Africanized bee appears to have done with its tendency to abscond. If that were to happen, the bee population would drop by 80 to 90 percent for a while, and it would be an economic disaster for people like John Miller, and all the farmers who depend on people like John Miller to pollinate their crops, and all of us who like to eat almonds and cherries and apples and lettuce and such. But eventually, resistant bees would develop, and from those bees would come a stronger national herd. Still, adds Evans, "I could never tell someone to let their bees die."

John Miller doesn't want his bees to die. But he's also got a healthy respect—awe, really—for bees that survive on their own. On a back road near his house in Newcastle, tucked in between the trophy estates that have overrun the place like so many behavior-challenged honey bees, there's a house with a tattered blue roof and degrading siding in a raucously untended meadow dotted with sheep and California poppies. There's a swarm in the roof there, Miller says, that has survived for a half century—through foulbrood and nosema, tracheal mites and varroa mites and perhaps even CCD. Miller's own property houses boxes and vats of antibiotics, miticides, and fungicides, but he's not so hardened that he can't admire the spectacle of nature taking its course. "I like to think they're survivor stock," he says: hardened bees with an infinite capacity to endure and regenerate, bees with mysterious properties of survival that have eluded the entomologists and the breeders and the queen-rearers, and especially the straight-up beekeepers.

But come to think of it, he hasn't seen that swarm for a while.

....
The Human Swarm

SOON AFTER MILLER'S NEW QUEENS COMMENCE THEIR reigns, he trucks his bees to North Dakota. It takes a month or so, but by mid-June all have hitched a crowded semi from a withering bee yard in America's populated, ever-replenishing West to the nation's empty interior. Miller arrives for the summer in June. He used to drive the Corvette; now he takes his Toyota at a more leisurely pace. He stops in Wyoming for dinner with Larry Krause, then pushes on to Greater Metro Gackle, where he places bees and waits to see what the summer's harvest will hold. June brings the flowering of the sweet clover, then alfalfa. July is more fickle.

I first visited Miller in Gackle the summer before CCD arrived. It had been a particularly cruel July. The temperature had hovered well above 100 for much of the previous weeks. Mid-month, a weather station on the state's southern border recorded a high of 120 degrees. Corn drooped knee-high, earless in the fields, the stalks edged a frayed yellow. Alfalfa florets withered in the meadows; locals wore expressions of stoic exasperation. But the day before I got there in early August, it finally rained, and the long-awaited moisture left the landscape a deep, heartbreaking emerald. After a long, hot month, the sloughs filled with runoff, waterfowl, and sudden, immeasurable hope.

I met up with Miller at the Bismarck airport, and we drove together to Gackle. In its subtle, windswept way, the land was breathtaking. The hills rolled to the horizon; the sky shone opalescent; great, billowing clouds built like temples to the ionosphere. The slopes that surged across the prairie looked like tallgrass snowdrifts, and in a geological sense, they are—the product of glacial ebb and flow, millennia of wind and water and ice marching across unbroken plains and then retreating.

North Dakota is, these days, a place of near-constant retreat. First the glaciers withdrew, pursued by the weather. Then the Plains Indians dispersed and the bison disappeared, run from the land. Then went the trappers, run out of quarry; the homesteaders and farmers who ran out of luck; the cattle who ran out of forage; the banks that ran out of money. After generations of defeat, this battered territory is, as Miller explains, "a place of modest expectations," where the aging farmer's boldest dream is to pay off the farm, move to town, and own a Buick. That is to say, it is John Miller's kind of place. Many flowers, few people.

Not even his family joins him now. When his kids were younger, they traveled with him; now they are off on their own and Jan prefers to stay in California, so Miller leads a bachelor life during the summer. If the winters weren't too harsh for honey bees and modern families, he'd stay here year-round. His life in California is dictated by global markets, eight-lane highways, and the springtime pollination dance of supply and demand. In North Dakota he and his honey bees stay put. The bees spend the summer feasting on a smorgasbord of flowering crops and wildflowers that burgeon on the borders and margins between fields; Miller spends the summer tending them and his

vegetable garden. "I see more traffic on a trip from the airport to
my house in California than I do in an entire summer in North
Dakota," he told me before I arrived. "I don't need to use my
turn signals here. Everybody knows where I'm going."

As we drove down the highway, it was clear that blinkers
were beside the point. The hundred miles of highway running
east from Bismarck to Gackle are straight, the homes along
the road infrequent. Almost every field along the way hosts a
haphazard-looking aggregation of white bee boxes. Year after
year, the state vies with California as the nation's top honey producer, and Miller's outfit ranks as one of the largest in North
Dakota, harvesting more than a million pounds a year. Still, not
every hive we saw belonged to him. Around Gackle, most do.
In nearby Jamestown they are likely to bear Zac Browning's
brand; in Medina they belong to Miller's local nemesis, a part-
time bee sharecropper who rents colonies from Florida for the
summer and who, according to Miller, dilutes his honey and
lets his hives go "rotten with hive beetle." Unlike bees, which
can forget as quickly as they enrage, a beekeeper knows how to
hold a grudge.

Miller had a yarn to tell about every bee yard and farm we
passed. Those bees over there belong to Zac Browning: "I com-
mingle my hives with him all the time." Look at that farmhouse:
a young couple with ten children who have single-handedly
brought the population slide in southern Kidder County to a
temporary standstill. "They go through gallons of honey." That
field full of cars? "Those are Kevin Klevin's. I haven't seen him
for a while." Kevin Klevin is the nephew of Jim Klevin. Kevin
used to let Miller keep bees on his farm, but another beekeeper—
one of Miller's ex-employees, in fact—stole him away. That
small red home hidden behind a hillock, perhaps a horizon's

length away from the road? A bachelor farmer named Duane
Trautman lives there. A few years ago, a Canada goose showed
up at the back door, bonded with the cat, and didn't bother,
when the cold came, to fly south for the winter. "Maybe," Miller
surmises, "the damned thing liked cat food." The goose stayed
for a few years, and then one day gazed skyward—hearing, perhaps, the distant gabble of former companions—and flapped his
wings and flew off without saying goodbye. Now Duane Trautman and his cat are alone again.

Loneliness is epidemic on the northern prairies. We turned
off the empty four-lane highway onto a narrow and even emp-
tier two-lane road. Each mile, exactly, the road intersected another thoroughfare—a paved street leading to a small town or a
graded gravel road extending to a home, but most often a rutted,
grassy two-track slowly returning to nature. This methodical
network of roads runs throughout the northern plains, a vestige
of the railroad surveys at the turn of the twentieth century and
a reminder that there was a time when North Dakota's population could support such orderly and optimistic dissection of the
landscape. Every so often, we flew past a small town with flak-
ing clapboard churches, rusting railroad tracks, and careworn
houses; some still had occupants, while others appeared to have
succumbed to slow neglect or even hurried abandonment, like a
hive left empty after the colony has departed. Finally we passed
a large and glimmering slough teeming with ducks and egrets
and red-winged blackbirds and approached a water tower that
peered above a large hillock adorned with red-white-and-blue
tires. They were organized to spell the word *Gackle*.

In both form and content, Gackle embraces every agricultural cliché that Miller's wintering grounds in the Central Valley
don't—the lonely dairy silo at the edge of town, the grain eleva-

tor, the rolling fields, the clapboard one-room library, the fluttering flags, the sign that informs visitors there are five churches that serve the town of Gackle (although the sign is not technically accurate anymore, because the Assembly of God building fell down, and after St. Anne's Catholic Church lost its priest the diocese sold the building to a hunter for $1000—leaving only the Church of Christ and the Lutheran and Baptist churches). We drove past a dusty grocery, and, in quick succession, the Gackle Community Café, the Gackle Senior Center, and Dani's Place, Gackle's only bar. Then the Krieger movie theater, which shows first-release films to weekend audiences that number in the single digits; a bedraggled Ford and farm implements dealership; a Tastee-Freez; a dairy-turned-firehouse; and a guy named Paul trimming a lovingly tended shrub. It was like a sepia, soft-focus campaign ad: morning in an America most Americans have never had the privilege to know.

We turned off the main drag. (No blinker, no need.) We drove up a gentle hill, past a remarkable procession of camouflage trucks—Gackle, with its generous sloughs, calls itself the "duck hunting capital of the world," or in more modest moments, the duck hunting capital of North Dakota. The mayor ran a camo-painting business on the side. Miller pointed to each dwelling on our route. We drove past a well-maintained home on our left: "I lent that guy two grain bins and he collapsed them. I sent him a bill and he never paid." A few houses down, another tale of woe: "A horse fell on that guy two years ago. He broke his ankle." On our right was a large house; I think it was made of brick: "That's a family from Washington, they're not from here, they have lots of kids and we don't trust them." Then a slightly unkempt dwelling: "This guy is a drinker." We passed a gray pickup truck: "I gave that truck away and I regret it to this day. It was a good truck." And then we approached Miller's place. Miller once claimed in an email that he didn't know his house number.

I am sure it has a street address . . .

ask anyone,

I live directly east, across the street from Melvin Muller, that's all you really need to know, unless you need further detail as in, he lives just north of Denning's house

so there.

Miller's house was as unpretentious as the next, although bee paraphernalia dotted the front lawn where others might have placed plastic deer or lawn jockeys. Inside there were comfortable if not terribly attractive leather chairs, piles of books on the floor, a few dirty remnant rugs, and in the cupboard, far more varieties of honey than spices. Being a proper gentleman bee farmer, Miller thought it best that a strange woman avoid the impropriety of staying in his "man cave," so he dropped me across the street at the large, comfortable house of Harry and Brenda Krause, who offered to be my hosts for the visit.

The Krauses were kind and unadorned. Harry had a craggy Germanic face and white hair; Brenda had soft brown curls cropped around her face and a sturdy frame. They welcomed me and showed me to the basement room where their grandchildren usually stayed, explaining that they'd built the place four years ago when, discouraged by high fuel, fertilizer, and equipment costs, and with their children all decamped to Minneapolis to make real livings, they'd leased their farm to a larger operation and retired. After I settled in, they offered me fresh-baked bread with honey. There was lots of honey in the cupboard, and all of it—except one tub of creamy honey from Utah produced by Miller's aunt Shirley Miller, "widow of David, and her slightly loopy daughter Eileen and son David Jr."—came from John's bees. Each year before the clover goes into bloom, Miller places his hives on his neighbors' pastures. To the east, his bee yards range twenty miles—the soil is good in that direction, but farmers tend to plant high-value crops like corn and soy that supply little in the way of nectar for foraging bees. To the west, his yards range forty-five miles. The soil in that direction is rockier and harder to till, thus better suited to raising clover and alfalfa for pasture, grazing, and haying. Thus better suited to bees.

Just as the first geese start rolling south—usually during the third week of October—Miller delivers a portion of last summer's crop to far-flung houses around Logan, La Moure, Stutsman, and Kidder counties. He pays his rent in honey and gourds from his garden. ("Brilliant gourds, exuberantly diverse. The old ladies love them.") Typically, he can do four honey drops an hour, far fewer if the farmers are lonely and want to talk. Most do. They talk of cattle prices and corn prices and sunflower prices and implement prices, and the loss of a grandchild or a husband or a dog, and "my God, how things are changing." Many now live in skilled care facilities—more every year. The old grow older.

I'll visit Tillie Dewald who used to bring sheets of honey cookies to the honey house.

And once I've left her room, smiling, I'll cry

Sometimes he can't bear it, watching lives wind down, and he deliberately delivers his rent honey on days he knows people won't be home. Sauerkraut Day in Wishek, when they serve German food and offer free blood pressure screenings, is always a good bet. It's been going on since 1925, and on the third Wednesday of October each year, farms empty out all over central Logan County. If nobody's home, Miller can blast through thirty properties in six hours.

Thirty years ago, Miller would have provided his neighbors with five-gallon buckets, but these days they're usually happy with five-pound jugs, or even small honey bears. That's because families in Gackle aren't what they used to be. There are bigger farms and fewer farmers, who have fewer kids, and the kids tend to leave for college and never come back. Since the middle of the twentieth century, the town, which was first surveyed in 1902 when the Northern Pacific Railway built a spur line nearby, has lost more than half of its residents. Today it is home to 275 senior-citizen farmers. Vacant lots grow wild; homes stand empty—if you're inclined to move to Gackle, you can buy a house for as little as ten thousand dollars. The school is the only public K–12 within forty miles. A few years ago it consolidated with the school in nearby Streeter, and Miller commandeered the bird's-eye maple flooring from the decaying Streeter schoolhouse to give away as a finisher's prize for the Streeter Centennial 5K "Strut-N-Skedaddle," a race celebrating the town's hundredth anniversary. No one objected to the loss of the school's floor. By the time I visited, the combined school for both towns educated a total of 110 students. Twelve had graduated from high school the previous spring; only four would enter kindergarten that fall. Ultimately, if the trend continues—and there's no reason it shouldn't—the school will end up consolidating with the one in Napoleon, the county seat thirty-eight miles away, which already shares a football team with the Gackle-Streeter school.

When that happens, there will be one public school serving an eighty-mile stretch of the state.

※

THESE STORIES OF ABANDONMENT ARE ALL TOO FAMILIAR IN North Dakota. The state's geography is particularly well suited to collapse. It lies at the very center of North America, far from the tempering effect of an ocean, and its "continental climate" brings brutally cold winters, cruelly hot summers, wrenching winds, and often negligible humidity and rainfall. Back when Gackle was surveyed, boosters of settlement in the Great Plains—which had previously been known as the "Great American Desert"—believed that cultivation of land would bring permanent humidity to the region. Rain, they said, would follow the plow. And so thousands upon thousands of northern European immigrants moved there, lured by abundant unsettled acreage and federal policies such as the Preemption Act of 1841, which offered public land for $1.25 an acre if settlers lived on and made certain improvements to their plots; or the Homestead Act of 1862, which promised 160 acres for farmers who occupied and cultivated the land for five years; or the Timber Culture Act of 1873, which offered 160 acres if ten of those acres were planted with trees. Others came for the dirt-cheap land offered by the railroad companies that hoped to lure customers to prairie depots like Gackle.

For a time, it appeared that the boosters were right. The years between 1890 and 1928 were unusually wet ones, and the state's population swelled with towns and farms that prospered as the nation's demand for wheat grew. Towns with populations as small as four hundred people often boasted the amenities of much larger cities: a grocery, a hardware store, a mercantile shop that sold everything from dry goods to kerosene lamps to ax handles, a grain elevator—possibly two—a livery barn, doctor's office, butcher shop, harness shop, and blacksmith. Also, often, a newspaper, hotel, billiards parlor, lumber yard, drugstore, restaurant, cream station, tractor and car dealer, dentist, movie theater, and dance hall—and, of course, a panoply of churches. But even in flush times, North Dakota's climate and population were hard-pressed to support such elaborately optimistic infrastructure. The state went through a series of booms and busts in the latter part of the nineteenth and early twentieth centuries. Between 1878 and 1890, the population mushroomed from an estimated 16,000 people to 191,000. By 1920, it had grown to 647,000. It peaked in 1930 at 680,000.

In 1928, North Dakota's luck turned. It was an unusually wet summer. Ann Marie Low, a farmer's daughter who lived near the town of Kensal, northeast of Gackle, and kept a lively and loving diary of her times, described a near-tropical climate that summer. "Crops and hayfields were lush; mosquitoes were thick and a continual torture to us and the livestock," she wrote. At the end of that summer, devastating hailstorms struck the central section of the state, destroying most farmers' crops. "The rest of the summer was a nightmare of slogging through either rain or clouds of mosquitoes to salvage what we could from the land." The next summer veered to the other extreme: the rain stopped entirely and didn't start up again for a decade. Summer after summer through the early 1930s, the heat was unceasing. Temperatures regularly measured upward of 110 degrees, sometimes climbing as high as 118 in the shade. It was so hot that horses dropped dead in the fields and bees stopped gathering nectar. In the years that followed, North Dakota farmers suffered calamities of biblical scope—drought, hail,

swarms of grasshoppers, months of winter cold during which
the warmest day was ten degrees below zero. And windstorms,
unceasing windstorms, bringing dust that drifted like snow and
coated clothes in closets and dishes in cupboards, windstorms
that came in so thick it was difficult to see even inside a house,
windstorms that blew so relentlessly that on white setting hens
in enclosed barns, Low reported, "not a white feather shows."

If crops didn't blow away, they baked in the fields, and as
the lean years continued, farmers mortgaged their homes, their
fields, their tractors, and even their old, wretched cows, in the
hopes of staying afloat. Most didn't succeed: more than forty-
three thousand farmers in North Dakota lost their land to fore-
closure between 1920 and 1934, and tens of thousands more
simply abandoned their homes, farms, and businesses. The Dust
Bowl eroded not only the land, but also the expectations that
North Dakota's dogged settlers had brought with them when
they settled there. Historian Elwyn Robinson called this sur-
feit of optimism the "too-much mistake"—"North Dakota had
too much of too many things too soon," he wrote in the 1960s.
"The pioneers created too many farms, too many towns, too
many schools, churches, and colleges, too many counties and
too much government, too much railroad mileage, too many
banks, and too much debt."

The population drain continued through the twentieth century. Profitable farms required more and more sophisticated
machinery and bigger and bigger spreads. (Today the average
North Dakota farm is 3,000 acres, nearly twenty times the size
of the traditional 160-acre homestead.) Farmers daunted by the
inefficiencies of small-scale farming or discouraged by the difficulties of making ends meet sold out to larger operations and
moved to town or to Fargo or Bismarck or out of state. First, a

handful of farmers would leave with their families, then a few more. Six would leave one year, three the next, seven the following. As they did, schools like the one in Gackle consolidated, teachers departed, and one by one, then in batches and bunches, counties began to revert to historic "frontier" conditions—a status defined by demographers as fewer than six people per square mile. Today large areas of North Dakota contain fewer than two people per square mile.

Only two states—Wyoming and Vermont—are home to fewer people than North Dakota; only Alaska, Wyoming, and Montana have lower population densities. Between 1930 and 2008, the nation's population grew two-and-a-half-fold. In that same time period, North Dakota lost 45,000 residents, declining from its 1930 peak of 680,000 to just shy of 637,000 in 2009. And while the population has stabilized and even begun growing again recently thanks to an oil boom in the western part of the state, the farm population has continued to bleed. In 1950, Gackle had 600 residents. At the end of the twentieth century, the number had dropped below 300. Despite the town's obvious (to me, anyway) rural charms, it's no mystery why such places continue to lose people: in 2000 the average per capita income was just under $16,000; the median age was sixty-one. More than 45 percent of the people who lived in Gackle in 2000 were sixty-five or older. Just 9 percent were under eighteen. "It used to be a hopping, be-bopping town," says Miller, but "now there are no kids. They leave for college and you never see them again."

WHILE MOST OF HUMANITY SWARMS TOWARD THE CITIES, Miller makes camp in the places they leave behind. This is an ideal setup for bees, but it poses a problem for their keepers, because although the bees do most of the work, their commercial keepers still need other humans to help them move the hives and harvest and process the honey, and there simply aren't enough. In the northern plains, humans, especially those of an age amenable to lifting fifty-pound hives, are in short supply. "I'll hire any schoolkid who will walk in the door," Miller says. "The problem is there aren't any schoolkids." Miller introduced me to his friend LeRoy Brant, who keeps his bees in Towner, North Dakota, in the summertime. Brant told me that he advertised for help in North Dakota a few years ago, offering a wage of twelve to fifteen dollars an hour. "I didn't get one phone call for six months." Hispanic laborers, so plentiful and controversial in urban areas today, have also proven difficult to keep around— many find it hard to leave their support network for the isolation of North Dakota.

So instead, Brant, Miller, and many other northern plains beekeeping outfits rely on labor brokers who arrange temporary visas for South African workers—mostly white Afrikaaner farmers and twentysomethings looking for adventure and relief from their country's erratic economy. Bee guys like to hire them because they speak English and have driver's licenses, and they also blend in well with the industrious German and Russian farmers who populate rural North Dakota. Most years, Miller imports around fifteen South Africans to tend his bees and process his honey. Some come back for successive summers and require little supervision. The green ones start in the honey house, "stapling together their fingers and boxes for bees," says Miller. Later they graduate to processing honey, then to handling the bees. They live with two or three others in six houses that Miller bought in Gackle as the original owners decamped for less arduous pastures.

On Friday nights, most of Miller's South Africans are at the bar, and after I settled in at the Krauses that August evening, Miller and I walked downtown to meet them. From all appearances, Dani's Place, the town's only watering hole, saw far less activity than the senior center next door. Shafts of late-day light streamed through the door and small windows, illuminating the dust and the beer-stained woodwork. There were five people inside. One was Dani, the bartender, who was tall, bald, and robust, with a puffy walrus mustache. The other four were Miller's Afrikaaner employees, Willie, Wessel, Conroy, and Jacobus— "Jaco" for short. Willie, in his fifties, was the father figure of the bunch, a solid, round-cheeked farmer from the southern Cape region who was struggling to keep his land and spent ten months of the year hauling American bees to make ends meet. Jaco, in his mid-twenties, was young, blond, affable, and soft-spoken. Conroy was still a teenager: tall and sandy-haired, he didn't say much. His half brother Wessel was twenty-one, the city boy of the group, with spiky dark hair and an edgy sociability. They had been drinking for a while, and as they ordered another round, Miller—as he is wont to do—disappeared, leaving me alone with them.

After a few awkward hellos all around, Wessel invited me to sit with him at a peeling two-top near the bar. He had just downed four shots of Jägermeister—a syrupy German liqueur reputed to contain elk's blood (it doesn't), and known to make people do stupid things (it does). He stacked his shot glasses as he informed me, with booming good cheer, that Miller had gone out back to talk to Barry, another South African migrant who had been coming to Gackle for years with his girlfriend Linda. Barry worked for Tommy Wagner, who farmed just down the road from Miller's honey house. Linda worked in the honey house, and the couple lived together in one of Miller's spare homes. Wessel lowered his voice and leaned in. This week, he told me, Linda had asked Barry to move out. Then Wessel raised his voice and leaned back and told me—out of nowhere— that he hated black people. I looked around furtively, expecting barbed stares from bystanders. But this was North Dakota. There were no bystanders, and furthermore, there were no black people—in 2000, Gackle was 99.4 percent white, and if that's not homogenous enough, it's also 75 percent German. Such fading prairie outposts are, for men—boys—like Wessel, imaginative reconstructions of South Africa as the creators of apartheid had wished it to be—an agrarian society of hardy northern Europeans, and not a black person for miles around. "I hate them," he told me again, and ordered four more shots. It seemed wise to depart, so I did, extracting promises that Wessel and Willie would take me along the next day to tour some of the bee yards.

I arrived at Miller's honey house the next morning dressed for beekeeping, but nobody else was there, unless you counted the usual straggler bees who came in with the honey and were in their death throes, wobbling across the floors and walls, clambering dizzily onto my ankles. I watched them wander the dirt parking area until Miller and Willie arrived with Jaco in tow. Wessel, they told me, had overdone it last night and was sleeping in. We gathered suits, smokers, and gloves, but as we climbed into trucks to head to the fields, the sheriff drove up, looking officious. The previous night, sometime after I left, sometime after more shots and more beers, sometime after Dani had kicked Wessel and Barry out of the bar, the two men had driven to Linda's house. Linda had called the police, Barry had broken a phone, and then Barry and Wessel had headed back to Main Street, where they trashed a bench that had been donated to the city of Gackle by the Future Farmers of America. They'd spent the night in jail.

This was not typical behavior in Gackle, and the sheriff was not pleased, so Miller spent some time reassuring him that the Wessel problem would be taken care of. Then Miller and I headed out in his big red pickup, followed by Willie and Jaco in a huge flatbed carrying a forklift and a pile of pallets. We visited a few bee yards and as morning bled into noon, Miller and I headed into town for lunch. The usual coterie of regulars was gathered at the Gackle Community Café, and they looked eagerly toward Miller as he opened the door. Seven or eight elderly men and women were holding court at a round table near the front. Miller said his hellos, shook hands all around, and beelined to a table in the back. He sat far from the others. "It's a seething pit of vipers over there," he said affectionately, nodding at the group. They didn't look very dangerous—geriatric farmers and their wives, flannel shirts and work boots and blue-rinsed curls and cooling coffee—but they appeared to have lots of free time. In this respect, Miller's boys had made the café society's day. It had only been a couple of hours since the sheriff stopped by the honey house, but by now the whole town knew that Wessel and Barry had gotten into trouble.

Small towns like Gackle are like beehives. They rely on a fine-tuned social balance that is, if not fragile, then at least fixed, yielding little. It was obvious that Wessel would have to go. There was simply no room for troublemakers who destroyed FFA benches and vectored unhappiness. So just as nurse bees escort sick or injured workers to the hive entrance, banishing misfits, Miller would have to devise an exit strategy for Wessel. At lunch, over grilled cheese and iced tea, Miller made up his mind. He would ship Wessel off to a beef guy he knew in

Iowa—beef guys can get by with a heavier touch—to see if he could make a fresh start in a town where all the FFA benches were intact.

Wessel's brother Conroy, who was quiet and pleasant and a hard worker who had done nothing wrong, would have to go with him. They came together; they would leave together. Miller knows what it's like when brothers differ. He often revisits the lessons of Jacob and Esau, Ephraim and Manasseh. His brother Jay is four years younger. For most of their adult lives, they worked as partners in the family beekeeping business. Jay ran operations in Idaho; John oversaw the California and North Dakota operations. This geographical separation was not an accident: the two men disagreed on most everything, but especially beekeeping. In 2008 their disputes proved particularly costly. Every fall, once the hives are stripped, Miller feeds the bees medicated syrup containing an ingredient called fumagillin, which helps prevent nosema. He must do so after the honey has been harvested, so as not to contaminate product intended for human consumption, but before the weather turns. If it's too cold, bees lose their appetites and won't eat the syrup. Early that fall, as it became clear that *Nosema ceranae*, the deadly new nosema strain, was spreading quickly through U.S. hives, the brothers disagreed about when to cut off the honey harvest to medicate the bees. John wanted to stop the harvest early and get the colonies "fat, heavy, and strong" for the coming winter so they could serve as pollinating units for the following year, not honey production units for the current one. Jay wanted to make honey. "The Idaho operation almost did a good job," Miller says bitterly. "Thus, the bees almost picked up the syrup. Thus, they were almost inoculated against nosema. Thus, they almost survived winter in good shape."

But of course they did not. A spring nosema epidemic cost the Millers three thousand hives and in early 2008, Miller and his brother decided to part ways. It was, says Miller, a "slow train wreck," long in coming. Jay kept some hives, and a real estate and cattle business he'd started on the side that John never approved of. John kept the majority of the colonies. He's fairly certain he's getting the poor end of the bargain. More bees, more headaches. So instead of going on vacation, instead of heading to the beach or the mountains, as normal Americans do, Miller spends much of the month of August pulling honey and counting red dots in his Frankenstein yard, the apiary where he tests various miticides. Each day in August, without fail, he visits the roadside semicircle of hives, monitoring the incursions of the varroa mite.

AFTER LUNCH, WE HOPPED BACK IN HIS TRUCK FOR A VISIT TO the Frankenstein yard. We pulled up under the shade of an old poplar a reasonable distance from the hives and put on our coveralls and veils. As we sat in the safe confines of the truck, a dark cloud spun past us. A swarm had departed from one of Miller's hives, leaving its safe rectangular shelter and heading into the unknown to find a new home. The churning brown eddy—tens of thousands of bees—smudged across the bee yard and came to rest on a cornstalk to reconnoiter. The plant bent with the weight of the insects. Miller was pissed, perplexed. Some swarms you can anticipate. If the hive is crowded and you spot peanut-shaped queen cells among the brood, there's a good chance that half the colony is fixing to pick up and leave. But it's awfully hard, when you have ten thousand hives, to open every brood chamber frequently enough to catch each developing swarm. Even smaller-scale beekeepers are often flummoxed by the onset of a swarm. "For years," wrote Langstroth, "I spent much time in the vain attempt to discover some infallible indications of first swarming; until facts convinced me that there can be no such indications."

Most often, swarms occur when a hive has outgrown its space in the height of summer. When this happens, when a queen is so prolific and her worker bees so industrious that the hive produces more bees than it can contain, the hive, in prosperity mode, begins raising a new batch of queens. Then, after the new queen cells are capped but before the new queen hatches, the old queen departs with a group of robust pioneers to find a new place to establish a hive. Most bees swarm at midday, so they have time to find shelter before night's coolness falls in. On the day that is "fixed for departure," writes Langstroth, the queen grows restless, roaming the combs instead of laying eggs, communicating her agitation to the bees, who gorge themselves on honey in preparation for their journey. "At length," he writes, "a violent agitation commences in the hive; the bees appear almost frantic, whirling around in circles continually enlarging, like those made by a stone thrown into still water, until, at last, the whole hive is in a state of the greatest ferment, and the bees, rushing impetuously to the entrance, pour forth in one steady stream. Not a bee looks behind, but each pushes straight ahead. . . ." As the swarm travels, it stops to rest on nearby trees, bushes, and walls, while the scouts look for a hollow tree, a rock crevice, or a chink in a building's siding to call home. Swarms look frightening, but they are in fact surprisingly docile. With no hive to protect and with stomachs full of honey for the long journey to their new home, they are less inclined to sting. Many beekeepers handle them without gloves or veil.

If bees swarm too early in the spring or too late in the summer, however, they tend to do so not because they are doing well, but because they are doing poorly, "driven to desperation," says Langstroth. It occurred to me, as we sat in the safety of Miller's truck watching the swarm spin away from us, that these bees, pushed from their home and desperate for a new place to lay down some comb, weren't all that different from Wessel and his compatriots. Wessel had explained to me, over his four shots of Jägermeister, that after the fall of apartheid the blacks had renamed the streets in his South African hometown with African names. Wessel's ancestors, of course, had performed similar acts of displacement. I couldn't help but think of Africanized honey bees—like Wessel, African-European hybrids, peripatetic, prone to swarming, and not above usurping the hives of others. Wessel was, like the Africanized bee, aggressive and not terribly well socialized, although we can blame genes, not alcohol, for the bees' behavior. And now both have been transplanted to the New World, where they have aroused no shortage of consternation.

Swarming—migration, in human terms—is part of the deal in human history, and while it serves as a natural means of regeneration, it is also a powerful force of destabilization. European settlers swarmed to North Dakota; years later they trickled away, leaving behind disused homes and underpeopled villages. In their place came Wessel, who had found his own home less hospitable than he liked and who came and went in a few short months, leaving North Dakota one FFA bench the fewer. It's not clear exactly why he derived pleasure from sowing such discord, but he had caused similar trouble, in smaller increments, all summer. Miller is certain that he erred in keeping Wessel around for as long as he did. Miller has never pretended to understand humans, though, so he'll excuse himself for those mistakes. The ones he makes with his bees are less forgivable.

The Frankenstein yard is where Miller seeks to foresee and forestall his mistakes, testing miticides, acids, and tick killers. It is where, in 2004, Miller came to realize that none of his previous go-to materials were working anymore, and where, in subsequent summers, he has tested new materials to control the mites. Late summer and early fall, when bee populations drop and mite populations rise, is the beekeeper's only window to kill mites on winter bees. By applying medicine at the right time, as the queen lays her last generation of eggs, a beekeeper can prevent varroa mites from multiplying within the brood combs and overwhelming the winter bee population.

So Miller starts, on the first of August, assiduously monitoring his Frankenstein yard, testing different mite-fighting preparations on different hives and entering the results of his tests on spreadsheets on an almost twenty-four-hour basis. Each of the test hives is numbered and placed in a semicircle. On the day I joined him, Miller pulled the top off each hive as we worked our way around. Most hives were healthy, the frames teeming with bees and dripping with honey. A few were in trouble. Those were bleak places to visit—dirty, bare, with few bees and little honey, like tenements with broken windows and graffitied hallways. Hive 411 was infected with chalkbrood, desiccated white larvae scattered below it. Hive 402 showed the telltale signs of varroa infestation: at the hive's entrance, a number of "ants"— sickly bees without wings—wriggled in desultory circles. Under the lid the mites crawled freely across the backs of the bees, and the brood cells that we pierced with a knife all hosted telltale red dots on the developing white pupae.

To monitor the incursions of the varroa mites, Miller places

stickyboards—white cardboard rectangles coated with Crisco—
under each hive. Each day he counts the number of mites that
have fallen to the board and enters it in a spreadsheet; the more red
specks on the board, the heavier the mite load. He counts the mites
in control hives where no medicines have been applied, counts
them in hives in which he has inserted approved pesticides,
counts them in hives treated with unapproved and off-label
medications. None of the honey in these hives is intended for
consumption—the Frankenstein yard is purely for mad-scientist
bee-medicine experiments and observation.

I joined Miller to count the sinister red dots in batches of
five, trying not to lose count through the netting of my veil,
the glare of the stickyboard, and the insistent humming of bees
whizzing past my ears, crawling on my arms, landing occasionally on my veil. There was something oddly meditative about
this process—the sweat dripping down my face, the buzzing
maelstrom of bees. The challenge of not scratching an itch and
still keeping count took on nearly existential dimensions. Most
of the stickyboards had only a few dots—40, 60, 150. Under hive
402, however, the board was covered in mites. I was charged
with counting that one, but sometime after five hundred, when
I had still covered only one corner of the board, I gave up. There
comes a point, in beekeeping, when even a spreadsheet is unnecessary to capture the magnitude of a loss. "In the dictionary under the word *collapse*," Miller said, "there's a stickyboard
with two thousand mites on it." In rural North Dakota, they
don't need a dictionary to understand the concept of collapse:
living off the land is always a gamble. Crops fail, colonies im-
plode, people leave, houses fall in on themselves, but somehow
the dwindling but still surviving residents find the proper balance of hope and fatalism that allows them to keep going.

ON SUNDAY, I JOINED MY HOSTS, HARRY AND BRENDA Krause, to attend services at the First United Church of Christ, a simple, sturdy, and unadorned church with white walls, white clapboard siding, and a broad wood-beamed nave. Miller, who typically attends Mormon services forty miles away in Jamestown, joined me, and we sat next to the Krauses and another local farmer. "I seen the cop coming out of your place of business," Harry Krause prodded Miller. Miller rolled his eyes. Brenda mentioned that the postmistress had asked if something was wrong with Steve Kleingartner, because he was getting lots of cards and it wasn't his birthday. Nobody knew the answer. After the service was over, they would surely find out.

There was a guest speaker before the service—Fred Kirschenmann, a local organic farmer and a longtime proponent of sustainable agriculture, who was to talk on the future of farming. He began with a statement of the obvious: the family farm in America's heartland is in decline. "There are seventy thousand farmers producing sixty percent of the nation's crops," he said. Only 6 percent are under age thirty-five. Almost 80 percent are fifty-five and older. "A century ago," he noted, "it was the opposite." Looking around me at the service, I had no doubt that what he said was true. There were a hundred or so people in attendance; only one or two appeared to be under fifty; there was one teenager, and not one younger child. The previous year's confirmation class was the last the church would have; there was no one left to confirm.

People are getting by in the heartland, Kirschenmann explained, either with help from their nonfarm income—a day job, a spouse's salary—or by creating economies of scale and

pesticide-and-fertilizer scorched-earth strategies that are ultimately unsustainable. Few Americans live on their farms anymore. Instead they rent them out to larger operations, because
the equipment is so expensive and fuel costs so high. Rural
communities, like inner cities, have ceded membership in the
nation's ownership society. The farmers around me nodded in
agreement. Kirschenmann, who owns one of the first, largest,
and most successful organic farms in the state, argued that only
a return to smaller, more varied and labor-intensive agriculture,
like his own farm, could bring the people back and revitalize
rural communities like Gackle and countless others in North
Dakota. But the trends are heading the other way.

After Kirschenmann finished speaking, Miller and his neighbors chatted. "How many of my kids went into bees?" Miller
asked Harry Krause and the men around him. "Exactly zero.
How many of your kids went into agriculture?" The farmers
felt no need to answer. "Did you want them to go into agriculture?" They shook their heads. Miller would like his business to
survive him. He would also like to retire. "I'd like to do something else with my life by the time I'm sixty," he says. "I'd like
to be able to see the exit door in five years and launch the next
generation." But he needs someone to launch. His children don't
appear interested; South Africans provide timely help but not,
unfortunately, a long-term solution. That lies, he hopes, in his
trusted manager, Ryan Elison, who came to work for him in
Idaho ten years ago and fell in love with bees. Poor soul! Elison
now runs much of the day-to-day operations for Miller, who
hopes to sell the business to him soon and then move on to a
second career "using my brain. I might want to be a paralegal,"
he says, only half in jest.

Big agriculture has not been kind to Gackle, which has

lost its kids, and thus its future, in a rural economy that is as unforgiving as the weather. The message was bleak, and after a more traditional sermon and a few hymns, we filed soberly out of the church. On the way home, we drove to Linda's house to see if she needed anything after the weekend's drama. But as we approached, Miller clucked and kept driving. Barry's car was parked outside. He had come back to Linda, and Linda had allowed him back, and Wessel would soon be heading to Iowa, to another unfamiliar home in another fading agricultural redoubt where people seek to endure in a world that is no longer so hospitable for them.

Barry wouldn't stay; Linda wouldn't keep him. But on that luminous and bittersweet August weekend, it was, perhaps, hard to let go just yet. We cleave to the way things are, not only to hold back a chaotic future, and not only because that is what we know. Gackle is a testament to the value of sheer persistence. There is value in returning to the one who loves you, in keeping the family farm going, in living where you grew up, in keeping bees when no amount of common sense and economic self-preservation can justify it. The colony may be collapsing in North Dakota, but not everyone is flying off. There is value, yes, and there is dogged romance in persistence. And John Miller is nothing if not a romantic.

I left Gackle that afternoon after church as menacing blue-black storm clouds boiled on the western horizon. A week later, Miller wrote me an email:

Upon your departure,

the skies erupted.

Remember how queer the sky appeared?

After your safe departure,

we received 2.80" of rain.

Zow!

Two days later, we clocked in another 1.30".

Zow!

Two days later, that being this very evening,

we received .65 in a violent temper tantrum.

Thus; a total.

January 1 through August 1, 7.21 inches precipitation.

August 2 through August 25, 8.25 inches precipitation.

The semi-arid region of the northern plains is a raucous place.

Unpredictability is predictable.

Soon, a frost.

No one knows, but you may bet around September 21.

By December 21, average daytime highs will be 21.

Average nighttime lows will be 2.

Tonight we hid the trucks in the buildings, anticipating violence.

It came, without hail.

Other areas were not so fortunate; receiving baseball sized hail.

No bowling ball hail, no watermelon hail.

But driven by wind, baseball sized hail will kill cattle,

and any human too damned dumb to get out of the weather.

....

Chapter Nine

Bittersweet Bounty

BUT IN THE END, THERE IS HONEY.

Before the thunderstorm, before the sermon, before the Jägermeister-fueled theatrics, Miller consulted a map dotted with red thumbtacks. Each tack represented a flowering meadow where he kept a couple dozen hives, and we planned to take the honey from one of those meadows. He promised a good meadow, one close by and wildly overgrown. In Miller's ideal world, the entire North Dakota prairie would be wildly overgrown. It would be overrun with impulsive, flowering weeds. It would belong only to alcoholic farmers who never get their haying done on time. The meticulous farmers, the corporate farmers, the uptight ones who cut their alfalfa before it blooms are no help to him. Neither are the ones who plow under their clover and alfalfa and plant in its stead acres upon acres of corn that brooks no weeds and carries no nectar and pollinates on the wind and provides little sustenance for a foraging bee. No, Miller prefers the sloppy guys, the ones who cut their hay late and thus let their fields explode in a riot of bloom.

But that year in Gackle, even the most neglected meadows were disappointing. As we headed east out of town, Miller pulled over and picked a violet alfalfa floret. The flowers looked healthy enough—in deep purple bloom. Miller put the flower in his mouth. I followed suit. The blossoms should have been sweet on the tongue, but they tasted like nothing, like dust. He squeezed the stem. If a plant is well hydrated, a tear of water should emerge. There were no tears. We hopped back in the truck for another mile, Willie and Jaco following in a flatbed truck, then took a right on a dirt road that led us to an overgrown swale on the far reaches of a nearby farm.

It was a perfect day to pull honey—calm, sunny, and warm. We stopped the trucks near a congregation of hives bunched haphazardly in a field of budding buckwheat and fading alfalfa, pulled veils over our faces, and lighted smokers to calm the bees. The hives were stacked four boxes high by that point in the summer—the bottom box housed the double-deep brood chamber with the queen; the three shallower supers on top contained the honey for human consumption. An excluder screen kept the queen from moving up to and laying eggs in the supers, ensuring that the upper boxes contained only honey, no queen or brood. The smaller worker bees, however, could travel easily between the hive and the honey boxes to build comb and deposit nectar and pollen—and as long as the flowers were blooming, that is what they did. But around this time of summer, as the light and blossoms faded, the bees shifted into survival mode, preparing to hunker down for a long winter with their honey provisions.

Miller had steeled himself for a disappointing harvest. August is never a fecund time, but this year, drought had accelerated the schedule. In early July, when the temperatures hit 105 degrees, the sweet clover went "poof." The alfalfa followed in short order. We were now harvesting the last of the season's bounty. Miller pried the top off a hive and placed a fume board on top of the uppermost honey super. The board had been doused with an acrid substance called Bee-Go, whose battery-acid stench defies description, though Miller kindly took a stab for me: "noxious, revolting, nauseating, eye-transplant; no anesthesia, chunk-blowing," he suggested. Suffice it to say, it stinks, and drives the bees down from the upper honey boxes into the brood chamber at the bottom, where they hunker down with the queen waiting for the malodorous moment to pass. Bee-Go deployed, he could then pull honey without depleting the hive of too many of its workers. The supers were dripping with honey, heaped with beeswax. Replacing the top, he hoisted the box onto the pallet. "This is beautiful," he said. "I mean heavy." Heavy is good in the world of beekeeping. Heft augurs prosperity. A light hive may be easier to lift, but it means that something is wrong, and so, if you are a beekeeper, it is the hardest labor that is the most rewarding.

Despite Miller's gentlemanly imprecations, I hefted one of the supers. It weighed around fifty pounds, dense with calories, and I waddled slowly to the pallet and let it down. Miller had already beat me there with another box, and after lifting one more—just to prove that I could—I happily stood by and watched as Miller and the South Africans did the hard work of robbing the hives. They stole the two uppermost supers from each stack, hoisted the boxes onto a pallet, loaded the pallet onto a forklift and onto Willie's large truck, then took the load to the honey house to see what sort of payoff they had reaped.

A honey house is a small processing plant where honey is extracted and placed in barrels or bottles for sale to the public. It usually has a concrete floor, a metal roof, and a sickly-sweet smell. The floors are littered with expiring bees, the air thick with honey and despair. Returning from the bee yards, Miller's crews hoist the supers from the flatbed to the "hot room," where the boxes stay for three days, heated to 90 to 95 degrees to liquefy the honey. They then remove the frames from the supers and put them through a machine that takes the caps off the cells. They place them in a centrifugal extractor, which spins for eight to twelve minutes, freeing the honey and also some flakes of wax. The honey and wax mixture is then pumped into a collecting tank. The honey is separated from the wax in yet another spinning contraption and piped into another large settling tank, from which it is emptied into fifty-gallon food-grade steel barrels. The air resounds with the noises of whirring machines, the shotgun crack of barrels expanding. Miller can produce as many as eighty barrels a day, each of which holds 660 pounds of honey. In a bad year, Miller produces around a thousand barrels; in his best years, he has produced upward of two thousand—nearly 1.4 million pounds of honey. Before varroa mite, he typically produced 120 pounds per hive; the average now is more like 100. That's good by American standards, but an Australian beekeeper is reputed to have extracted 629 pounds per hive during a particularly enthusiastic eucalyptus flow.

Once the honey is packed, an employee of Miller's—when I visited, a woman named Mona did the work—classifies each barrel for sale, measuring the water content and assigning numbers depending on how dark the honey is. The lowest numbers denote the whitest honeys, such as those produced from clover and alfalfa, which are the most valuable because they tend to have milder flavors, and honey packers can mix them with darker varieties to achieve a consistent, supermarket-friendly color. After marking the number, color, and moisture on the barrels, Miller stores them, thus classified, for loading into the trucks the packer sends each fall. It is then that the bee's life's work translates into dollars—though not, unfortunately, into enough of them. Honey prices have fluctuated wildly over the years and Miller says it typically runs five years from trough to peak: $0.10 a pound in 1970; $0.50 in 1975. In the five years between 2005 and 2010, prices went as high as $1.45 a pound and as low as $0.95. At the bottom of the trough, Miller loses money on every barrel of honey he produces. But no matter; to him, making honey is about more than annual profit. It is an annual miracle.

✼

HERE'S WHY, LEST WE FORGET: HONEY IS THE DISTILLED NEC-tar of blooming flowers. It is collected by bees, lots and lots of bees. To make a pound of it, the 50,000 or 80,000 bees who live together in a hive at the height of summer will travel a collective fifty-five thousand miles and visit more than two million flowers. A hive can collect more than thirty pounds in a single day when the stars align and the nectar gushes. One worker bee will visit fifty to one hundred flowers on each trip from the hive, in the process collecting and dispersing pollen from flower to flower, allowing the plants it touches to reproduce. In that sense, bees carry the future from tree to tree, and honey is the reward for their labors, nectar distilled by desire and duty into something more. Floral perpetuity is the transaction; bees are the middlemen; those who take care of the bees are also its beneficiaries. Vegans struggle with the question of whether they are allowed to eat honey: is it an animal product? Way back when, the Jews struggled with the same question; the rabbis resolved it in favor of the sweet tooth. "That honey is a vegetable product, was known to the ancient Jews," wrote Langstroth, "one of whose Rabbins asks: 'Since we may not eat bees, which are *unclean*, why are we allowed to eat honey?' and replies: 'Because bees do not *make* honey, but only *gather* it from plants and flowers.'" Could they have followed any other logic?

Honey is composed of glucose, fructose, and water, in addition to at least twenty-two other complex sugars, such as maltose, sucrose, kojibiose, turanose, isomaltose, and maltulose. That combination of sugars is what makes honey honey; the acids, pigments, proteins, and minerals found in smaller amounts are what make clover honey taste so very different from, say, onion honey. The average honey bee will produce about one-twelfth of a teaspoon of the stuff in her lifetime, returning home from each trip laden with half her weight in nectar and pollen, then transforming that raw nectar into honey through a unique digestive alchemy in which she ingests and regurgitates it a number of times. As she does so, she adds enzymes that help break down the complex sugars in the nectar into simple sugars. She then places the processed nectar in unsealed honeycomb cells, which other worker bees fan with their wings until much of the water evaporates. The water content of fresh nectar may be as high as 55 percent, but within an hour it reduces to 40 percent. Once the "ripe" honey is sealed, the moisture content falls below 18.6 percent. Ripe honey will not ferment and, if properly sealed, can be stored for years, decades, even centuries, without spoiling. The typical moisture content of unadulterated honey, which is 36 percent denser than water, is between 15 and 18 percent; Miller's North Dakota honey typically comes in between 16.4 and 17.4 percent. If the water content is much higher than 18 percent, chances are it's been diluted with other substances or taken from the hive before it is ripe. Good honey, like good wine, gets better with time. "Old honey is more wholesome than that freshly fathered by the bees," Lorenzo Langstroth explained.

It is easy to tell good honey from bad: good honey flows from the knife in a straight stream, forming a bead as it lands on a surface. Should the cascade break into separate drops, a second stream of honey will temporarily sit on top of the older bead, forming a layer. If the honey has too much water, it will break into droplets as it falls, pooling as it hits bottom without taking form. Good honey never separates in the jar, though many varieties will crystallize into a creamy, granular solid as they age. Tupelo honey never crystallizes; acacia, sage, and star thistle rarely do. There are more than three hundred different types of honey in the United States. The taste and color of a particular variety depends on the flower from which it came. Polyfloral honey—also known as wildflower honey—comes from many types of flowers, too many to be identified. Mass-produced honey is generally blended from a mixture of two or more floral sources. Monofloral honey comes from the nectar of one floral source. If it is called alfalfa honey, for instance, it means that the bees were located near fields of alfalfa at the time they were in bloom, though it is functionally impossible to ensure that every bee in a particular hive has visited only alfalfa plants during the period when the honey was produced—that no rebellious forager snuck away for a nip of, say, buckwheat.

Those in the bee business talk about different honey "varietals" the way oenophiles discuss wine—eyes closed, tongue on the roof of the mouth, appraising "notes" and "nose." Orange-blossom honey, according to Miller, leaves a floral taste on your back molar, a "citrusy finish" that goes well with food and is never too pushy (the bees, however, get cranky during the orange bloom, because the nectar flows like a fire hose and then, bang, shuts off). Buckwheat honey, favored for some inexplicable reason by Orthodox Jews and Muslims in New York and the Middle East, has a cloying "farm smell"—a "big, sheepy nose," according to Miller. One of Miller's employees likened the aroma to that of "mouse pee," and I tend to agree. It's good in coffee; too strong on toast. Clover honey is another favorite—light, delicate, pure, the color of late-afternoon air. Some consider creamy clover honey, harvested from the irrigated valleys of Idaho and Wyoming, to be the beluga caviar of honey. It's the ace in the pocket the smart beekeeper holds to make sure his relationships stay civil.

There are nearly as many honeys as there are blossoms, though not all are coveted by humans, or even by bees. For all the economic value attached to almond pollination, the honey produced from almond blossoms is bitter and unpleasant-tasting to humans and bees alike. Almonds bloom at the same time as apricots in California, and bees much prefer apricots; almond farmers are well advised to keep their plantings far from any neighboring apricots, lest the bees forsake their cash crop for a sweeter flower. Onion honey is "bitter, dark, and nasty"; bees detest pollinating the plants, and a beekeeper must leave ten colonies in every acre of onions to ensure that the bees visit the flowers in sufficient numbers. The hives stink for weeks afterward. Sunflower honey has an unpleasant aftertaste. The canola bloom gives bees a bad temper—no one knows why. The honey has a tenderly aromatic flavor but granulates in about twelve hours.

The best honey plants aren't always the best plants for other human purposes. Miller's favorite honey of all time comes from the yellow star thistle plant. The star thistle is a "terrible, noxious, invasive, nasty weed," he says, which proliferates along roadsides and is toxic to horses. It is so hated by farmers that in

California, state agriculture officials have released a wasp that lays eggs that kill the bloom, so star thistle honey guys just don't get the production they used to. Botanists suspect that the weed hitchhiked to the New World with alfalfa seeds from Spain, and it can now be found all over the West; the stuff Miller likes comes from a specific microclimate in northern California right along Interstate 5. It is really good; I can attest. Its honey tastes the way flowers smell, like violets, like honeysuckle, like, Miller says, a "wall of sunshine." Good star thistle honey just about never granulates: "I have a jar of 2001; a real vintage year . . . and it has about twelve granules in it . . . five years old!!! amazing." In the South, they swear by orange and tupelo honey; in Alaska and Washington state, they covet northwestern fireweed, gathered from the magenta blossoms of lance-shaped plants that flourish in the open clearings of the Cascades, the Olympics, and the Coast ranges in the wake of forest fires. It is mild and clear, and the light dances through the jar. Langstroth liked wild red raspberry honey from the "hill country" of New England. "When it is in blossom, bees hold even the white clover in light esteem," he wrote.

Not everything a bee gathers provides such pleasant experiences; honey produced from rhododendrons, mountain laurel, sheep laurel, and azaleas may cause a condition in humans called "honey intoxication." Symptoms include excessive perspiration, dizziness, weakness, vomiting, and in rare cases, heart arrhythmia, convulsions, and death. Most honeys produce more beneficial effects, however. Honey is a natural antibacterial agent, used for centuries to treat burns and wounds. There are hundreds of studies exploring its benefits: it has been suggested that it can help control diabetes, Alzheimer's, osteoporosis, stress, skin conditions, sexual problems, and scores of other maladies.

Back in 1707, the English writer Sir J. More listed a few other
benefits he believed honey to provide: it

> *openeth obstructions, and cleareth the heart and lights*
> *of those humors which fall from the head; it purgeth the*
> *foulness of the body[,] cureth phlegmatick matter, and*
> *sharpeneth the stomach; it purgeth those things which*
> *hurt the clearness of the eyes, breedeth good blood,*
> *stirreth up natural heat, and prolengeth life; it keepeth*
> *all things uncorrupt which are put into it, and is a*
> *sovereign medicament, both for outward and inward*
> *maladies; it helpeth the greif [sic] of the jaws, the*
> *kernels growing within the mouth, and the squinancy;*
> *it is drank against the biting of a serpent or a mad dog;*
> *it is good for such as have eaten mushrooms, for the*
> *falling sickness, and against the surfeit.*

Its boosters make fabulous claims, yes, but honey is a fabulous
thing. Though sometimes, sadly, what purports to be honey is no
such thing. There is currently no legal, federally regulated "standard of identity" for honey, and "funny honey"—products sold
as honey but that may have been "stretched" with water or corn
syrup or sucrose or glucose or worse—is widely sold across the
United States. Corn syrup, which once sold for less than a third
the price of the same amount of honey, is particularly difficult to
detect because it is structurally similar to honey. Some products
labeled as pure honey contain up to 80 percent corn syrup. Thus
labels claiming "100% Pure" are only that—labels—because the
government has asserted only a minimal role in grading honey or
setting and enforcing standards. A coalition of beekeepers and
honey packers have for years been requesting that the FDA in-

stitute stricter rules governing the definition of honey, but the agency has so far resisted, classifying honey purity as low on its list of food-safety priorities. In 2009 the state of Florida passed a law prohibiting chemicals or additives, including corn syrup, in products labeled as honey. American honey producers—or most of them, anyhow—are desperate for a similar federal law.

One day, Miller took me with him to the gym he uses when he's in Modesto. He cranked some classic rock on his iPod, ran the treadmill for a while, then hit the weights while I entertained myself on the elliptical trainer. There was a dollar store next to the gym, and afterward he rambled up and down its aisles looking for the honey shelf. The honey was placed much too high for his liking—because honey never spoils, there's little incentive to push it off the shelves—and there wasn't enough of it, and what was there was of dubious provenance. The label said it was honey, and it looked like honey—a plastic bear full of misleading amber liquid. But if you turned it upside down, bubbles rose rapidly to the top—the faster the bubble, the wetter the honey; the wetter the honey, the larger the chance it is adulterated. Good honey—dry honey—has a glacial bubble. You could wait days—multiple seconds, anyhow—for the bubble in Gene Brandi's sage honey to rise to the top; ditto for Kevin Ward's star thistle and John Haefeli's high-altitude clover. Not the funny stuff. The bubbles in the dollar store veritably raced upward. Miller was irate—*heartbroken*— to find such inferior products in the aisles of America's bargain stores. But he was not surprised. As long as the laws remain as they are, there isn't a penny of incentive for him to sell pure honey, "versus whatever they scraped off the floor in a dog kennel in Florida." Nonetheless, he does—which is why he needs almonds.

The United States produces around 165 million pounds of honey a year. Americans consume 400 million pounds a year, and the balance comes from places like Argentina and China, which can, thanks to lower labor and capital costs, dramatically undercut U.S. honey prices. For years the nation's biggest supplier of honey was China, whose product cost about a third of what homegrown honey goes for. While U.S. beekeepers need to earn more than a dollar a pound just to break even, Chinese honey has at various times in the last decade sold for as low as thirty-five cents a pound.

But in 1997, a nasty epidemic of foulbrood blew through Chinese apiaries, slashing honey production by more than half. In response, Chinese beekeepers turned to a drug called chloramphenicol—the cheapest and most effective antibiotic they could find—to cleanse their hives. Chloramphenicol is a highly toxic drug used as a last-ditch treatment for life-threatening infections in humans, but it is banned by the U.S. Food and Drug Administration for use in livestock, including bees, both because of its toxicity—even small exposures have been linked to a deadly blood disorder called aplastic anemia among a small percentage of those who take it—and because residues of the drug remain in hives for years after its use. More than ten years after the epidemic in Chinese apiaries, detectable levels of chloramphenicol can still be found in honey from hives exposed to the drug. Two other powerful antibiotics—ciprofloxacin and enrofloxacin, which were also used to treat foulbrood in China and can cause deadly reactions in humans exposed to even small amounts—have also been found in Chinese honey imports.

In 2002, after European and Canadian food safety agents detected and confiscated dozens of shipments of chloramphenicol-tainted honey, the FDA banned the importation of all Chinese honey. But then an odd—if not entirely surprising—thing happened. Shortly after the ban was enacted, millions of pounds of honey began entering the United States from countries that had no record of producing surplus honey for export. Australia, for instance, imported little honey and exported negligible amounts to the United States in 2000. But after the ban, the level of honey imports to Australia rose by more than twentyfold—to nearly 4.5 million pounds in 2002. All of that honey is thought to have originated in China—and most was then shipped to the United States labeled as Australian honey.

Australia wasn't the only country with suspiciously high levels of newfound honey exports. Vietnam, which was a non-producing, nonexporting country prior to the ban, became the number-two honey exporter to the United States after Canada. Singapore—an entirely urban island-city which has no bee-keeping industry—exported 2.9 million pounds of honey the year after the ban was imposed, becoming the fourth largest exporter of honey in the world in a matter of months. Of the top twelve honey-exporting countries in recent years, seven—Vietnam, India, Malaysia, Thailand, Russia, Indonesia, and Taiwan—export more honey than their domestic bees produce. Even after the ban on Chinese honey was lifted, those shady practices continued because steep "antidumping" tariffs were imposed against Chinese honey in 2008.

There was, for a time, very little risk involved in launder-ing honey. In the last few years, however, the U.S. Customs and Border Protection service has begun stepping up enforce-ment, testing barrels of incoming honey for antibiotic resi-due and even analyzing pollen and soil residue to determine the honey's origin. (There's a name for the study of pollen in honey—melissopalynology—and very few practitioners.) But there are limited personnel to pursue honey-laundering cases and there are bigger fish to fry, so large amounts of adulterated or contaminated honey still make it through the customs gaunt-let. Suppliers suspect that 50 percent or more of all imported honey has been transshipped from China through another country.

And so another bee metaphor: honey sellers, like bees, are borderless. Bees fly all over the meadow to supply a hive with nectar; crooked importers ship their honey around the world to avoid tariffs and fines. It is hard, without sophisticated labo-ratory instruments, to ascertain that honey from Thailand is not honey from China; it is equally difficult to ensure that late-season alfalfa honey doesn't also have a touch of buckwheat in it. For the same reasons, it's well-nigh impossible to ensure that honey is truly "organic." You can refrain from using Terramy-cin to keep the foulbrood at bay; you can refrain from using fu-magillin to keep the nosema under control; you can refrain from using Apistan or coumaphos or amitraz to kill varroa mites; but unless your apiary is secluded on an island free of agricultural chemicals there's no way you can ensure that your bees haven't visited a hayfield sprayed with trifluralin, or a neighbor's rose garden treated with Roundup, or even—God forbid—an aban-doned Coke can on the side of the road. Honey bees are, in the words of Florida apiary inspector Jerry Hayes, "flying dust mops." Bees forage where they will, bring home what they en-counter.

❋

BEES ARE OPPORTUNISTS—THEY GO WHERE IT'S EASY. A BEE-keeper's job is to locate the bees in a place where they can do their job well. Lorenzo Langstroth understood this. He noticed that in some localities, bees accumulated large stores of honey, while in others only a mile or two distant, an apiary would yield "but a small profit." "Every bee-keeper," he opined, "should carefully acquaint himself with the honey-resources of his own neighborhood." N. E. Miller also understood this. One of his gifts, his daughter-in-law Rita wrote, was "an instinctive understanding of bee territory"—the flowering plants, the length of the blooming season, the topography. Location was everything: it determined whether a hive would starve, or produce merely enough to survive, or produce a surplus that a beekeeper could sell. A bee yard had to be close to water and roads, be sheltered from the wind, and get early morning sun—but none of that mattered if there wasn't a sufficient supply and variety of nectar-producing plants.

Earl Miller, and Neil Miller, and John Miller, too, understood the importance of location to the production of honey and the prosperity of their bees, and thus their operation. From 1976 on, Neil and John kept track of the performance of each bee yard in their bee book, a hinged board with enormous cardboard pages that turned like a collection of hanging carpets in a rug shop. (These days, the tablets have been replaced with spreadsheets.) Each page represented an individual apiary and was marked with a series of data points, such as the location name (for instance, the Wilbur Hauff yard); origin (where they were before they arrived in Gackle—the apples in Washington? cherries in Stockton? a nuc yard in Newcastle?); and the dates they were placed in and removed from the yard. At the end of the season, Neil and John Miller would scrutinize each graph to see how the bees had fared and to make sure the crews didn't leave any hives behind when packing up for Idaho. Then they would roll the graphs up and throw them in an attic above their office. This decidedly musty and mouse-turd-laden archive—John Miller calls it his "Dead Sea Scrolls"—provided a remarkably detailed record of the land around the family bees.

In 2008, he dug those scrolls out at the behest of Marla Spivak, the entomologist who developed the Minnesota Hygienic bee, and Chip Euliss, a U.S. Geological Survey biologist and hobby beekeeper based in Jamestown, about forty miles away from Gackle. In the name of science and spring cleaning, Miller unloaded the scrolls into the back of Euliss's Chevrolet Suburban. Euliss's specialty is integrated landscape monitoring, which involves examining how land use changes affect the broader ecosystem—for instance, how extensive crop cultivation or floodwater storage projects might affect wildlife habitats. By accessing thirty years of climate and land-use records down to the smallest parcels, the team hoped to determine what type of landscape produces healthy bees. This is not necessarily earth-shattering information—just as Langstroth and N. E. Miller had their own formulas for bee-yard success, so do most serious apiarists—but remarkably, no one had actually conducted a controlled, long-term study on the subject.

So Euliss and Spivak consulted with Zac Browning, John Miller's sometime collaborator, who was based near Euliss in Jamestown, to compile a recipe for an "idealized bee neighborhood" that could support a hundred hives. This included flowering plants from spring through late summer, water, shelter, and proximity to roads. In North Dakota, it is also beneficial to locate one's bees close to Conservation Reserve Program (CRP) land that the government pays farmers to set aside to prevent oversupply and keep commodity prices from plunging. CRP lands are typically either fallow farmland sown with native seeds to restore soil, or wildlife refuges or restored prairies— places where flowering plants abound and bees can find easy nourishment. It also behooves the beekeeper to steer clear of large fields of corn, soy, and short-season grains—crops that provide little, besides the occasional hedgerow or crop border, for bees to eat, and lots of pesticide hazards. The invention of short-season corn and soybean varieties has made these crops viable in places like North Dakota that were once too cold to sustain them, and the world's hunger for animal feed and biofuels has made them more valuable. Good for the farmer; bad for the beekeeper.

Once the team determined the factors a beekeeper considers in placing his bees, they set up experimental apiaries in various landscapes and asked Zac Browning, the team's guinea pig, to place some of his hives in three "good" locations and three "bad" ones, then follow those bees through the pollination season to see how they fared. By cross-referencing Browning's bees and Miller's scrolls with USGS and USDA data on nearby horticultural patterns, the scientists hoped, in essence, to determine the secret of a good apiary—to replace a beekeeper's "gut feeling" about a bee yard with more quantitative measures. "The secretion of honey in plants," wrote Langstroth, " . . . depends on a variety of causes, many of which elude our closest scrutiny. In some seasons the saccharine juices abound, while in others they are so deficient that bees can obtain scarcely any food from fields all white with clover." In more quantifiable terms, asks Jeff Pettis of the USDA Beltsville Bee Research Laboratory, another member of the research team, "What makes a bad location bad? Soil moisture? Forage? Pollen protein content?" Through their study, the team hoped to discover that elusive formula.

There was a big problem with Miller's contribution to the historical side of the study, however. Miller, it turns out, is too compulsive a beekeeper. Scientists need control groups—bee yards that haven't thrived—and if Miller found that a bee yard wasn't thriving, he got rid of it. So all he had, over time, was a record of good apiaries. "He ruined the experiment," joked Spivak. Nonetheless, the team hopes to break new ground, especially as they move forward with Browning's bees, in determining how weather and forage affect a hive's nutritional health going into the "national season" of winter and spring pollination, and how that in turn affects its health coming out.

This is important because more and more scientists have come to believe that, in addition to all the other hypotheses— nosema, varroa, pesticides, exotic viruses—nutrition may play an important role in the inexplicable and intolerable hive losses of the last five years. Entomologists have come to believe that bees require a more varied diet than monoculture can provide. In 2006, for instance, when CCD first appeared, there were devastating dry spells across much of the country; 2007, when beekeepers lost another third of their hives, was another difficult year. Some researchers are suggesting that adverse weather could not only limit forage, it could also affect nutrition in ways both obvious and subtle, such as producing tiny changes in pollen grains that render them less nutritious.

Most large-scale beekeepers had, in the years leading up to the crisis, come to rely on low-cost corn syrup to help bees survive the lean times before the pollination flows. They'd pumped syrup into the hives from three-hundred-gallon tanks with gasoline nozzles, as you would at a filling station. More and more research, however, has suggested that bees may be suffering from the same kind of malnutrition afflicting humans who eat processed junk food. The problem is compounded by the lack of natural forage. Sprawl, monocrops, flawless lawns, weedless

gardens, and a general decline in pastureland have made it hard
for bees to find a suitable diversity of nectar and pollen sources.

Bees, it turns out, need natural places. "Nature deficit disorder," as Dennis vanEngelsdorp coins the larger nutritional problems facing bees, is easy to cure: "Make meadows, not lawns."
Lawns are "green deserts," plied with pesticides and devoid of
flowers. Monocrops flower only briefly and leave bees equally
bereft, nutritionally speaking. But in meadows—wild meadows,
untamed, unsprayed meadows, meadows where flowers flourish
all summer in ever-replenishing weedy bloom—there lies the future. In meadows lies the salvation of the bee.

Bees need meadows. They need nectar, pollen, honey. They
need the things that bees were meant to eat. This is not a new
revelation: "Few things in practical beekeeping are more important than the feeding of bees; yet none have been more grossly
mismanaged or neglected," Langstroth wrote more than 150
years ago. "In the Spring, the prudent beekeeper will no more
neglect to feed his destitute colonies, than to provide for his own
table."

Miller has reached a similar conclusion. He used to use tan-
kersful of corn syrup to keep his bees going between blooms,
but after his varroa debacle of 2005, he figured he should
rethink his approach to nutrition. Many commercial beekeepers
sell most of their honey and feed their bees high-fructose corn
syrup in its place. Miller used to, but he doesn't anymore; anec-
dotal evidence suggests that beekeepers who have left honey in
the hive rather than pumping in corn syrup, and have provided
pollen supplements to their bees during lean times, have seen
fewer losses. So now he uses only sugar syrup and leaves plenty
of honey in the hives for the lean season. "Once winter begins
and the hive is dormant, no amount of fairy dust can make it

prosper through the winter," Miller explains. So in late summer he must decide how much honey to harvest and sell and how much to leave in the hive to sustain the bees over the winter. He will feed them some sugar syrup in spring as they wait for the almonds to bloom, but in winter they will eat honey.

As Miller contemplates the approach of winter, so do his bees: as the days shorten and nectar and pollen sources begin to fail, the colony contracts. First, the hive makes a judgment whether the queen is strong enough to survive the winter, and if she is, cuts back on drones, which consume lots of honey but contribute little—besides sperm—to the well-being of the hive. By early October, the hive's nurse bees dispense with the drones altogether, stinging them or gnawing at the roots of their wings and legs to drive them from the hive, then opening the developing drone cells and dumping the remaining drone pupae out the front door. "If not ejected in either of these summary ways," writes Langstroth, "they are so persecuted and starved, that they soon perish." That's just the way it is this time of year. "Nature is unforgiving," Miller writes.

Now, the scarcity model prevails.

Days shorten.

Height of sun-angle is lower.

Temperatures drop.

Soon, with autumn fast approaching, the queen stops laying eggs altogether. The last eggs she lays hatch into "winter bees," which must live for four to six months, long enough to raise the spring brood that will replenish the hive when the flowers blossom again. Now the colony organizes for winter in earnest.

Foragers gather propolis, the resinous material that they use to seal and caulk cracks and holes in the hive, shoring up the structure for winter. Pollen gatherers seek goldenrod and gumweed to sustain the developing brood. Nectar gatherers find their task increasingly futile. Finally, as the cold hits and the nectar flow ceases entirely, the remaining bees and brood contract in a cluster close to the bottom of the hive, where it is easiest to stay warm and safe. They fill the space once used to rear young bees with stores of honey and pollen.

It is from this stockpile that beekeepers take their own sustenance, and each fall, like Miller, they must make a calculation as to how much they can safely steal. Leave too little honey, and the bees emerge from winter in a weakened state, easy prey for varroa mites and the multiplicity of viruses that spread through the almonds each spring. Or they starve, each bee consuming less and less until the honey is gone and the colony dies. Miller likes his hives to weigh 130 pounds going into winter—75 pounds of honey (most beekeepers aim for 55–60 pounds); 55 pounds of bees, wood, and hardware.

This weight is considered "heavy" by many fellow beekeepers.

Some beekeepers will actually strip honey from wall frames in brood chambers,

expecting to replace that weight with syrup.

Others, particularly my good friend Larry Krause of Riverton, WY maintains there

is no better feed than honey for bees.

He also takes his hives into winter "heavy."

I know, I offload the semi he sends down to Placer County each winter.

In normal summers, Miller can achieve the weight he wants and still have plenty of honey left over to sell, but in a summer of oppressive heat and drought, or one of too much cold and rain, he pulls his harvest boxes early so that his bees can stockpile the season's remaining bounty inside the brood chamber, the hive box where the colony spends the winter. It means another disappointing year for honey sales, but when the summer forage disappoints, that is the choice a beekeeper must make. Good forage—good honey—is everything for a beekeeper. It is the difference between prosperity and bankruptcy, between the industrious hum of hardworking foragers and the melancholy stillness of a dying bee yard.

It is, perhaps, what makes beekeepers such lonely figures. Beekeepers don't share locations. They can't—there aren't enough flowers to go around. That's why Mona, the woman who once worked in Miller's honey house, no longer does. Mona was a friendly enough woman, square-shaped, with a deep but somehow unconvincing belly laugh. But soon after my first visit to Gackle, she approached some of Miller's neighbors there and asked if they'd allow their fields to be plied by "local" bees owned by Mona and her husband Ernie, instead of by Miller's traveling bees. About ten landowners agreed, and Miller felt beyond betrayed. For months, maybe years, he preferred to call Mona "Satan" rather than to speak her given name, though he now sort of regrets being so childish. Ironically, the locations had been underperforming for several years. Still, it was a battle that Miller hadn't asked to fight, a bitter lesson he didn't need to learn. Sometimes it hardly seems worth it.

But then there is honey—the still-astonishing sweetness, such pleasure on the tongue. We sometimes forget to mention, when discussing the problems of modern bees, that they produce a wondrous thing, the sweetest natural substance on earth, as varied as the flowers that bloom. And that skunks, bears, other bees—and humans—will go to remarkable lengths to share in the bounty.

Toast, any bread is merely a means to an end.

The end is transporting as much honey as gravity and theory enables from jar to mouth; without actually putting a lip lock on that one-pound jar.

It's just physics.

If no one is looking, snorking from a honeybear is perfectly legal.

Miller loves honey; he pours jugs of it over his food. He often loses money with each barrel he produces. But ultimately he participates in the creation of something unquestionably good. He makes honey.

Chapter Ten

....

Next Year, Right?

THE SUMMER OF 2009 LOOKED TO BE A FECUND ONE IN
Gackle. The previous fall had been wet, the winter snowy.
Miller was building a new honey house, but by December drifts
had covered the building's exoskeleton, and work ceased. In
spring the prairies were sodden. It rained through April, then
May, then June. The yard surrounding the honey house, where
the backhoe had harrowed in the fall, melded into a frightful
ooze. But the moisture was good for flowers, so Miller didn't
mind. "Lots of water in North Dakota," he wrote.

Huge puddles, close together.

Several of the houses have water in the basement. Not
unusual, but

still a pain.

These conditions are, of course, a precursor to a three
Cadillac Crop!

I'm thinking Kelly Green El Dorado, Floptop, White Ostrich
Leather

interior, just because I can.

These conditions also pre-curse world-class mosquito populations, and

deer ticks by the trillion.

Stuck trucks, and broken equipment are also promised.

Deer ticks and stuck trucks, he got. It kept raining. Miller was getting excited.

the sweet clover will be mirror high on 4th of July

truck mirror, that is

Yellow Gold, Dakota Tea

why pretty soon ol' John's a millionaire

But July was less searing than usual. "Beautiful, temperate, five degrees below average," he wrote. This began to be a problem. It seemed warm enough for the clover to bloom, but the clover, apparently, disagreed. "Our moisture is adequate," he wrote, but his clover was not.

This season is not a sweet clover year, and I have no clue why not.

Last September, we had three well-timed rains. A sweet clover plant germinates in the fall, setting a tap-root for fall. Next year, walla! Sweet Clover.

Not so this year.

With so much bad weather, the delays in completing the honey house didn't really matter, because there was no crop to run through it when it was finished. Miller took to calling it his "Lost Summer," and contemplated commissioning a batch of hoodies with the epithet written across the back. As the delightfully cool summer wore into a prematurely cold fall, the season's disastrous repercussions in the northern half of the country grew clear.

Our crop sucks.

Krause's crop sucks.

Krause's neighbor is ⅔ cleaned up; and has not extracted one barrel of honey. . . .

Bees are going to go through another bad wreck in 2010.

As read first here; shitty crops = shitty bees . . . it's a six-month-long slow-motion wreck.

Careening down the slippery slope to ruin; I am.

The bees weren't getting out of the hives. It was too cool; it was too rainy. Miller's "dancing ladies" were "set to starve their keepers and themselves." And because the bees weren't foraging in the cold and rainy September, they didn't pick up their nosema medicine. Nor did they do so in the cold and rainy October that followed. By November, as Miller packed up the hives to return them to the cellars, his spreadsheets told him that things were very bad—not that he needed a spreadsheet to know that his hives were going into winter without enough honey. They were an average of twelve pounds lighter in 2009 than in 2008, and all he had to do was lift one to know its stores were insufficient.

Though many of the factors that determine a beekeeper's

fortunes are utterly beyond calculation, you can predict a few things, and here's one: a poor summer begets a poor winter. Miller was going to have to prepare for a bad one, as were beekeepers across the northern tier. The cool, wet summer left a poor honey crop throughout the Midwest. The early, cold fall killed off any late forage that might have allowed bee operations to recoup. By the end of 2009, honey production nationwide had dropped by 20 million pounds. It was the worst crop on record, the lousiest anyone could remember.

The result was, by now, not at all surprising—another year of staggering winter losses. An unusually cold winter across most of the nation—temperatures in Florida hovered below freezing for two weeks—stymied winter honey flows in southern climes and killed off brood and young bees everywhere. In northern climes the cold snap further exacerbated the problem of insufficient honey stores, because the colder it is, the more bees have to work to keep the brood warm—and the more they work, the more they need to eat.

Between January and March 2010, Miller lost around half his hives, some to varroa mites and CCD, but most to plain winter starvation. Nationwide, 34 percent of all managed colonies were lost, though beekeepers in North Dakota fared worse because of the cold summer there. Miller was able to meet his pollination contracts only because he'd now factored major losses into his pollination business model, setting aside a large reserve of hives in case of disaster. It had taken him some time to accept that he must plan for disaster year after year: "I had been resistant to that because of pride, self-righteousness, denial, stupidity, not wanting to lose many bees," he told me. But he'd finally faced the fact that he was going to see a lot more death than he liked, and that he needed to get used to a "low-level grind of hive failure that I think is with North American bee-keeping permanently." Nobody is happy about that. Few in the industry have figured out how to make money when each lost hive costs them sixty dollars extra in labor, feed, and replacement queens and packages. "It's unsustainable," says vanEngelsdorp.

But Miller can't dwell on such thoughts. After the losses of 2010 he cursed the weather, castigated himself, dusted himself off, and went about the business of keeping lots and lots of bees. Because though he lost half of his colonies, the other half survived, and those hives, Miller says, were really good ones. "We sent some dynamite bees up to Washington state for the apples," he told me. He's not sure why they did so well. But he's grateful. It is no fun to lose money, but it is fun to take care of bees. "Which would the bee guy rather have?" wrote Miller.

30% of his outfit dead; or 30% reduction in pollination prices?

Answer: NEITHER!, of course, we are bee guys; we want it
both ways.

By now it should be obvious: bee guys are not reasonable people. They love bees. Bees grab them; say "take me." When their bees are sick, it affects them profoundly. Perhaps the affection is mutual—the Germans believed that when a beekeeper died, the bees must be told or they would fly off. More likely, it is a one-sided passion. But no matter. Nectar seduces bees to pollinate flowers; bees have seduced humans to take good care of them for millennia. Thus Miller loves nothing more than putting on his "full battle gear," puffing the smoker at the entrance of a hive, and prying the top open, ever so gingerly, with his hive tool. "Let all your motions about your hives be gentle and slow.

Accustom your bees to your presence: never crush or injure them, or breathe upon them in any operation," wrote Langstroth.

Miller can be churlish and immature, a terrible Mormon and a neglectful husband, and, if he is to be believed, an occasionally ghastly businessman of bees. His motions, metaphorically speaking, may not always be as gentle toward humans as he would like. But with bees they are. They are gentle, compassionate, inquisitive. He can't wait to see what's going on under the lid of the next hive. Ask any beekeeper: bees are addictive—their purposefulness, their solidarity, their endless complexity. Miller loves nothing better than the sight of a teeming frame of bees, of sealed-up honeycombs and brood ready to hatch: "Ah," he says, "that's prosperity right there."

But beekeeping, as an industry, has not prospered. Just as mites and disease have ravaged the profession, so have demographics. In 1946 Americans, whose sugar had been rationed during World War II, kept nearly 5.8 million managed bee colonies. By 1970 that number had dropped to around 4 million. That was B.V., before varroa—well before—and it was a confident time for the industry, which had finally found a cure to the longtime scourge of American foulbrood. It was as easy then as it would ever be to keep bees. Still, people left the profession in droves. They left because they moved to cities. They left because there were suddenly so many better ways to make a living. They left because cheap sugar and corn syrup and saccharine and supermarket honey provided easier ways to sweeten tea and toast. They left because keeping bees was something difficult in an age of convenience. There was no logical reason for modern Americans to keep bees as a profession. Those who remained did so only because they really, really wanted to.

Miller left once. In 1974, when he was twenty, he departed

Gackle after an arduous summer and drove to Idaho in twelve hours flat—a record that held until 1999, the first year he owned the Corvette, when he made the drive in 11:45. As with the Corvette, it was another time of mutiny. "Gackle had emptied out as fall came," he wrote, "and I just quit." He wanted a normal life: "Friends. Independence. Irresponsibility." He went to work in an Albertson's supermarket and then did a semester at Ricks College, a Mormon school in Rexburg, Idaho, but was asked to leave because of "unacceptable behavior involving cigarettes and alcohol." He transferred to Boise State University for a year, joined the student council, threw a bunch of parties, nearly got arrested, was dismissed from the student council, then did get arrested and spent a weekend in Ada County Jail. It was, he says, an education. "I learned that I did not want to be in jail. Ever." Another semester, this time at Brigham Young University, cured him of college for good: "I damned near suffocated," he said. He went back to bees. He didn't know how to get along in the world, but he did know, even then, that bees provided "never-ending intrigue." Better than jail; better than booze; better than college; better, ultimately, than any other future Miller could imagine.

It is too easy to compare bees to their keepers, but I will do it once more. "I once furnished a candy-shop, in the vicinity of my Apiary, with gauze-wire windows and doors, after the bees had commenced their depredations," wrote Langstroth.

> *On finding themselves excluded, they alighted on the*
> *wire by thousands, fairly squealing with vexation as*
> *they vainly tried to force a passage through the meshes.*
> *Baffled in every effort, they attempted to descend the*
> *chimney, reeking with sweet odors, even although most*

*who entered it fell with scorched wings into the fire,
and it became necessary to put wire-gauze over the
top of the chimney also. . . . As I have seen thousands
of bees destroyed in such places, thousands more
hopelessly struggling in the deluding sweets, and yet
increasing thousands, all unmindful of their danger,
blindly hovering over and alighting on them, how
often they have reminded me of the infatuation of those
who abandon themselves to the intoxicating cup. Even
although such persons see the miserable victims of this
degrading vice falling all around them into premature
graves, they still press madly on, trampling, as it were,
over their dead bodies, that they too may sink into
the same abyss, and their sun also go down in hopeless
gloom.*

As with Langstroth's candy-addled charges, beekeepers see
the "hopeless gloom" that lies on their chosen path, and follow
it anyway. Miller likes to say that there are two things in life:
greed and fear. But he knows as well as any that there's also
passion. "A bee," Kahlil Gibran wrote, "is a messenger of love,"
of the evolutionary dance between stamen and stigma, flower
and flower. Bees will do anything for nectar; beekeepers will do
anything for bees. Like bees plunging headlong into the deluding sweets, like drunks in quest of their next fix, the beekeeper
obliges, instinctively, whatever the cost. Unlike bees, though,
beekeepers are human—they have a choice. We should be grateful, then, that they have chosen to do something so imprudent,
so daft. The world would not function without them.

But for all his folly, the beekeeper has had to make some
concessions to reality. The toll of pathogens and chemicals and

rapid-fire migration has forced bees to evolve far more rapidly than they would have in a state of nature. And beekeepers have had to evolve along with them—to become survivor stock, or else to become something other than beekeepers. Beekeepers are more difficult to influence than bees, since they reproduce at a rate of one generation every twenty-five years or so, not one generation per year. They too have the problem of resistance, though it is mainly having too much of it, not too little; they are resistant to messing with what's always worked for them. Some beekeeping experts—mostly the kind who don't keep thousands of hives—would like people like John Miller to stay home with their bees and keep them away from the disease-vectoring almonds, to banish all chemicals from the hive, even to shun mass production altogether. That's not likely to happen, so long as we want to keep our supermarkets teeming with produce. There simply isn't another way to feed the multitudes who want to eat such foods. Big agriculture requires big beekeepers. "John and I are trying to make a living and keep twenty people making house and car payments," says Pat Heitkam. It's not so easy to "live on roots and seeds" when you've got a real business to run.

Still, beekeepers have evolved. They've moved from skeps to top-bar hives to the Langstroth hive, where they've roosted, for the most part, because who wants to mess with something so simple and elegant? They've moved from black bees to Italian bees, Carniolans, and Buckfasts, and on to Minnesota Hygienics. They've moved to trains, then highways, then into almonds and cherries and cranberries and blueberries. They've moved from honey to sugar syrup to corn syrup and back to honey. They are looking askance at chemical mite medications and searching for more sustainable options for fighting mites, such as breeding for resistance and using natural materials.

They are avoiding certain crops that are associated with a high degree of loss and hassle. John Miller yanked his bees from the California oranges in 2008; Dave Hackenberg followed suit in Florida in 2010. He now takes them to Georgia, where he places them in the woods, well away from industrial crop pesticides. There they feast on titi shrubs, gallberries, and raspberries, on the wild things that bloom throughout a southern springtime. "They're the best bees we've had in we don't know how long," says Hackenberg. "We're going gangbusters, just big colonies of bees."

Beekeepers are also learning to be less reticent about their contribution to the world, and to work together better, starting advocacy organizations like Project Apis mellifera, on whose board Miller sits, to push for better research and to educate Americans about the importance of bees and bee habitats. Miller fears they have learned too late—that they have squandered their fifteen minutes of fame.

Folks have moved on.

We are so yesterday.

So last century. . . .

He worries that beekeepers have evolved too slowly, "a room full of old men"—senescent, like worker bees that have outlived their usefulness. When bees get old—after they hatch and then labor as nurse bees inside the hive and then venture out to serve as foragers—after they have lived a full life, they begin, through natural exertion and time, to lose their vigor. They get shiny and raw. The fuzzy filaments of youth fall out and their supple skin grows tight and hard. Their wings get notched and ragged. They wear out. "They appear to die rather suddenly," writes Langstroth, "and often spend their last days, and some-times even their last hours, in useful labors." That is the way a bee should die. But the way they have gone lately—wingless, or mummified, or quivering in a paralytic seizure, or simply gone, unmoored and disappeared—it's just not right.

Losing so many bees isn't financially viable, and it isn't fun. John's father, Neil, is philosophical about the continuing losses: "If I was young I would probably do the same thing over again," he told me. "I guess I've been around long enough to know that if you get one problem solved another one will come along." He had his struggles with pesticides and mechanized mowers in the 1960s; his boys now struggle with mites and disease. When that's in hand, they'll be "waiting for the next problem," Neil says. In the summer of 2009, John thought he had his bee prob-lems licked. "I thought it would be a good season," he says. "I had those three Cadillacs ready to go." And then it kept rain-ing. What to do? Like a bee to nectar, the only thing is to move forward. "We'll do better next year," he says. "Next year, it will be different."

He is being ironic. Because then on comes next year—this year, now, which has started off well enough, with enough rain but not too much, enough warmth but not too much. It could be a good year, as long as the predicted midwestern grasshoppers don't materialize—grasshoppers that rain down like green con-fetti, eating flowers and larvae, devouring every scrap of vegeta-tion, every leaf, stem, and flower, carpeting highways and fence posts, eating cotton shirts right off clotheslines. Grasshopper counts increased more than tenfold last year, leaving conditions ripe for the worst outbreak in nearly three decades. So if this year isn't better, perhaps, then, next year will be. "Next year, for sure, right?" Miller writes.

Because he knows: beekeeping has its rewards. In the almonds one February day, in a brief season of reprieve between die-offs, Miller checked his bees. There had been a dreadful killing frost the night before, and early in the afternoon the temperature finally climbed to 42 degrees, the threshold above which the first scouts might venture out to look for pollen. It continued ascending to 54 degrees, when the first foragers emerged. Then, when the mercury hit 65, every food gatherer in the hive poured forth, spreading out among the almonds, dancing from blossom to blossom. The year before, the bees had been so sick that you could walk through the hives without a bee suit. But this year—this year was different. You could see it; you could hear it; there was life.

Miller drove his truck along a dirt road and stopped between two endless rows of almond trees. He shut off the engine to listen to the humming sound of thousands of honey bees at work in the blossoms. "Hoo hoo! You guys go!" he shouted. "Look at 'em buzz."

ACKNOWLEDGMENTS

First and foremost I must thank John Miller again and again, and yet again, for agreeing to star in my book. His generosity with his story and his life, with his bee suits and veils and jokes and insights and star thistle honey and sweet mandarins and baggies of almonds and Honey Stinger chews—it has all been astonishing and humbling.

Thanks also to Pat Heitkam for sharing his queen secrets, for his edits and wise words, and for hooking me up with that Benadryl; and to Marla Spivak for the patient explanation and the liquid-nitrogen ice cream. Larry Krause is every bit as nice as John Miller says he is. Linda Stander was a fun and informative road trip companion and an excellent photographer, and is really good at pulling out stingers. Jan Miller has shared her home with the legions of bee tourists who pass through and has put up with us with grace and good humor. Harry and Brenda Krause took such good care of me in North Dakota that I didn't want to leave; my daughter naps daily under the flannel frog blanket Brenda sewed for her.

Thanks also to Denis Anderson, Dennis vanEngelsdorp,

Justin Schmidt, Jeff Pettis, Jay Evans, David Miksa, Dave Hackenberg, Joe Traynor, Neil Miller, Richard Adee, Frank Swiggart, Roy Tighe, and John Thoming for sharing their stories, work, and time with me.

Tammy Horn's *Bees in America* was an invaluable resource on the history of American beekeeping. Singeli Agnew's "The Almond and the Bee," which appeared in the *San Francisco Chronicle Magazine*, offers a perceptive overview of the symbiotic relationship between bee guys and almond guys. Ron Miksha's *Bad Beekeeping* also provided a wealth of gritty detail about the life of a modern-day beekeeper.

Jean Nordhaus, my mother, has been my first and best reader from the time I could spell my name—I couldn't have a more exacting or engaged audience, and every word I write bears her rigorous and graceful influence. I thank my dad, Bob Nordhaus, for his keen eye and his unswerving support and encouragement; and my brother Ted for his insight and guidance—for keeping it deep. Carol Byerly is a good friend and her passion for history is contagious; her engagement with my first draft was nothing short of heroic. Hilary Reyl's friendship, literary companionship, and far-flung fondue dates over the years have been a cherished gift to me.

This book grew from a magazine piece that ran in *High Country News* in March 2007. Greg Hanscom originally commissioned the article and John Mecklin did a masterful job of developing and editing it—I am grateful to them and the *HCN* staff for supporting this project in its infancy. And thanks to Jean Weiss and *Delicious Living* magazine for introducing me to John Miller in the first place.

I am so grateful to Sarah Burnes for her steady encouragement, and to Dan Baum, whose enthusiasm for the original pitch egged me on to aim big. Florence Williams, Lisa Jones, and Hillary Rosner provided a rousing lunchtime support group. And a big huzzah to Becca Heaton and Shaun McGrath, for letting me lounge on their couch while I wrote.

My agent, Stephanie Cabot, championed the book even as the global economy collapsed around us; Michael Signorelli shepherded the manuscript with enthusiasm and a steady, respectful hand. Meg Knox's editorial eagle eye helped me produce a far more elegant and cohesive text.

My husband, Brent Barkett, is as miraculous and conscientious as any honey bee—no shiftless drone, he. During the time I wrote this book, we also moved out of our house, renovated it, moved back in, had a baby, and said goodbye to our dear dog of fourteen years. Brent was his usual tranquilo self through all of it, the eye of our personal hurricane. And I thank Delia and Milo, our own little brood, for making me laugh every single day.